The Unholy Path

of a

Reluctant Adventurer

Rosie Kuhn, Ph.D.

To Kim,
I love you tons!
Rosie

The Paradigm Shifts Publishing Co

FIRST EDITION

Cover design by Ponder at http://www.ponderhome.com

Production and editing by Lynne Krop at The Write Well
http://www.thewritewell.net

The Great Little One. Copyright 1996 by Rosie Kuhn, Ph.D.

Book text in Times New Roman, headers and sub-headers in Cambria
and *The Great Little One* in Gentium Book Basic.

Names, places and dates have been changed to protect personal privacy.

Quote by Kenny Loggins, 1993, *Outside from the Redwoods*,
Shakespeare Festival, California, from the song, Leap of Faith.

Children. From The Prophet, Kahlil Gibran (1970).

Library of Congress Control Number: 2011927980
Publisher: The Paradigm Shifts Publishing Company
Eastsound, Washington
ISBN 978-0-9835522-0-8

For my grandchildren:

Even before their little feet hit the planet, I want them to appreciate
the ground of their being
and
the wings of their desire.

The Great Little One

Every beautiful morning of every beautiful day, The Great Creator arrived at his workbench to begin His meticulous work. He promised himself a long time ago that by sunset of each day He would complete the creation of one new being for His wondrous Earth.

And after many millenniums, today is the day He set out to create me.

Funnily enough, He began with my nose. "What a strange place to begin," I thought. "I hope it will be the nose of The Great Wolf who is so courageous and has such a keen sense of smell. He can pick up the scent of his dinner from a very great distance."

When the Creator finished my nose, it did not feel at all like I expected.

"It's just a tiny little nose," I thought. "It's hardly big enough to smell even the tiniest of rose buds."

When He began to make my eyes, I thought, "Well, perhaps I will be given the mask of the pesky Raccoon who always sees his way clear of the most difficult problems; or maybe I will have the eyes of the Great Eagle, who sees the smallest details from way up in the sky!"

But when He finished my eyes, I could see just a tiny, tiny bit of light. How could Creator give me so little sight with which to see his beautiful world? How am I to do great things on his Earth if I cannot see?

I began to feel very frightened and unsure about how much I really wanted to be one of The Great Creator's earthly creatures. "Maybe this isn't such a good idea," I thought.

"Ears! What about ears!" I thought excitedly. "Oh, I want the ears like the Great Elephant, so I can hear all the wonderful voices and sounds of all creation. I want to hear the wind blow through the treetops and the water trickling softly over rocks in the brooks."

The Great One completed my ears and they were not the very large ears I had in mind.

"No, No, No! These are not ears. These are just tiny, teensy-weensy holes on the side of my head, nothing through which any kind of real sound could come. What's going to happen to me if I can't see or hear? Where will I live? How will I find food and a safe place to sleep?"

It took The Great One a very long time before He began to create my front paws. He seemed to be putting a great deal of thought into them.

"Please give me claws such as those of The Great Grizzly Bear, so I will have the strength and power to defend myself. I could feel brave and courageous with claws such as those."

But the Creator gave me tiny little paws. "Oh, how on Earth will I manage? My little eyes can hardly guide me from trouble and my front paws can't possibly get me out of harm's way."

"Perhaps the Creator has plans for my tail. Perhaps it will be as powerful as that of The Great Beaver. I could swim with a tail like that and I could make a stupendous slap on the water to warn of this great animal's approach. With a tail like that, I could feel proud and important."

The tail I received was just as puny as my tiny nose, my tiny eyes and my weensy paws. I was so sad and scared. I did not understand what purpose I would serve the Great One being such a tiny little being. What good could I bring to the world?

Perhaps, it will be my hind legs that will give me importance. Perhaps they will have the power of the Great Turtle. With her powerful hind legs, she digs really deep holes in the sand to deposit her eggs. Then she buries them so carefully to protect them from harm. Perhaps that is His great plan for me.

The Great One's idea of powerful legs and my idea of powerful legs were very different. He did not give me the legs of any mighty creature I'd ever seen him create.

"Oh dear. My hind legs are just as tiny as the rest of me. I feel humiliated. I feel no greatness, no strength, courage or power to do anything upon the Creator's Earth. What in the world has gotten into Him that He could come up with such a design for me? I'm pathetically small, virtually sightless and useless. If I knew how to cry, that's exactly what I would do!"

After a very, very long pause, The Great Creator sighed with delight. Then He said, "There Little One; you are now perfect and complete. You can now serve the purpose I have in mind for you."

I was confused. "My purpose?" I asked. "I actually have a purpose? Please Great One; tell me what purpose it is you have planned for me on your wonderful Earth. I feel so terribly small and helpless. Without much sight or any real power, I couldn't possibly be any good to anyone." Maybe as a tasty morsel for one of your bigger creations. I thought to myself.

The Great One smiled and said, "It is your small stature that gives you the power and the might to do the job I have in mind for you. And, your great work will not be on this Earth but deep, deep within it. There was a great flood upon the Earth a very long time ago. I hid the Human Beings down in the Earth, away from the waters that would kill them. It is now time for them to return to the Earth's surface. My plan for you is to dig a tunnel from the Inner Earth to daylight so that the Humans can return to their homes and live among the trees, rivers and sunshine once again. I have made you the Earth's Guardian too. You possess the wisdom of all the healing herbs and roots within the Earth."

I sat there, overwhelmed by The Great One's words. I couldn't believe that the Great Creator would have chosen me for such an important task.

The Great One explained further, "Though your nose is tiny, it has the keen ability of the Great Wolf. It can smell the tiniest of rosebuds many miles away. It will always lead you towards the flowers. Though your paws are small, your claws are not, and they have the strength to dig the tunnel. Do not believe that you lack power and greatness just because you appear small. For your size, you possess the strength of the Great Grizzly Bear!"

"But why don't you have the Grizzly dig the tunnel?" I inquired.

The Creator smiled beautifully and laughed. He replied, "The Grizzly is far too large to do the work that only a fellow your size could manage. No, I am quite sure that you are the one to fulfill the task."

I was becoming more and more curious, and asked, "You have given me ears that are hardly ears at all. How am I to hear the wonderful sounds of your Earth?"

"I have buried your ears deep within your thick fur to protect them. You will find that your hearing is very powerful indeed," said the Great One. "I considered giving you bigger ears but they would get in your way and fill with dirt. That would not be very pleasant for you at all. You have also been given the ability to feel the Earth's vibrations through your whole body. These vibrations will alert you to any danger that may come your way."

I said to The Great One, "I thought a tail such as The Great

Beaver might be helpful. The humans will know where

I am when I slap my tail. How else will they know how to follow me in the darkness of the tunnel?"

They will know the greatness in your heart and they will feel your courage and the care with which you lead them. You are very much like the Great Turtle in that way." He said.

Still not satisfied, The Little One asked, "Without the sight of the Great Eagle, how will I see the enormous distances I must travel to bring the Humans Beings up upon the Earth?"

With infinite patience, The Great One replied, "You have within you a tremendous power. It is the power of intuition and though you cannot know of it through your eyes, your ears, your nose, or yours paws, it is the greatest of all your senses. It will give you great strength and power. Intuition sounds like a tiny voice deep within you. Though it will sound tiny and quiet, it will be Me guiding you safely wherever you need to go."

The Little One felt wonderful. He realized that just like all of the other Earthly Creatures, he too had been given the very tools needed to fulfill his purpose on Earth. "You are everything you need to be," said The Great Creator. "Be happy and know that you are perfect just the way you are."

And The Great Little One, feeling content with himself, came to understand his own special purpose on Earth.

The Creator, content with His day's work, laid The Little One down into His soft, warm Earth. "Take very good care of yourself. Sleep well, for tomorrow will be the beginning of your new life."

The Great Little One nodded, curled himself up among the soft green moss and fell fast asleep.

The Great Creator set out for his place of rest too. For tomorrow, He would begin to create another earthly creature just as wondrous and glorious as The Great Little One.

Chapter One

Navigating by Your Inner Compass

Spiritual teachers and self-help gurus encourage navigating by our inner compass, not by someone else's inner compass. What they don't tell us is that the magnetic force of any compass is not only influenced by the magnetic weight of our own compass, but also by the electromagnetic influences in the surrounding vicinity of the compass. Anything that has a magnetic or electrical charge will pull the compass needle off true north. What this means is that generally we are steering by the magnetic influence that surrounds our inner compass and us, not by our true inner guidance mechanism.

Steering one's ship by someone else's compass rarely works. Each vessel has its own weight and way of moving through the water. Each adventurer has to consider these elements before journeying into unexplored territories. This requires some exploration of what true north is, as each one of us has a different true north and each one of us has a set of charts and coordinates by which to steer. If you don't know what your true north is, you'll never get where you want to go.

As children and often as adults, we are ignorant of this very important piece of knowledge. We make assumptions about where it is we are going and how we will get there. We observe fellow travelers and those who've gone before us, thinking if we do just what they do, we'll achieve our destiny. We are unconscious to a large degree of this process and because of that we don't take into consideration the influences of other people's magnetic forces and the environment within which we live.

So, as a child, I didn't know that my true north was something that belonged only to me, not to my mom, dad, or my sisters or brothers. I just didn't know! I set a course, like my mom, like Donna Reed and Harriet Nelson—the role models of my generation and the magnetic influences of my environment of Middle America—and went for it. I got in my little boat and set sail, anticipating a wonderful romantic adventure and arriving at a destination of security, stability and invulnerability. This destination revolved around being a mother and having a life full of love and happiness, just like on *Leave it to Beaver*, *Ozzie and Harriet*, *Father Knows Best*; all of the major family TV shows of the fifties and sixties.

Though that was the course I intended to sail, the fact is that I've been involved in an enormous quest, undreamed of as an adolescent girl, whose only envisioned adventure was to be swept up into the arms of Prince Charming, carried off into the sunset to live happily ever after. Yet, each incredible adventure provided me with opportunities and challenges to be the kind of person I could never dream of being.

What Happened to My Dream of Happily Ever After

Rarely are we able to understand the unfolding of our own story until we seize the opportunity to look back and see what it was all about. Divorcing and giving up custody of my children; moving to Nova Scotia, Canada; crossing the Atlantic Ocean on a seventy-three-foot schooner; acquiring three master's degrees and a Ph.D. and writing a book on self-empowerment. I never saw any of it coming.

The intention of this book is to share a story, *my* story as a reluctant adventure on a path far beyond the constraints that could have bound me to conventional religion; well, to conventional everything. I would say that there are very few aspects of my life that have remained traditional, no matter how hard I tried to hold onto the ways of my family, culture, gender and identity that I always hoped to live into—and I do mean always!

My hope that my life would follow the illusionary path of my mom and father were dashed by the constant sea of consciousness awakening me to follow my true course not found on charts designed by someone else.

I say illusionary path of my parents because they held a fantasy life that looked secure, stable and beautiful. The fact is there wasn't as much substance behind the façade of that fantasy and not much integrity that I could discern. They played by the rules and won on many levels, but my sense is that their souls did not fare well at all. Alcoholism and pill popping were strong indicators, as was the lack of emotional availability. As adventurers, they were lost at sea.

If my parents were lost in the sea of unconsciousness, what chance did I have? More importantly, how would I find out that I could be just as lost as they were? Once I realized I was lost, maybe I had a chance to find my trajectory and final destination, whatever that might mean.

Like most children when born into a family, I would have to orient myself to my surroundings, using my own compass and my own navigator, my choice-maker. Even before my head popped out of mom's birth canal, I had had many experiences that began to direct me on my path. Instinctively I would begin to sense what felt safe, what felt good and what felt nourishing and nurturing.

My sense of the Spiritual/Human form thing is that life is going to throw curve balls at us for as long as we are on the planet only in service to what we want to accomplish, what life lessons we've come to complete and what life purpose we've come here to fulfill. Some call it Earth University. Being a life-long student myself, Earth University has been a most challenging program and my teachers far exceeded my expectations. They have been impeccable in driving home the objectives of the course. Only the students, somewhere in the midst of the course, will understand for themselves what those objectives are.

Parents

In the spiritual sense of the word, my parents were impeccable teachers for me. Though loved by so many people around the world, their way of parenting from my perspective sucked! Rarely were they interested in *me, my* thoughts or *my* perspective on life, love or on religion and spirituality. I didn't feel seen or heard by them. Being the sixth born of nine children made it difficult to be seen. I felt invisible to everyone. It was most painful though being invisible to my parents.

Both of my parents were second generation Americans. Their families came from Germany in the 1800s and lived in Detroit. My matriarchal grandfather was a butcher and my patriarchal grandfather was a house painter. My dad became the prize of the family by becoming a doctor.

My dad, Richard Kuhn, never was considered handsome. He was somewhat short and pudgy. His most prominent physical feature was his nose—it was large. As a physician and a decorated hero in WWII, he had quite a few amazing adventures in his life. He was the Surgeon General of the Disabled Veterans Association. He also had a horse in the Kentucky Derby many years ago.

My dad had many hobbies. He had an orchard of fruit trees and a tractor on which he loved to play. He had racehorses, so he'd go to the track after his time at the office or hospital. He had a farm where he'd go when he wasn't at the racetrack, on his tractor, at the office or the hospital. If we wanted time with dad, we had to go to one of these places with him. Once there, it wasn't as if you were with him, because he'd go off and do what he wanted to do, leaving us to do whatever we could find to do. There isn't much for a kid to do at a racetrack.

My mom, Rosalie Velton, was considered a beauty, especially by my dad. Even after nine children, she kept her girlish figure. I think that he was always in love with her until the day he died. She never finished high school because she had to help support her family when her dad died; she was only twelve.

She married my dad when she was twenty-three and because birth control was not an option for a Catholic girl in those days, she had her first child within that first year of marriage while her husband was away at war. My dad returned three years later to his wife and a young toddler, my brother Dick, who later in life shared with me that he didn't like Dad from the first moment he laid eyes on him.

I believe my mom married for position and security, not for love. I can't say I saw much real love from my mom toward anyone really and not to my dad, specifically. It would have been good to see that. There was a *restrained affection;* something I inherited as a defense mechanism. For a Catholic woman this may have been her form of birth control. Any true affection could be construed as an interest in making love, which too often led to pregnancy.

My mom was unavailable in that she was either in her beautiful and peaceful rock garden, cooking, changing a baby, going to visit friends, going to the country club, going to the Altar Society at Sacred Heart Church, out to dinner with Dad or driving one of us here or there. There was no down time for Mom and very little quality time with those of us at the further end.

Though both parents went to church every Sunday and spoke of faith, being generous and charitable, I was confused by what seemed to be a lack of honesty, integrity and Christian-like behavior. Like many adults, I witnessed that they did not practice what they preached, or what the Catholic Church preached; they did not keep their word. Dad said mean and angry things to his children and spoke derogatory comments about people in Detroit. He used the N– word for black people. My mom didn't show much compassion towards her children. Quite often, she was like a martyr, having sacrificed a great deal of herself for the sake of her faith and her role as Mother. This was a grave disappointment. I could not count on my parents to show up in integrity, love and respect toward their children, at least the way I believed it should be.

Mom and dad took many vacations together. Annual trips consisted of Mardi Gras in February, the Kentucky Derby in May and Florida in the winter. It didn't matter what was happening for us, nothing got in the way of those events. My parents missed every one of my glee club concerts and musicals because of the timing—the rotten timing!

Early on, I began the *restrained affection* towards both of them. As much as I wanted to believe, they were the best parents in the whole world—something I think every child wants—I was left with the sense of coming up empty, lonely and confused.

There was very little physical abuse. What it was, was soul fragmenting and psychic abuse. I believe my sisters Mary Therese, Patrice and Annie got the worst of it. My dad's mom was obese and he didn't want his children to be fat like she was. He wanted his daughters to be slender and beautiful, like my mom, and when their bodies began to grow in ways that was not appealing to his eyes he'd criticize and say demeaning things, believing that through shaming, he could control the outcome. They grew up believing they were flawed and weight has been lifetime issues for each of them.

I was wounded deeply one evening when I witnessed my dad attempt to peroxide Patrice's hair and do whatever he could to change the course of nature. To me, Patrice was the most beautiful of us all, but he couldn't see beyond what for many teenagers is normal weight gain and acne. He couldn't love his daughters unconditionally. I don't believe he ever forgave us for being less than perfect.

Some of the abuse was just plain emotional, brow beating, especially of my brothers. "You are NOTHING!" I would hear my dad yell to Dick or Michael. "You will never amount to anything – NEVER!"

I had the good fortune to be small and beautiful. I also learned early to stay below the radar when my dad was drinking. It wasn't until the older children had left home that I became more visible and vulnerable to attacks.

I learned recently from Mary Therese that I was the favorite child because I was so beautiful. She resented that I would get attention and some preferential treatment. She didn't know that I felt just as empty, isolated and invisible as she did. My essence-self wasn't any more visible to my parents than Mary Therese's was.

I don't remember ever hearing my mom stand up to my dad for us. I don't remember hearing her say she loved us just the way we were. She did what she could to appease my dad and rule us with a seething silence that felt like death was coming to get us. I learned to stay away from her and at the same time, I so wanted to be loved by her.

I think that perhaps this is how I came to see past the worst of people to their essential loving and innocent self. My radar was continually searching for authenticity and connection. When it was realized, even for just a few brief moments, any problematic behavior was erased. I saw the best of them and forgot the rest, until it surfaced again.

As soon as the youngest child, Annie was out of the nest my parents became snowbirds, spending half the year in Florida and the other half in Michigan. My dad traveled back and forth weekly so he could see his patients in Detroit then fly back to Florida to be with my mom. He liked being busy.

While my mom was alive, I always struggled to be the daughter she expected me to be, while at the same time struggling to be in integrity in my own life. Though she may have loved me, I don't think she really liked me, so struggled as best she could to accept me as I was. Rarely were there moments of connection and true caring between us. I'll carry this regret to my grave.

My mom died when she was eighty years old, but shortly before she died, she began to open to the possibility of maybe seeing me as a unique human being rather than who she thought I was supposed to be. I have to tell you honestly, the morning she died, just after I called to wish her a good day, I got into my car to drive to work. The song from the *Wizard of Oz* broke through from my unconscious: "Ding dong the witch is dead, the witch old witch, the wicked witch, ding dong the wicked witch is dead." It sprung out so spontaneously I was caught off guard with the degree of relief I felt with her passing. For just a brief moment, I chastised myself for such a horrible response to her dying. Then I allowed myself to experience the relief of decades of struggle to be accepted and appreciated by Mom. It's a horrible thing for a child, even an adult child to live with the rejection from a parent.

My dad would always talk about a storybook character, *Uncle Wiggly*, who was always in search of adventure. He would share that he was off to have another *Uncle Wiggly* adventure. For Dad, it seemed that the more I became the qualities of being that he valued; adventurous, courageous and curious about life, the more emotionally abusive, critical and distant he became.

I caught him off guard, a few days before he died, when I flew to Detroit from California to spend some time with him. I entered his room at the University of Michigan Hospital. Not expecting to see *me*, he looked up at me from his bed and said, "This moment is worth a million bucks." He was so happy to see me. Two mornings later, just before I left—never to see him again—his parting words to me, while I was stirring his *Cream of Wheat* cereal were "What are you doing, you brilliant son-of-a-bitch?" Compliment? Sarcasm? Ridicule? Abuse? I didn't know quite how he meant it. I took it as his way of acknowledging me the best way he knew how.

I'm grateful that I got through this Earth School Course—*Freedom from Criticism, Neglect, and Other People's Truths*, for as I left the hospital that day I was free of any attachment to his considerations. I would have loved to hear what every child longs to hear from their parents, "I'm really proud of you!" And I accept that part of the curriculum in his particular course was learning how to acknowledge my own successes and be proud of myself without expecting it from others.

I could smell a lack integrity and dishonesty a mile away. My parents' impeccability led me to decide to be different from them. My requirement was to live life impeccably in responsibility, accountability, integrity and dignity. My Global Positioning System (GPS) was set for these coordinates. At the same time, I was only human and have struggled to be impeccable, in integrity and accountable. I've gotten off course far too often than I care to admit. I'm no saint, as many people will be glad to tell you.

Living in a family is like living in a fishbowl. As fish, you don't know to distinguish yourself from the water in which you swim. The water may become toxic, but you, the fish, are part of the toxicity too, not because you made it that way, but because you can't separate yourself out. You can't know that you are not the water, the bowl or the toxicity. You can't know for a very long time.

Guiding Lights

I had eight brothers and sisters—five of them older than myself. Perhaps I would have had a lot less confusion had I had fewer siblings to observe and wonder whom to emulate.

There were times when I loved my brothers and sisters so much, especially Helene and Michael. When I was young, I loved to be around their charm and charisma. I felt part of a magical unfolding of a prince and princess, witnessing the makings of royalty; from my vantage point, that's how they were treated. They both had an air of fun and playfulness about them and they didn't seem to mind having me around. I felt a sense of a kindred-spirit with them both; more so than with my oldest brother, Dick, who was ten years older than I was and much more detached from the family.

From my very young eyes, Mary Therese seemed to carry deep anger and sadness. It made sense, though given the continuous bombardments of messages that said, "*You are not enough!*" Patrice, who was just two years older than me was fairly closed off; it was her way of staying safe in a very mean family. She eventually became my best friend. The funny thing was that even though I felt a closeness with these individuals I wanted more of a sense of belonging, but none of them, and I need to include myself here too, had a sense of truth or an ability to care about what made us feel safe in that knowing way. What they spoke and how they acted were two very different things. It wasn't safe to share in a vulnerable way, not really with anybody.

As a family, we didn't look mean, bad or dysfunctional. We were the Kuhn Family—Dr. Kuhn's Family. At the country club, when my dad would take us all out for dinner, everyone would ooo and ahhhhh. Here comes Dr. Kuhn with his beautiful wife and darling children. How wonderful! I assumed, since we looked like the ideal family, we must *be* the ideal family. This was very disorienting and confusing. As a kid, how could I make sense of my feelings that this is a crazy-making family in relation to what we look like to the outside world? Somebody had to be wrong here and since I was just a child, I guessed it must have been me. If I were wrong then I would have to change *me* in order to fit in, to be loved, to belong. Very early on, I took it upon myself to change me in service to making things right, so people would be happy and I would feel loved.

I think parents in general underestimate the wisdom and brilliance of their children; how they can continually assess their environment and attempt to create balance and harmony in a chaotic world. Meanness, sarcasm, practical jokes, as well as the slugging, biting, pinching and scratching were some of the ways that we worked out our unconscious and unspoken anxiety and anger. Other than the instant gratification that comes with a punch in the arm or a practical joke played on one of the younger siblings, there wasn't any explanation for this behavior. We didn't hate each other. We just didn't have any other way to be with the invisible craziness of our reality.

Though I believe I was inherently kind and caring, my little choice-maker decided that in order to avoid being poked, scratched or socked in the arm, I should choose to be a good sister. What that meant to me was do what others wanted me to do. *Be kind and loving so people won't harm you.* It's a coping mechanism, a survival strategy for staying out of harm's way. I became more vigilant to ways that I could be helpful to others and truthfully, it felt good to be kind. I just would have liked more kindness in return; perhaps we all did.

What the Future Holds for Me

Looking up to siblings who are five, six, or even ten years older gives one a sense of destination. "That's what it's supposed to look like in high school; the boyfriend, choosing colleges, etc." It was my Atlantic crossing; getting from elementary school to junior high to high school. I can't imagine making that crossing without waypoints or role models. Sometimes for me, having five role models gave me an opportunity to pick and choose whom I wanted most to emulate. The dilemma was who held true north, which person in my young life demonstrated the qualities of being that would most support my own sense of truth and lead me to my perfect world—whatever *my perfect world* meant?

When I was ten years old, while at Dominican Camp, on Kelly's Island in Ohio, where my parents sent us a few times, I met a girl from Windsor, Ontario, Canada. Her name was Cathy McCabe, and I was able to visit her for a weekend at her home shortly after our return from camp. Her dad was a physician, like mine; they were Catholic, like us, and there were six children in their family. I truly enjoyed being with the McCabe's. They seemed to care about each other. The house seemed peaceful and calm. Dr McCabe was playful, loving and available with his children. The kids weren't afraid of their dad and they weren't punching each other. I wanted to live with them!

This one short weekend with the McCabe family was a telling moment that was wonderful, yet created further confusion. My compass needle began to point in the direction that the McCabe's were going, but the vehicle I was in, the Kuhn Family wasn't on that trajectory; we were headed in a very different direction. How could I get more of what I experienced with the McCabes? How would I connect with my own family members when they weren't connectable?

Attractor Fields as David Hawkins discusses in *Power vs. Force*, generates a type of energy field that makes one attracted to that individual, group or fields. I couldn't find mine. From kindergarten to junior high, I could not find a sense of belonging. Dick was always in trouble with my dad. Though given amazing opportunities to succeed—my dad pulled some strings so he was admitted into Notre Dame University—his anger at my dad had him flunk out, not once, but twice. This behavior was not a match with my attractors.

Helene played the demure beauty. Charming, feminine and smart enough to get into St. Mary's University. She had a boyfriend in high school and had many friends around her. From my perspective, she was social and active as the perfect teenage girl. Her downside, from my point of view, was that life revolved around her. As the oldest daughter, she was the princess and everything she wanted, it seemed, was bestowed upon her. Because she was so special she could flake on her commitments, change her mind at a moment's notice, leaving disappointed and frustrated siblings and friends in her wake. Her ways hurt me a great deal and I did not want to hurt people if I could help it. I learned from Helene to be more vigilant about how not to hurt other people.

Michael was a real character. He was handsome, athletic, charming, fun and playful. He was a practical joker and much of what he did was funny to a kid, but not to grownups. Throwing eggs on people's houses, allegedly running Mom's car into the river, many things. I wasn't tricky enough to be like Michael, nor did I find that his success rate was good enough to emulate. He played football and always thought he'd get a scholarship as an athlete. That didn't happen.

Michael called me his A.F.S., his All Time Favorite Sister. I loved that he called me that because it made me feel special. He liked me and liked me doing stuff for him, but he wasn't around much if it wasn't convenient for him. He flaked on me as much as Helene did, but I loved him anyway. I see now how I cultivated a high degree of tolerance for people flaking on me.

Mary Therese was four years older than I was and from my perspective was cloaked in a dark and victimized veil. It makes perfect sense to me as she was burdened with the responsibility of us younger siblings. She took it upon herself to make sure that we were fed and warm. No one knew that she would get up in the middle of the night to change a diaper or provide a bottle of warm milk. No one knew, so no one could acknowledge her and deeply appreciate how much of her childhood she had sacrificed. Nobody knew and nobody cared.

Mary was the one who sat me down and told me how people have intercourse and where babies came from. I remember her in that moment as being very gentle and soft with me in that very important moment. She was also with me on my thirteenth birthday, when my period started. She really had a certain knack for compassion.

Patrice learned that the best way to avoid criticism and abuse was to hide out in her room. That was her way of avoiding painful jabs that continually flew through the air from any number of people. Her room was kind of a safety zone. No one went in there much, as she didn't have a lot to say. But, I liked being up there. It was quiet and peaceful. We became close friends. We understood each other in our silence.

Patrice found her place as a majorette in the high school marching band. I was really proud of her. She'd found her niche and seemed truly happy. I wanted that! We'd lost connection when she left for college in California. I actually felt abandoned by her when she left, but didn't have a name or sense of what that meant at the time. In college, Patrice was happy being on the swim team and the diving team and enjoying life. It would make sense that by leaving the house, she could leave behind the destructive memories and that life would get better. I certainly hoped that was true.

My younger brothers and sister, Christopher, David and Annie played important roles in my life too, but not in the same way as those who came before me. I didn't look to them to find my way, not for a long while anyway.

Christopher was just a year younger than I was. We were never friends. He had his own life, his own schedule and aside from supper, he wasn't around much. He was independent and loved the outdoors. I envied his freedom and his joy. But, like my older brother Michael, he became bullying and sarcastic to his sisters and to David. It's interesting that the form of meanness and bullying wasn't like an angry meanness. It was always delivered as if it were funny. Regardless of how it was delivered, it was painful.

David had an interesting life. During the winter, before he was two years old, he'd fallen six feet off the break-wall in front of the house onto the frozen river, and he fell down the stairs twice too. He had at least one concussion and knocked out all of his little teeth. From the beginning, people didn't expect much from him because of these falls, as if he'd been knocked stupid or something. He was given a great deal of attention and people felt sorry for him.

I always felt a lot of love for David. He's always had a loveable and kind nature about him. He was five years younger than I was and we didn't spend much time together. Like Christopher, he too was a kid who loved the outdoors. He didn't seem to hate girls as other boys did and was as much a brunt of Michael and Christopher's pranks as the girls in the family.

David became an alcoholic by the time he was thirteen, but nobody knew it then. He smoked marijuana from an early age too. Now in his fifties, he's recovering successfully from his addictions to drugs and alcohol.

Annie, six years younger than me, the last child to be born, was my nemesis. She brought out the very worst in me. When I was approximately eight years old, my mom hired a live-in housekeeper. Her name was Mary Boise. She spoiled Annie rotten. Annie could get away with anything, which pissed me off to know end. My righteous, *angelic* nature was so angry with her for being mean, self-centered and taking advantage of every opportunity to get her way. To me, it was wrong for her to be this way. I probably envied that she would use those tactics and get what she wanted.

While I was angry with Annie for being the way she was, she was angry with me for excluding her from my life (as best I could). She was hurt and felt abandoned by me. All I can remember is that I had no interest in being around her whatsoever. I did not like how she treated people to get what she wanted. It took both of us well into our forties to begin to get over who we were in that family. We've since become very good friends.

One by one, brothers and sisters left home to go off to school, leaving Annie more alone and feeling victimized. She didn't get to have all of the fun experiences that the older kids got to have. She couldn't share in any of the fun stories that were told around the dinner table. She held this against us all for a very long time and her poor me attitude didn't help create friendships with any of us.

Annie shared with me how she manipulated my parents into getting what she wanted through a practice of being the victim of "I never got to ..." And they were so burned out on parenting they would give into her every whim. Nothing she received made her feel more loved. It only contributed to her list of ways she wasn't loved.

What was obvious is that we were living with something that was unnamable, which was my parents alcoholism, my dad's anger and abuse, my mom's unwillingness to stand up for her children and I don't know what else.

No one stood up for anyone. You always had to watch your back. You never knew when you were going to be kicked in the head, slugged in the arm, smashed with a snowball or baseball, biting, scratching, given hickeys or tied up by your underpants. Sometimes this was all very funny, but mostly it just hurt. I have to admit though that I delivered a few good blows myself when I could.

I would say confusion and anxiety were my constant companions. It was like living inside a pinball machine. Parents, priests, nuns, sisters, brothers, housekeepers, sin, punishment; I had no way of knowing what was true, because there were so many *truisms*. I assumed that everyone else had a sense of clarity. Everyone else knew where they were going and how to get there. My sense of self kept bouncing off my perceptions of what other people were saying and doing. I'd want to be aligned with people (especially my parents), but that didn't seem to make them happy and it didn't seem to make me feel any more loved or lovable. How does one decide what's right?

As best as I could, I followed the directions; observed what it took to be a good girl. I did my best to make the men in my life happy. I gave up knowing anything beyond my dream of getting married and having children.

Humor as an Antidote

One of the very best aspects of being a member of the Kuhn family was that we had such a great sense of humor. Patrice was pegged with being the funniest of us all; however, each one of us brought our own special flavor of wit to the mix. A comment would be made by someone, and then another sibling would add something clever and funny. Someone else would add to the mix and another would follow from there. Soon, laughing would be joined by tears. We've all kept our sense of humor and tend to find things funny that other people would frown upon. Funerals more so than weddings would have us rolling in the aisles. This was a great gift to have received from my family.

Addictions Galore

David wasn't the only one of us that had substance abuse problems. Each of us had our own abuse issues. My sisters and I, especially Annie suffered from eating disorders. My obsession was with *not* becoming fat. People remember me saying at the early age of five, "I want to keep my figgor (figure)." I didn't want to be fat and to that end, I counted calories as soon as I knew what they were. I didn't realize that that was as much of an addiction or obsessive/compulsive process as eating can become.

From as early as I can remember there was always some talk of diets and not becoming fat. My grandmother was obese and I'm sure my dad was afraid that his kids would perhaps have that gene. His worst fears were realized with three of his five daughters. Mary Therese and Patrice were big women, but not necessarily obese. The worry and the talk of them being fat was constant. Annie, at one point weighed nearly three hundred pounds.

Actually, I don't know what Helene's specific addiction was. Dick smoked cigarettes before he was sixteen. Michael used humor, sarcasm, and practical jokes to deal with his frustration. Each of us found our own way to deal with the anxiety of not knowing what the heck was occurring that had Mom and Dad drink so much; Dad being angry and sarcastic with his kids and why Mom seemed depressed. It was unlikely we would find out while living under their roof.

Fun with the Kuhn Family

Though I lived in a crazy-making home there was exquisiteness to the life I was given. I remember as a small child knowing the purity of love and beauty of the Divine presence that surrounded my life, and was my life. I remember seeing the sun break through the clouds leaving streams of light shining down to the Earth and knowing that the angels and God were peering down on me.

We grew up on Grosse Ile, an island on the Detroit River, at the mouth of Lake Erie and across the river was Canada. We had a big, beautiful home with lots of outdoor space in which to play. We could roll for what seemed like forever down the slope of lawn, stopped by the rust covered rickety fence at the water's edge. The beauty was tangible.

Almost every day of my childhood, I experienced sunrises in a way that brought a sense of magic and awe. The morning sun reflecting off the river provided many hours of delight as I lay on my bed entranced by the fairy-like sparkles on my bedroom ceiling.

In those same hours came the hum of the outboard motors on the back of the small wooden fishing boats. People from Detroit came down-river to rent boats at the boat livery to fish for carp, perch and catfish.

The Bob-Lo boat, a white, triple-decker boat silently ferried people from Detroit to Bob-Lo Island, an amusement park in the middle of the Detroit River. Maybe twenty times a day it would pass in front of our house. During the night, the Bob-Lo boat would be lit up with thousands of white lights, and though it traveled through the Livingston Channel a mile away, we could sometimes here the dance-band playing. I never tired of seeing the Bob-Lo boat.

There was also the sound of huge pistoned freighters that also traveled through the Livingston Channel. They were lake freighters, traveling around the Great Lakes. I could feel the CHA-CHUNK, CHA-CHUNK through my whole body as they passed in front of the house. It was a fascinating feeling, one that connected me to the huge ships far across the river.

The incessant conversations of mallards and canvasbacks, the geese and swans that lived along the shore were also familiar to my morning imaginings. I remember seeing them all as beings with as much personal importance as myself.

My life was rich with sounds and views of the natural surroundings. I languished in bed as long as I could, mesmerized by the cacophony of sound and light.

Thunderstorms with their huge crashes of thunder and blinding lightning were terrifying to me. We watched the storms crawl across the sky through the glass walls of the front porch that looked out over the river. I could feel the rumblings reverberate through my body. It was during those times that I'd see a peace and aliveness in my mom. She loved to watch these storms. She wasn't afraid. She wanted us to see the magnificence and beauty in the lightning strikes that hit the water and the rainbows that would appear magically afterward.

Winter was my favorite time of year. We had a lot of snow then, and the river would freeze so solid that someone could drive a car or a tractor onto the ice to shovel off an ice rink.

Before the snow would layer itself onto the ice, miles and miles of open space was ours on which to skate. The quietness and the freedom to explore were delightful. Sometimes you wouldn't have to move your skates and the wind would push you for as far as you wanted to go. Of course, the effort it took to get back home was exhausting. It was oh, so worth it, especially if my mom had a fire going and some hot chocolate waiting.

Winter brought freshness to the air and the remarkable change in scenery. We had lots of space to sled, toboggan and build snow people. Being outside always renewed my spirit. I didn't realize until now that this has never changed. It has been the most significant contributor to the places I've chosen to call my home, and I'm grateful for having the relationship I've had with nature.

Difference of Boys and Girls

I envied my brothers their freedom to *be*, to explore and adventure into places where girls weren't allowed to go. For hours, they'd be off spearing pike or carp, catching turtles or just fishing. Later in life, they were invited to go duck hunting with my dad. Between the unwritten rules of what I was allowed to do as a girl and some of the things I didn't really want to do, like tearing wings off flies just for the fun of it. I limited my tomboyish nature to activities that were more acceptable.

It's an interesting dance we do with ourselves when caught between two worlds. It's curious to notice now what I allowed myself to like and not like despite my true nature to explore and to adventure into the world. I limited my knowing and my exploring by focusing on what I was supposed to want. I loved playing football with my brothers and I was fairly good at it. Baseball games happened every evening after dinner. With all of the Catholic families on our road, we always had more than enough team members. My dad built a tennis court, so tennis was one of my favorite things to do. Golf was something I was supposed to like because we belonged to the Golf and Country Club. We had to go to junior golf every Friday during the summer. I hated it. Patrice, on the other hand always won at least one trophy on awards night. She loved to play golf.

Yet, the fulfillment of my soul by the stuff that girls were made of; playing with dolls and such just never worked for me. I never got the intrinsic value of dressing them up, undressing them then dressing them up again. I did love my baby-dolls and loved to play house. I rarely allowed myself to know my independent nature. It went against the grain of family. If everyone wanted what he or she wanted, how could our parent's deliver to each of us? They already spent so much of their time catering to the needs of their children; to acknowledge our wants and allow them to be spoken was seen as being selfish and self-centered. At the time I came along, my dad was forty and my mom was thirty-four. They were already burned out. Early on, I learned somehow to feel guilty for asking for anything. Over time, I had to decide to forget who I was and what I wanted. I figured that it was required of me as a member of a family—to be as easy to live with as possible. Of course, this didn't mean I was easy to live with. It just meant that I developed it as a survival mechanism to avoid rejection and ridicule and hopefully to gain immunity from pokes, jabs and pinching.

Fun

There were special times that we had with our dad that made life worth living. We would drive into Detroit with him on the occasional Saturday to go shopping at Hudson's and have Coney Island hotdogs at Dooley's, a small, corner diner near my dad's office. On Sunday's he would always go into town to the hospital to see his patients then go to St. Mary's church where he was an usher and eventually became a Deacon. We loved to go with him, because while he did his rounds, he'd park us at the hospital cafeteria where we would have roast beef, mashed potatoes and gravy and real butterscotch sundaes—for breakfast! I have never, ever been able to find that same butterscotch flavor of those sundaes. They were the absolute best!

Church was always just church, but because my dad was privileged and special (he donated a lot of money to Old St. Mary's Church), we were able to go into the choir loft and sit with Eddie, the organist. Between services, Eddie would let us play a little on the huge pipe organ. After church, we'd go down into the rectory and say hello to Father Nader. He was one of the nicest priests I ever met. Sometimes we were allowed to count the money from the collection baskets. We were Dr. Kuhn's kids and we were special!

In the 1950s, a doctor always dressed in a white shirt, black suit and drove a big, black Cadillac, or at least that was my dad's style. It was a big, ol' hunkin' car that could easily fit six little kids in the back seat. On the way home from church, after all the morning adventures in town, my dad would usually smoke his cigars and listen to the ballgame in the front seat, while in the back seat we were free to be goofy kids, as long as we didn't bug dad too much. I remember the cigar smoke as a good smell, but also really horrible when enclosed in the car with the windows rolled up. I'd feel sick to my stomach, but it never stopped Dad from smoking his big stogies.

Quite often, on the ride home from Detroit, I was troubled by the rows of houses that all looked the same. There was dreariness when passing by the Rouge Steele plants. They were dingy with a lack of soul. I didn't understand. I felt sad for the people who had no views of the river or didn't have a real lawn to speak of. This is when I was too young to understand what middle class or working class was. I thought everybody was supposed to live like me—whatever that meant in that moment. It didn't make sense that these people lived the way they did and we lived the way we did. Why would they choose to live here and not on a beautiful island?

I wondered if there was love in those homes. What were the people like? Did they have fun? Did they play music? I couldn't tell by the outside of these houses. All I knew was that when I'd pass those houses I'd feel a melancholy sadness. This confusion still rests within my child-self who's never gotten over what the real world looks like.

Boating

After church, during boating season, my dad would load us all up on our forty-foot Chris Craft and head out for a boat ride. Sometimes we had a barbeque and sometimes we would ride to a restaurant that had a dock where we could dock the boat, have supper and then ride back home. We loved to sit on the bow of the boat with our feet dangling over the sides. We loved the spray of the water splashing on us. There was so much exhilaration in those days. These boat rides took us away from the everyday events, the rituals of life, the humdrum of all of the things we were supposed to be and supposed to be doing. They were times to have pop and potato chips, and just be kids. I felt less constricted and more alive. Somehow, the oppressiveness of life was lifted. We just had fun!

The other real opportunities for fun with my dad came with trips to Niagara Falls, Atlantic City and New York City. I was too young to go on these trips, but I was able to go to Florida when I was six! These were opportunities for my dad to give my mom a break from her throng of kids; though she always had help with live-in housekeepers, she still needed a break.

These trips with my dad gave him the appeal that we as children really loved. He gave us a lot of freedom to play and have fun. In Florida, we had the pool, beaches, fishing, hotdogs and macaroni and cheese every day of the week, if we wanted. We played together as a family and had so much more fun than at home, where everyone went their separate ways.

Trips to Florida occurred two weeks before Christmas arriving back home on Christmas Eve night. This gave my mom time to do all of the Christmas-y things. Depending on how things were progressing at home, Dad would delay our homecoming by taking us to the hospital and then to the Sacred Heart Convent to sing Christmas carols. We would arrive home moments after Santa Claus had done his magic in the living room. Those were the most magical times of my life.

It's so fascinating how parents can be so available sometimes and so unavailable at other times. I learned to appreciate the good times when mom could be warm and available, and put up with the bad times when she was cold and withholding.

I wondered if it was my mom who created a lack of fun. She had a sternness that ruled by a look in her eye. She could kill me in an instant with one of her looks. Too many times, I died in the moment when she threw her dagger of disdain at me. I'm not the only one, but it fragmented my soul terribly, living in shame so much of my life for just being me.

I spent many hours wishing my mom would die or just decide to move away. I never wished that on my dad. I knew that if they ever split up I'd want to live with him. He was never angry with me the way mom was.

Almost as if checking off a list, item by item, those dream moments of life in a big family disappeared. Rarely were there bedtime stories read by mom or dad, no reading aloud to share stories or for the purpose of learning how to read. Aside from those summer Sundays out on the boat, there was very little interacting with parents in a playful way that I can remember. By the time I was ten my dad was fifty and my mom was forty-four. I believed they lost interest in doing the fun things they had enjoyed with my older siblings. It's as though the life I had been promised was all make believe. No wonder I spent so much time wanting to grow up and have kids of my own. I wanted to give them all the fun stuff I never had with my parents: sledding, skating, skiing, bedtime stories, dancing and singing. I wanted nothing more than to create the life for my children I couldn't create for myself. This is what I lived for.

The Withering Soul of a Child

My career as a budding young Catholic led me to follow in the footsteps of my five older siblings. I watched them prepare for their first Confession and their first Holy Communion. I was instilled with a sense of awe and wonder. I couldn't wait to grow up and be just like them. They seemed at times to embody the epitome of Jesus Himself as I imagined Him to be. How could I not want what they were about to receive.

I remember being about four years old and being left behind when my mom and all of my five brothers and sisters went off to mass. In my heart, I imagined that inside the little Sacred Heart Chapel they were graced with the face of God, the saints and all of the angels. How could I be denied such an experience? My mom said I was too young and that I would not be able to sit quietly throughout the service. Of course I would, I thought. Why wouldn't I? I imagined that being once again in the presence of my Divine Father would bring me back into my pure essence, into peace and joy and love. What else could I be in God's house?

Eventually that memorable Sunday came when I was granted an audience with the Lord. I wore a dress with the scratchy crinolines, my little black Mary Janes and an excitement that could not be contained. My mom brought all six children with her to church! I remember that the chapel was crowded, so we went up into the balcony, where we had a front row pew. The organ was right next to us and our Aunt Rosie was the organist. OH, MY GOD! I saw so much that morning. I saw the most beautiful statue of the Blessed Virgin Mary I would ever see in my whole life. There was nothing more real to me than knowing that *this* statue was *her*, not just a pretend fake or an icon. *That* was Mary in all her blessed being, radiating love: oh, so much love.

I saw statues of Saint Theresa, angels and archangels. I saw the priest in his regalia, vestments of wonderful, rich colors. I saw my brother Michael, who was an altar boy. He sure looked angelic, not like the brother he was at home.

I saw Jesus on the cross. This image of Jesus always pained me, especially when I heard over and over again that he died for our sins; my sins. My sins? What sins? I was four years old. I hadn't done a single, bad thing in my whole little life. Okay, I did talk in church, which was a venial sin. Of course, that didn't begin to happen until I began going to church. I made up sins when I started going to confession. That was lying to a priest; that was a big sin!

My mom was right. I did a good deal of wiggling and squiggling that first day in church. The crinolines around my waist made me uncomfortable and were driving me crazy! The priest spoke in Latin, which made no sense to me at all. The sermon was far from coherent to my innocent ears. I was bored, bored, bored. And from the virtuousness of those years, I was disheartened to find that space in the chapel void of the Grace of God that I had so longed to be in. That Sunday was the beginning of the end of my innocence.

Only God Knows

I was so excited when it came time for me to enter Sacred Heart School. It brought my innocence to the forefront. I was prepared to take on the holiness of those who went before me. I wanted so much to have the light of Jesus enter my little heart; anticipating the peace and love always promised me. But my memory tells me that it wasn't more than just a few days into first grade that we began to get the teachings of Sister Mary Denata on the ever-present, all-knowing, all-seeing, all-powerful and wrathful God, the description of which changed my young life forever. As I recall, sitting in the first row of desks near the window, guilt and shame took root inside me almost immediately: Mortal sins, venial sins, and The Original Sin, into which we were all born. There was no escaping this reality and my innocence was left behind. Though I knew I was a very good child, this horrible feeling that there was something very wrong with what this nun was teaching followed me for a very long time.

We were told that only God knows what you are supposed to be in life and if you do something other than what God wants for you there will be repercussions and a great deal of suffering. Imagine those words landing on the naive ears of a six-year-old child. This was a traumatic moment in my life—one that set me on a course fraught with fear and despair for the rest of my childhood; honestly, until I finally got married at twenty, my life was troubled with worry that God had other plans for me.

Sister Denata talked about God's will and that it was He Who had chosen our vocation for us. If I didn't take on this vocation, I would live a most unhappy life as retribution for not listening to God. For me, at six years old, and many years thereafter, vocation and religious occupations were synonymous. So, for the next fourteen years I was scared to death that God wanted me to be a nun.

Up until that moment, my innocence was still intact. God was all good and loving and He wanted only to shower me with love and kindness, to hold and nurture my sweet little soul, ensuring that I would be safe and protected from harm for all of my life. The moment Sister Mary Denata spoke those words that only God knows; I became confused, swirling into a world of dogma too huge for my six-year-old mind. What scared me most was this fear that God would want me to be a nun. My image of the nun-life was prison-like, dried-out, lonely and family-less living mostly with mean, unhappy, unfulfilled women. That was not what I had in mind as a life worth living.

During this first year at Sacred Heart, I heard the very same teachings my brothers and sisters had heard, but I had no recollection of conversations from them indicating their fears and worries. I don't remember hearing them talk about guilt and shame, though sinning was always a major issue around our house, but that had to do with outright wrongdoings, like stealing cookies, swearing or talking in church. I began to believe it must be me; that I must be unworthy of love and value. Shame and guilt had become my constant companions. I was confused and afraid to talk about my thoughts. Between my home life and school, there was nowhere to turn for comfort or counsel. As I recall, my parents were not approachable or at best the approach was precarious, depending if they had been drinking, which I did not figure out until I was well into my teens.

There's a story about my Aunt Jeanie who considered going into the convent. She decided against it, married my Uncle Ray and had ten children. When the youngest was only months old, Uncle Ray was killed by a falling tree. Aunt Jeanie's life was full of suffering from then on. As a child, I wondered whether the perils of her life were caused by her decision to be something other than a nun. It was one of those stories that always had me wonder whether I was doing the wrong thing. After all, I could end up like Aunt Jeanie.

There was no manual or spiritual language for the care and operation of my spirit or soul, only catechism classes filled with stories and parables that never made much sense to me. I learned to pray for what I wanted and I prayed for forgiveness for sins that seemed fairly insignificant in the scheme of things. Either prayers were answered or they weren't. If they weren't answered, did that mean I didn't deserve or I didn't pray hard enough or what? Like with Santa Claus, I was either good or not good enough—what a rotten way to figure out how worthy or valued you were in the world.

This was very bewildering for me as little girl who was encouraged to wish on stars and to dream for what I wanted, only to have my dreams dashed on Christmas morning. If God didn't love me enough to answer my prayers and Santa didn't think I was good enough to get what I asked for, how does a little Catholic child know she is loved and valued? What I figured, given this reasoning, was that I had little value and worthiness. I should be grateful that anyone would want me around. I believed this to be true for many decades.

I decided that it wasn't safe to be me, the me that was always in a state of love, always; I learned that I had made Jesus die on the cross for sins I didn't even know I had committed. I learned I needed to be very careful with every thought, word and deed, because something I was doing was causing me to sin; I just couldn't figure out what that was. I learned that to survive in Catholic school and in a Catholic family, I would have to let go of my own knowing of a loving God and trust that what Sister Mary Denata was teaching was accurate. I never actually bought it, but I tried very hard to be good. I was terrified to be anything, but good!

As an aside; just the other day, I was thinking about some of my wants, and thought, "Well, I know I'm a good person and I do good things—where are the rewards?" And the phrase from the song Santa Claus is Coming to Town came to mind "so be good for goodness sake." Be good because you choose to be good, not to be rewarded for being good. I never heard that in that song before—how Buddhist!

This is one of those magnetic influences on my compass—not a good one. Veering off course because of a fear of something is how most of us operate. We can't get to where we want to go while avoiding potential fears. That's one of those learning objectives of Earth University. At times, we may have to sail into the stormy seas, learning that we have the skills not only to survive, but also come out better for having gone through it. It might be scary, but it's what we have to do.

So, I would say the moment when Sister Denata essentially found me guilty of sin and gave me a life sentence of remorse and regret, was one of the most significant moments that led to my loss of innocence. Fear and anxiety trapped and held me to a promise I made to God that I would be good and caring and do as I was told. There is a loss of will when this comes from authority as opposed to again, being good for goodness sake. When you feel trapped in the circumstance of your life, no matter how old you are, sublimation, suppression of your essence of being will be a huge repercussion. Who knows any better at six years old?

My family upbringing paralleled my religious training. Both were autocratic, unsympathetic, and oppressive and promoted shame, guilt and self-denial. This was a very toxic environment within which to find myself and there was no way out.

Actually, when I was just two years old, polio was the epidemic of the time. I was diagnosed with polio and since the hospital was full and my dad was a doctor, they sent me home to die. My mom told me many years later that she prayed for support: "Please let me get through this loss of my child."

What I think is that at two years old I'd had enough of the Kuhn's and knew there wasn't enough room for me, so I created an exit strategy – Polio! But, when I heard my mom praying I interpreted that as "Well, maybe there is enough love here for me. I guess I'll stick around." I was foiled by my own lack of experience. Damn it!

The Challenge of Being Seen

I was considered a gorgeous child. People would come up to my parents and tell them how beautiful I was. These comments never landed inside. They ricocheted off the veneer, never reaching the essence of me. I didn't feel more beautiful than anyone else in the family. Aside from the fact that my mom had portraits done of Annie and me, there was no preferential treatment given to me that I was aware of. Although people saw me in my physical form, I felt unseen on the inside. I felt like I was yelling and screaming from the inside, "Here I am. I'm in here. Look, in here!" But to no avail. I was invisible to the world.

Mary Grace and Sister Mary Carolyn

There were only two adults I can think of who saw me; truly saw me. Mary Grace was one of three nannies we had while I was growing up. Rachel was our first nanny who left when I was about four years old. Mary Grace came next and then came Mary Boise.

Rachel was the best of the best for the older kids, while Mary Grace was the best I think for Christopher and me. I think I was eight when Mary Boise moved in and primarily focused on David and Annie. From my perspective, she spoiled Annie and was abusive to me. Regardless of how much we talked to mom and dad about her they wouldn't fire her.

Mary Grace was a nurse at the hospital. My dad knew her from there and suggested she come and work for the Kuhn Family. With Mary Grace, I was a real person. Kindergarten for me was in the afternoon, so after all of the big kids went off to school Mary Grace and I had a ritual. She would give me a bath in the tub in my parent's bathroom. She would have me step from the tub to the toilet seat where I would stand while she dried me off. She cleaned my ears with cotton swabs every day, whether I needed it or not. I liked that this was an indication of love. She'd sing to me "Mare's eat oats and does it oats and little lambs eat ivy. A kid will eat ivy too, wouldn't you?" This was in 1959. She also sang, "Fly me to the moon and let me play among the stars." The experience of those brief moments every morning was the best of my day. After that, I went back to being invisible and withdrawn.

Something happened that had my mom fire Mary Grace. It was a mystery to us kids, but I blame my mom for taking Mary away from me. She couldn't have done anything bad enough to warrant being fired. My dad hired her to work at his office as one of his nurses so I was able to see her there, but it was never the same. I so loved the joy and playfulness that she brought into my life. I held out for that kind of recognition and unconditional love; that it truly existed somewhere out there.

Years later, I'd written to Mary Grace and visited her at her home. She was the same good-natured sweet woman. I let her know as often as I could that she was my lifesaver. Being a good Christian woman, she never said a bad thing about my mom. She was true to the end.

With Sister Mary Caroline, my fourth grade teacher at Sacred Heart School, she seemed to like me too. Some of the kids said I was the teacher's pet. So rather than feeling good about being seen and acknowledged I felt guilty. I also wondered whether it was because my dad was the Doctor for the nuns at Sacred Heart that she was treating me special. It was so hard just to feel good about being me.

I tried to believe that Sister Mary Caroline saw something special in me, well, actually saw me, but in some ways it was too dangerous to risk believing this to be true. I didn't know the ramifications of being a teacher's pet, it seemed to alienate me from the kids in my class and I was already challenged by that. It's such a dilemma, to desperately want to be seen and at the same time not want to stand out, for fear of retribution from, well, from lots of different sources.

The loneliness, the isolation and the angst: See me, but don't let others see that you see me. Oppression from the outer world teaches us to suppress our inner knowing and wisdom. We come not to know that we know. We have to play small and dumb down to survive within the community. Others have to do other things to survive, but my way was to keep my head down and stay below the radar. What a quandary. I'd say so much of my energy went to dealing with this internal process that there was little left to actually care about learning anything. I really didn't care about any of it. All I cared about was avoiding social annihilation in the ways that I figured worked best.

Social Annihilation

My oldest brother, Dick, was ten years older than I was, so when I was four years old he was already fourteen. My little ears picked up the arguments between Dick and my dad. It was a power struggle for a very long time, probably until my dad died. Dick and my mom always were close because they were together until my dad returned from the war. Dick bucked dad's authority every chance he could.

Observing and witnessing Dick from a four or five-year-old perspective provided interpretations that were challenging to integrate. He had many friends. We had a pool table in the basement and he had his friends over a lot, it seemed. This was the way it was suppose to be—lots of friends and social time.

It wasn't until I was in my forties that I realized I was actually an introvert and wasn't comfortable around people. So, trying to emulate my older siblings who were much more extroverted than I was created self-retribution for not being what I should be. Be that, be that, be that … The *be that's* pointed to being what I should be and not what I was. So much of who we are as adults, or who we try to be, comes from this very young time in our life. And it seems that whether you have siblings that you try to find yourself through or you are an only child, there is still something or some no-thing that could really help you get it right, especially if you don't have a Mary Grace or Sister Mary Caroline. For me, I felt lost and hopeless.

I Couldn't Find My Niche

At school, no one seemed to want to be with me, not the cool kids, anyway. As I said, I was lost. For the first two years of grade school, I hung out with Patrice and her friends. She didn't seem to mind at all. At the beginning of my third grade year though, she wisely shared that she thought it was time for me to find my own friends. I totally understood and agreed, yet as I moved away from her safe circle, I just came up empty, like entering a sea of the unknown. I had little idea how to create friends. That's one of the blessings and non-blessings of living in a big family; there is a well-made circle of people to be with regardless of the circumstances. At home, rarely was there a moment when someone wouldn't be sharing the space with you.

But at school, I *was* alone. Inside my head, I drifted, like one of those kids who hangs out on the edge of the playground hoping to be invited into a game and maybe, just maybe find a sense of belonging.

The girl I called my best friend, Jan Coolsaet, somehow found herself playing with the kids in the next grade up. So, I followed Jan into this group and was accepted enough. To this day, I don't know what it was about the girls in my own class that had me distance myself from them. Most of them I'd been through kindergarten with. I liked them enough, but it didn't seem to matter. I isolated myself from them, perhaps before they would isolate from me. They weren't bad or mean, but for some reason I felt vulnerable with them. That never changed.

My friendships rarely settled into deep friendships. There was always a sense that I had to be cautious, careful, follow some protocol that wasn't explicit to be a member of whatever group I was in.

Nearing the end of sixth grade at Sacred Heart School, my only friend Jan announced to me that she was leaving Sacred Heart to begin seventh grade at the Grosse Ile Junior High School. I felt abandoned and thought I couldn't be left behind with any real friendships at Sacred Heart. I was isolated enough and if Jan left, I'd feel invisible. So, I went to my parents and made a case for transferring to the public school as Jan had done. Since my parents usually wanted to keep up with the Coolsaets and to save money on my tuition I figured, I had a very good chance of it happening. I just couldn't bear the thought of being isolated and alone for two more years in a school I hated.

My parent not only transferred me, but the rest of the younger one's too. For some reason leaving Catholic school gave me a huge relief.

There must have been moments of fun and innocence—I think to myself as I sit here writing and rubbing my forehead. How much of that time did I feel a sense of belonging, of truly knowing I'm loved?

Fast-forward forty years. At a high school reunion, I found myself sitting in a circle of people that at the time were the outsiders, those that didn't play by the rules. They smoked pot, skipped school and, well, weren't probably going to make much of themselves. These people were now shamans and creative types and seemed to be living much more fulfilling lives; they were people with whom I would love to spend more time. I see now that the context of right place, right approach to life for me was about going to college and meeting the right guy—the whole prince charming story. I missed out on knowing myself the way these people seemed to. Life took me on a more cautious and circuitous path to bring me to that moment, connecting to people I could relate to, who had more soul and were more grounded than I ever anticipated. I wished in that moment that I had allowed myself to know what I wouldn't let myself know when I was young. It just felt far too dangerous to step off the path of my parents' path that was set for me. It was an unholy path.

Lip Synching

One place that I did find my niche was with my sister Patrice. She loved to lip synch to musical numbers. She and I sang, The Rain in Spain Stays Mainly on the Plain, from *My Fair Lady*. Lots of wonderful time was spent leaping and dancing and singing with the music. Quite often, when my mom would have family over for dinner, we'd come into the living room and have a talent show. Dick would play the banjo, Helene would play the piano and Patrice and I would do our lip-synching. This was one of those times we had a lot of fun together as a family.

Adolescence

I learned to be me through the community and the family within which I was raised; eight brothers and sisters, parents, Grandmother, housekeepers and a handyman, George, who kept things on the outside of the house running relatively smoothly. Witnessing how people operated, especially my parents, I observed and decided that chores were work, and anything you were asked to do was work. And from a kid's point of view, work did not equal fun and wasn't supposed to be fun. Basically, if my parents didn't want to do it I didn't want to do it either.

I interpreted my parent's resistance to contributing to community events and projects as a sacrifice of their well-being. I watched them dread being asked to serve on another committee for the church, for Girl Scouts or the athletic association; with nine children, there could be any number of possibilities for my parents to engage in community service. I picked up on their overburdened, over committed attitude and developed the belief that *you let other people do the work because they like to and they don't have anything better to do.* I can see how this attitude spilled over into my own adult life, deciding that taking care of my individual needs before the needs of my community just made sense. I can rationalize this any number of ways for myself and have been very successful in doing so until ... now.

The fact is, my parents burnt themselves out on all different committees and organizations well before I was old enough to understand what burnt out meant. They had given tirelessly of themselves in so many ways in the community, on top of parenting toddlers to teenagers, chauffeuring everyone to dance lessons, football practice, swimming lessons, on and on and on. Being born child six of nine, I wasn't around when they had the energy and the fun of participating in all kinds of community activities. It's fascinating how we come to decide what we decide.

I hated being a teenager and I hated everything about this time of my life: school, making friends, everything! This was the very worst time of my life. It was something to endure in order to eventually get married and have children.

Everything I intended to be I wasn't: I was liked, but I wasn't popular, I wasn't good enough to be a cheerleader, which I really wanted to be. I wasn't pretty enough to be voted for homecoming queen and my prom dates were not the most popular people in school. I felt like a loser and lived in hope that maybe someday this would change, and at the same time afraid that they wouldn't.

I was on the Student Council throughout most of my junior high and high school years, though it didn't buy me much popularity or specialness. It was something to be part of, and at the same time, I wasn't that interested in politics. I was also the president of the ski club in my senior year; somebody had to do it. I didn't really care about anything accept getting and having a boyfriend. The rest was superfluous.

There was little parent contact; they were drinking every night from 5:00 p.m. until they passed out. At one point, my dad was drinking a bottle of Grand Marnier nightly. Life at home was not much fun.

Being outdoors, especially in the winter was great. And because most of my male friends were on the cross-country team I began running with my friend Beth Beckett, whose really cute brother just happened to be on the team too.

I guess that was another whole part of my life. When I was twelve years old, the boy down the street, Daniel Beckett would come over and shoot hoops on our tennis court. One particular moment, while I was sitting on a swing watching Daniel throw the basketball over and over again into the hoop, something happened. It was as though cupid had shot me with his arrow and I fell madly in love. From that day on for almost twenty years I had a hopeless crush on this guy – yes, I said twenty years! I knew nothing about him other than he played basketball and ran on the track and the cross-country team. It was a hopeless crush and unrequited. I had no way out of this. I had crushes on other boys too and went steady with a couple, but Daniel was the BOMB!

Are You Thinking

Growing up in a dysfunctional family I learned not to feel or think, need or want. I wasn't allowed to question authority, to be curious about why people think the way they think. My curiosity was squelched in elementary school, by the Catholic Church and by my dad who would yell, "Do what I tell you to *DO*!" I was too intimidated to think for myself, so I didn't.

I remember one day, when I was in eighth grade, my math teacher, Mr. Zook, became really frustrated because the students in his class weren't coming up with the right formulas or answers. In sheer exasperation, he shouted, "Come on people, think!" I didn't actually know what he was talking about. I could say quite honestly that I didn't know how to think. I figured I hadn't learned the formula he was asking for and neither had anyone else. I didn't realize he was asking us to use our mind in some capacity beyond memorizing stuff. But at the same time I was deeply affected by his level of attachment to what we weren't doing – thinking.

That afternoon, after getting off the school bus, Patrice and I were walking up the road to home. We were both quiet and focused on the small hill we were climbing. In front of Betsy Keller's house, I asked, "Do you ever think?" Patrice's reply was quick and to the point: "Nope." She said. "Thinking makes me depressed." This was another one of those life-changing moments when I realized that there was something else I could be doing with my brain, but I didn't yet know what that was. Nothing else was said about this thinking thing, but from then on, I was curious about how I was using my brain. I realized that I was living as if I was in some movie, and all of the lines were given to me by books, parents, siblings, friends and the Church. I got my cues from what other people were doing. I knew I spent much of my time day dreaming about Daniel Beckett and other boys, creating thousands of scenarios all ending with me being swept away in a happily ever ending. Mr. Zook's words have stayed with me forever, and thank God, forty years after that day in his classroom, I was able to thank him for that gift.

Outward Bound

In 1967, I was fifteen years old. After playing tennis one afternoon with a fellow from high school, Steve Rothwell, he shared with me what he had done on his summer vacation. He had gone to Outward Bound, a wilderness adventure school that teaches self-reliance, collaboration and survival skills by living in deep wilderness for four weeks. These programs have existed since after WWII in the US and Europe. Steve's four-week program was out on Hurricane Island in Maine. I was completely enthralled and inspired by his story, the program, everything. I wanted to go. I don't ever remember wanting something for myself so much as to have that single moment of knowing that I had to make this experience happen.

Steve's story: collaboration, team building, needing each other, belonging, developing a working relationship with nature, living with nature, understanding it in such a way that you develop a marriage. It's not something to be endured, but to engage with, find harmony in while deepening a relationship with oneself. I was starving for connection. I longed for something that through Steve's sharing was realized. I wanted what he got through his experience at Outward Bound.

I did some research and found out that the previous year Outward Bound had created their first program for women in Minnesota. I applied and was accepted.

My mom wasn't happy about this and I can't tell you why. She just did as little as possible to support me in making this happen. There was no encouragement to find my own path. There was no interest in why such a program would draw me the way it did. Neither she nor my dad asked me questions that would have brought about the kind of engaged connection I was seeking through this wilderness adventure. Either they didn't care or they didn't know to ask?

For my sixteenth birthday, I don't know what I was expecting for a present, but there wasn't a wrapped gift from Mom or Dad. Later, after dinner and big disappointment that there weren't any presents, Mom said in a *don't think you are so special* kind of a way, that the flight to Minnesota was my birthday present. I guess it didn't even occur to me how the flight was going to be paid, but I found out.

I immediately experienced guilt, but quickly recovered. I wasn't going to let her ruin or take away my dream. I just wasn't going to let that happen.

The next two and a half months I engaged in an exercise regime that would have me meet the physical fitness requirements for Outward Bound. I would have to be able to swim at least a mile and run two miles and be in good enough shape to hike, handle a ropes course and an obstacle course. I was already running two miles daily so it was just the swimming I'd have to work on. The Coolsaet's down the street had a pool and I was allowed to swim whenever I wanted. That was very cool!

Into the Wilderness

The Minnesota Outward Bound Base Camp is on the border of Minnesota and Canada. It is or at least was secluded in total wilderness. Hurricane Island, where Steve went focused on sailing, which would have been my first choice, Minnesota's School focused on canoeing and rock climbing, neither of which I had done before.

Our canvas homes had wooden floors and three sets of bunks in each tent. They were the kind of tents that if you touched them when it was raining they would begin to leak and would continue to do so until the rain stopped. I slept in a soaked sleeping bag many nights during that program and none too happy about it.

The first session of the year, which started in late June, was only the second year for women to attend Outward Bound. I felt privileged to be one of the first groups of women ever to go through an Outward Bound Course. I felt like a forerunner, a trailblazer. I was curious and ready for the adventure, though I had no idea what that would entail and demand of me.

There were eleven girls in my group who came from all parts of the country. There were a couple that had some experience in the outdoors, but most of us were citified, rather than from lifestyles that are more rural.

The directors and leaders were excellent. I felt safe. They made it very clear that being in such a school in the wilderness meant that danger was very possible and that it was important always to be aware of what's going on in the environment. Though there was a lot of fun to be had, there was also a lot of care to be taken.

The first two weeks were spent close to base camp learning the skills of orienteering, map reading, canoeing in rapids and portaging (carrying our canoes, backpacks and gear between lakes). We learned to rock climb and rappel down the side of a mountain, survival skills and more. We got up every morning at 6:00 a.m., ran two miles then went for a dip in the very cold lake. After a week, it became a wonderful experience. All of this was preparing us for our two-week canoe trip and our solo adventure; a two or three night stay in the woods all by ourselves, alone, outfitted with a sleeping bag, a tarp, six matches, three fishing hooks and line and our journals.

"What can I get away with?" was one of those questions that had been part of my internal dialog my whole life. Growing up with housekeepers, older siblings and an attitude that work is to be avoided at all cost, my approach to volunteering and initiating for the sake of the community really hadn't occurred to me before this time in the woods. Obviously, when teamwork is so critical in such an environment it was bound to come up.

Early on, it was clear to the leaders, Jan and Marlene, that I wasn't pulling my weight. I remember one of the discussions they had with me. They brought to my attention that I wasn't contributing my share to the group, that I did as little as possible. They encouraged me to take a larger role in supporting the well-being of my group. I didn't see the value in contributing more if I didn't have to. I didn't get the concept of enjoying the effort for the efforts sake, you know, being good for goodness sake. There were girls that wanted to do even less than I did. They made me look good! Yet, I knew I could do more and should do more if for no other reason than to see what it was like. That was part of Steve's story that so compelled me to take this journey in the first place. It was an opportunity to show up differently in order to experience myself differently.

Surviving in the Wilderness

Learning to read maps and work with a compass was a big part of our education at Outward Bound. One particular test of our competence in this area came when our group of six was dropped off one morning on the side of a road, with sleeping bags, a tarp, a first aid kit and enough food for two days. Our leader pointed to a spot on the map and said, "This is where you are now." Then she pointed to another spot on the map and said, "This is where we will meet you before 6:00 p.m. tomorrow. If you aren't there by 6:00 p.m. we'll call out the search party." They weren't kidding!

Each of us took turns leading with compass and map. We collaborated at times, but generally, it was the leader who made the decisions. I mostly stayed at the back of the pack, uninvolved in it all, until it was my turn to lead. Then, I was out in front, leading with clarity and purpose. It felt good!

When every tree and every ridge looks the same, it's really difficult to know if you are going in the right direction. Though it was possible for us to reach our destination by nightfall, we found ourselves lost, and spent the night in the woods. I thought this was going to be easy!

The next morning we packed up our stuff and prepared to move out, hoping to reach our destination by noon. One of the girls began to fall ill. She was covered with black fly bites – hundreds of them! It was clear that she was having a toxic reaction. We were told that if someone gets sick, three people stay with that person and two people find help.

I was never so clear in my life that I wasn't going to be staying. I was annoyed that this girl hadn't dressed properly to avoid her circumstance. I always wore a turtleneck shirt tucked into my jeans with at least one sweater on top if not more. I always tucked my pant legs into my socks. This was the best way to avoid black fly and mosquito bites. Even with all of this layering and bug repellant, those little critters bit me all over the place. This woman only had on a man's white cotton undershirt on with her jeans. The bugs were very happy to have fresh meat so available.

Had I stayed I would have felt trapped in a circumstance in which I didn't want to be. My frustration would have been of no use whatsoever.

Since I had done such a good job of leading the day before, I was chosen to go with another girl, Sarah to get help. Thank God! Sarah was one of two girls that I actually liked in our group, so I was happy when she chose to go with me.

When you think you know where you are going, and you are going there with a companion you like, things aren't so bad. It wasn't until 4:00 p.m. that afternoon that Sarah and I reached our destination. We yelled hoping to be heard by the other groups and our yell was reciprocated. We were so happy! It turned out though that we weren't on the right lake. We were on a connecting lake, but one that the group just happened to be exploring. They were just getting ready to head back to base camp when they heard us. If we'd been later by even a few more minutes they wouldn't have heard us, and then there would have been two lost groups of girls.

When we got back to base camp that evening, Sarah and I reported as best we could where we thought the other girls were. We'd hike through a logging area so that was helpful in locating the girls. It wasn't until the next day that they were found. The one girl had to be carried out of the woods. She was paralyzed by all the bug bites. After a few days in the hospital, she was back to normal and rejoined us in our preparation for our two-week trek.

After this adventure, the trek was a piece of cake. Canoeing and portaging between lakes was what we did. We explored two hundred miles of wilderness in two weeks. It was pristine, breathtaking and serene. The sound of loons when there are no other sounds around is an ephemeral phenomenon unto itself.

Our solos were just two days and two nights long. Once you were placed on your island, there was nowhere to go. It was just a matter of setting up a shelter, getting wood for a fire and scavenging for food, perhaps catching a fish, if you were lucky enough. I was warm enough and dry enough. I'd lost my fishhooks the first day so fish was out of the question. We had all the water we wanted because the lake water was so fresh. I tried eating some wild lettuce, but really, I wasn't hungry enough to eat it. It so happened that someone had stayed on the same island before so a shelter and fir boughs for a bed were already in place. I did a little bit of housekeeping, went about losing my fishhooks and settling in to my tiny home.

This part of the adventure was in some ways to be the pinnacle of the whole wilderness experience, but it wasn't that challenging. Aside from a couple of beavers passing by and the leach that swam by my little rocky ledge, those two days were fairly quiet. I didn't have any big revelations about myself. I was just there.

I've asked myself a few times why share this story about Outward Bound; what was so significant about this time in my life? I guess it was important to share with you what it was like to be sixteen and realize for the very first time that I had a desire strong enough to do whatever it would take to make it happen. I also wanted to share how Steve Rothwell's story inspired me to act. Rarely, if ever up to that point had I chosen something outside the box of the reality presented before me. I was a country club kid who was to aspire to playing golf. I pushed hard for this trip to happen, though I had no idea what it was about. I pushed against my mom who just couldn't understand why I would want to go into the woods, canoe and rock climb. I didn't understand it either. I just knew it was a course that inspired me to act; do the necessary things to be accepted and enjoy the journey.

I also wanted to share that nature doesn't allow much room for confusion and anxiety. You have to pay attention, follow rules and work together as a team, even if it's a team of one.

Lastly, I did not realize how critical a wilderness environment would be in my life. The sense of connection I have with water, trees, rocks and land, it's never dissipated, not in the least.

For many years after I had extensive dreams of being back at Outward Bound, again. It's amazing how such an experience can impact a life. It says that in the brochure, but I didn't believe it.

Life back on Grosse Ile didn't seem to appear much different when I returned from Minnesota. Aside from my dream life, which continually reminded me of the adventures possible, I went back to being the same old me.

1968: Age Sixteen

Patrice left for college in California and I began my junior year of high school.

I had a fun group of friends that year. The boys and the girls all goofed around together. We didn't do drugs or any bad things; we were just good friends. But things shifted soon after my friend Sarah and her boyfriend, Dominic broke up.

Dominic began to show interest in me and I liked him too. We had a lot of fun together. One evening, after the group of us had been watching TV at my house and everyone was leaving, Dominic and I had our first kiss. You *know* what it's like. Dominic was kind of holding back, while all of the others were heading out the door. There was that sense that something was going to happen and yet, I didn't really believe it was happening; that he was interested enough in me. It was in the hallway of my parent's house. It was one of those moments when you can feel the electricity in the air. We were leaning against the wall, talking about something when he took my hand and leaned in and kissed me.

Life is never the same after a first kiss. I waited a lifetime for that moment. It was everything it promised to be. Dominic was cute, fun and caring. What more could a girl ask for?

While we went steady, we had a wonderful, playful friendship. It was good. I remember watching Neil Armstrong's walk on the moon with him, his mom and his dad in their living room. I guess it wasn't good enough because after eight months he broke up with me. I was caught completely off guard when he told me he was breaking up with me. He said it wasn't me, it was him, and it wasn't for another girl. Shortly thereafter, he and Jan Coolsaet, my best friend, were inseparable.

I took my pain to church and to God. I prayed as if I'd never prayed for anything in my life. This was the first time I really asked God for what I wanted; not like Outward Bound. I didn't take that to God. I wanted Dominic back and I figured God was the only being that was going to make that happen.

I Guess No one is Listening

No response, no change, no relief. Silence.

I didn't take this as a sign that Dominic wasn't right for me; I took it that God wasn't listening, not unlike my parents. I began to decide that God and the Catholic Church was not benefiting me in the least. The Church, from my experience only wanted to control my soul. Every Sunday at Mass, the words spoken made me feel guilty for just being me. "Lord have mercy, Christ have mercy, Lord have mercy." Have mercy on me? I didn't do anything that required mercy or forgiveness. It was as if they were trying to take away any sense of personhood I had left! I wanted a sanctuary where I felt loved, where there was peace, where I could nurture hope. I wasn't finding it in church, at home or at school.

Without my parents knowing I checked out the local Presbyterian Church where many of my friends and their families went. It was friendly, loving and not intimidating by all the talk of sin. I also tried out a Catholic Church in Trenton – the next town over the bridge from Grosse Ile. It was better, but still did not provide any real sense of connection. So, as best I could I avoided going anywhere on Sunday mornings.

Depression: Age Seventeen – the Descent & Sexuality

After Dominic broke up with me, I was alone. I'd always been a follower of the high school cross-country team and often supported the coach on race day. I knew the boys pretty well except for Peter, who always distanced himself from girls. He never appeared social or slightly interested in girls, until one day after Christmas vacation, he started talking to me, as if he were interested. Confused, but appreciating the sincere attention we started to date. We had fun together, enjoyed each other's company. He initiated me into a world larger than what I knew by introducing me to Eric Fromm's book *The Art of Loving*. There were ideas in that book that were way above my head, but for some reason, it was important to Peter that I understand. He was gentle, caring and very patient with me.

Boyfriend over Parents

Later, in our junior year, Ralph Nader visited the University of Michigan. He talked about population explosion and the environment. After seeing Mr. Nader, we were inspired to make a difference. Peter and I decided that we would make a pamphlet for our community, spelling out all of the things people could do to make a difference for the planet. Over the summer we typed it up (on electric typewriters) and made thousands of copies with one of those old mimeograph copiers that you applied ink to and cranked the handle over and over again. Mrs. Withers, Peter's mom was a great support.

We distributed them to all of the households on the Island, by bike and car. My parents were critical of what I was doing. They didn't ask what I was doing or why this was so important to me. They asked sarcastically what the point was of making this brochure. Why was I spending so much time over at the Withers' house? Well, for one thing, I felt loved by Mrs. Withers. She was always so happy to see me. She loved her husband, her two boys and her life. I always enjoyed visiting her home.

"Brick in the toilet? The next thing you'll want us to do is give up using the toilet all together." These were my dad's sentiments about my project. My mom would just look at me with her evil eye and walk away; however, when the Detroit Free Press called wanting an interview with me about the brochure, my mom told them how proud she was of me. This was not how it felt. I actually didn't know what it felt like to have my parents be proud of me. The quality of that experience never actualized. I think I would know what that would feel like.

Scared Shitless

Making out with Peter, one night I had an experience that rocked my world. In the middle of some wonderfully heavy petting, all of a sudden, as we were making out, in my mind, Peter became a woman. It lasted only a moment, but it really scared me. Physically, Peter was a bit slighter than I was; he was an all-state champion wrestler who kept his weight low for his weight class. It wasn't that I tried to imagine him to be a woman, the experience just overtook me and I was overwhelmed with the possibility that I was homosexual. What else would have me experience that?

How do I talk about such an experience with my boyfriend or my parents or even girlfriends? My parents were out because of the whole Catholic thing, making out thing and the … well, they were never the kind of people that I felt safe to confide in. I eventually talked about it with my best friend Beth and asked to talk with her dad, who I trusted, but with whom I rarely talked.

When I told Dr. Beckett about my experience and my fears, he assured me that it was just something that happened. He had watched me be google-eyed over his son Daniel for four years, plus all of Daniel's friends who'd be over at the house. He was sure I wasn't homosexual.

But the thoughts didn't go away. At school, I'd walk down the halls looking at girls wondering if I was attracted to them. I never felt a sexual attraction to girls and was always attracted to boys, but I was very confused about what I did feel and why I had had this experience. Am I looking at girls because I'm attracted or because I'm wondering if I'm attracted? I couldn't tell. I had a boyfriend and was attracted to my boyfriend. I'd go back and forth, but it was years before I was able to construct a reality that made me understand such experiences.

Peter started hanging around with Marie, a cute new girl at school. She was one of those girls who made chocolate chip cookies for the boys. She was also in the honor society with Peter, which meant she was a great deal smarter than I was. I'd see her walking with Peter or inviting him to her home, without me. She didn't seem to care that he had a girlfriend. He began spending more and more time with her and less time with me, and though I don't remember us ever breaking up, he became less kind and caring and more distant. This created a lot more confusion for me.

We were still working on the pamphlet project, though he wasn't there much. On summer vacation, he worked in the car factory in Detroit.

As our senior year progressed, even though he was with me, he was also with Marie.

Emotional Breakdown #1

Ski Trip, February 1970 – After a great day on the slopes we were all sitting around, just watching people dance and drink. This abstract thought popped into my head from nowhere, "We are all here, spending time doing what we do until we die. We are doing what we are doing just to kill time and then we die. This is our reality" This one single thought threw me into a tailspin—another tailspin. In that brief moment hope disappeared, and all I can say is I wanted to die. If that's all there is, let me get it over with now! Fears of being homosexual, the betrayal of Dominic and Jan, Peter being my boyfriend, but not; parents being unavailable and now clearly alcoholic; it all came crashing down. I wanted to die. The proverbial two-by-four struck hard! I was down for the count!

This was in the 1960s, not a time of easy access to therapists, counselors or social workers. There was no one to talk with except Peter, and he was becoming less available.

I quit going to church, which put a larger chasm between my mom and me; I quit glee club because of rejection by the teacher and because the spiritual/Christian music sung by our glee club was creating more anxiety, the whole nun thing and all. Somehow, death and church were related; and I stopped most of my school activities because everything was reminding me of my fears, my disconnection, isolation and lack of worth, value and lovability.

I could find no truth, but my own experience. I found no one to talk with. I found relief only by giving up the concept of God and everything the Catholic Church stood for. I gave up the idea that there was anything or anybody outside myself that would help me in anyway. It worked to relieve that suffering. Giving up trusting an authority figure of any sort meant I no longer had to worry about being a nun. That was a huge relief. With a sense of truth found within, my knowing certain, I dealt with internal and external turmoil all by myself.

Soon after, I was home one Sunday morning, when my mom asked if I was going to go to Mass. I couldn't lie. I told her I didn't find any value in going to church, that I wasn't going back.

Telling my mom I wasn't going back to the Catholic Church brought absolute death to my childhood. I faced her eye-to-eye and spoke words that would change our relationship forever. My brothers and sisters who decided not to go to church just stopped going. I don't remember ever hearing her talk to any one of them about their choice not to go to Mass. For some reason, when she confronted me I had to tell her the truth.

There wasn't any discussion about what I believed in. She wasn't interested in what it was like being me choosing to leave the safety and the sanctity of the Church. What she saw was that I was defiant and for that, she was angered and unforgiving. After giving me the evil eye, she walked away and didn't speak to me for three weeks. She didn't know that I felt suicidal, hopeless and lost and that leaving the Catholic Church was my way of following my own truth, to save myself, my life. She just didn't know.

My need to be in integrity with my truth would not allow me to be in a church that did not nourish my soul, which confused and upset me, and where I did not feel understood, nor could get straight answers to my questions.

In some ways, I have always been willful. I have had to live what is true for me, regardless of the outcome. At that age, from a spiritual perspective I became lost; lost enough to want to end my life. My spiritual journey meant casting myself from my family, out on the sea of the unknown, again, unsure of whether I would sink or swim. I released all my ties to anything that smacked of Christianity, the only form of spirituality that I had.

Dark night of the soul also set in, and what made sense at the time was to take on a life of being agnostic, being with "I don't know." I went to a mode that supported a secular structure. No God with a white beard, just a Universe that was vast and beautiful, unfolding from a single explosion, the Big Bang! What my truths were regarding spiritual issues became a non-issue for the next fifteen years.

Carolyn Myss talks about the aspect of our self that needs to confront our tribal authority in order to move into adulthood. We are actually called to do this many times through the cycle of our lives. In the face of what others have spoken as true and to stand toe to toe, face to face and state what is true inside of our selves is courageous at least. It may mean death; it may mean imprisonment. It may mean abandonment, or mean being ostracized, cast out of your family or community.

In the Catholic traditions, martyrs are born the day they die for their religion or spiritual beliefs. In the face of death, they know their God and live in peace, even at the moment of death. The degree to which an individual is willing to know their truth and face the world with that truth demonstrates the degree to which they are willing to live in courage, even fearlessness. The suicide bombers that brought down the World Trade Center on 9/11 died for their beliefs. So did thousands of others. For me, courage is the willingness to act in the face of fear. Fearlessness is a state of being that knows no fear. Tracy Goss and many others speak of dying before going into battle. Letting go of the outcome of our desires and living in peace in the moment, even at the hour of our death.

Parenting is a great venue for practicing truth, courage, wisdom, and patience. All children, at some age, begin to do and say things with which parents disagree. It is an amazing opportunity to distinguish when they are acting as a parent and when they are acting from their unresolved issues. Too often parents are not parenting; they are just being people, people with children, dealing with their day-to-day issues. There is effort and discipline in actually practicing parenting skills, just as there is discipline in practicing any relationship skills, be it management, relationship, or how to be healthy in your body.

When conflicts arise, parents too often go to "I'm right, because I'm the parent and you're wrong because you're a child and don't know any better." There is little room for exploration of ideas, a place where there is no right or wrong, just different points of view. It takes courage for parents and for children to come to this place of intimacy and vulnerability, sharing their view, their truths.

Letting go of power, will, and control issues is a great practice. Living in the possibility of connection and relating, is something all of us desire and long for, but most don't know the way to that place.

I knew I was depressed. I knew I was suicidal. I didn't have a clue how to be in this reality. I felt a pressure in my head. Thinking and hoping it might be a tumor that would explain my fear of being homosexual and the depressed sensations, I asked my dad if I could get an x-ray of my brain. I told him of the sensations I was having of pressure in my brain and that was all that was safe to share. The next day I went into the hospital with him and he set me up for a chest x-ray! A

CHEST X-RAY! I felt so unheard and powerless to get my parents to take me seriously.

The chest x-ray was clean, which somehow proved that I didn't have a brain tumor. I appreciated my dad's attempt to nurse my concerns; however, it did not touch the wounds of isolation, confusion, betrayal and wanting to die. I went about continuing to be in this terrible funk, hoping something would change.

One of the most profound things I ever heard allowed me to understand how I was able to be who I was. I was thirty-four years old and I was at a workshop with Virginia Satir, a great woman, teacher, family therapist and humanitarian. She said that, in dysfunctional families, you are not allowed to think, feel, need or want. Not allowed to think, feel, need or want. Wow! Stunning! This explained why I didn't know my feelings; I had numbed them out in order to be present to others. I rarely argued with people because I came to believe that their point of view was probably more valid and generally mattered more than my point of view.

I had learned not to want things because my wants were generally usurped by my brothers and sisters, and my mom and father. I had learned to be quiet and nice, to swallow my anger, to be pleasing and generous.

It worked for me in so many ways, into my marriage, throughout my marriage and out the other side. But the bottom line was that I lost my self. And, feeling by feeling, thought by thought, want by want and need by need, I'd have to remember.

For the longest time, I didn't want to hear about all of this spiritual woo-woo stuff. I wanted to be at the mercy of God and others, in a good way, of course. I wanted to be a member of a church. I wanted to be a member of a family, to get married and have my husband support me. I wanted to be told what was true and have the faith and conviction that it was the truth.

From a very young age though, the way life appeared didn't support some ideas that must have been pre-established before I came into the world. If you believe in life before birth, you know what I'm talking about. But, the way people were being, mainly family and religious people, did not resonate with the reality of love and compassion that I never questioned.

I was trying to figure out why things were the way they were and not the way I assumed they would be. Why was I confessing sins that I didn't feel were bad? In mass, the congregation asked for mercy and forgiveness. I didn't experience myself needing forgiveness because I hadn't done anything wrong. Why were all of the adults in church asking for forgiveness? "Lord, I am not worthy." I was worthy! I was good, loving and lovable. There were no answers to my questioning mind, for to question the dogma was an indication that I lacked faith and then it became just another sin to be confessed.

How many of us have this deep, deep knowing of our connection with the Divine, but the structure of family, church and community doesn't allow free expression or free exploration of this truth within each of us? My longing to share this loving knowing went unknown and unseen for decades. Eventually finding such an environment where each person's individual reality can be explored authentically allowed me to come to the place of knowing myself and my need to write and articulate the formation of this process, developing what I now know to be called spiritual intelligence.

Like the butterfly that is encased in its cocoon, it needs to push and use effort to work its way out. In that process of relinquishing its home, struggling to liberate itself, blood is coursing through body and wings making them strong and straight. It is strengthening and empowering itself to take flight. If a kind person in their pursuit to help free the butterfly breaks open the cocoon, they will actually participate in killing the butterfly. It needs to fight for its life in order for it to live its full powerful presence, being strong enough to fly vast distances.

All of us, at one time or another, need to fight for our lives. For us to have convictions worth living for, dying for, strengthens our knowing of our truths, our essence. We feel congruent with our authentic self and know we are worthy of our own thoughts, feelings, actions, and beliefs. Depression in our society is an acceptable form of suicide. However, the acts of self-deprecation that brings about depression do not serve our highest good, our highest truth. It veils the light, suffocates and smothers the world of possibility. It dis-empowers the soul and spirit from being heard and heeded. We too need to struggle against the walls of our cocoon to find liberation in the breeze.

College

In 1970, because of my grades in high school and my SAT scores, which were embarrassingly low, I entered Northwestern Michigan College, a junior college in Traverse City, Michigan. It was one of the few schools that accepted me, and it was far enough away from my parents that I had some freedom from the oppressive environment of compromise and suppression of my true self as I only imagined it to be.

I began to find friends again. I worked part-time as a switchboard operator and was a member of the student council. The first two quarters focused on everything except my studies. My depression began to lift; I felt acknowledged and appreciated by teachers, friends and my boss. I was beginning to have fun.

Unexpectedly, one day in December, Peter called. He was missing me and was just calling to say hello. I was lonely and I knew deep down he loved me, so he came up for a weekend. This started the ball rolling again of losing myself not only to his needs and wants, but to my desire to be taken care of, dependent on someone else to tell me what to be and how to be. My short-lived self-reliance fell away. I lost my virginity soon after.

Things didn't last long with Peter, but my weekend visits to see him at Michigan State University (MSU)—three hours away—took me into the magnificence of a huge, vast learning institution that had so much to offer. I fell in love with the campus and knew I wanted to go to school there.

There were complications, of course. My grades were very low and MSU had just changed their policies for allowing first-year students to transfer from junior colleges, unless they were entering into specific three-year programs. That was not me; however, I could attend for one quarter, finish my requirements at a junior college then enter State as a junior.

I took it one-step-at-a-time, hoping that one quarter would lead to two or three quarters. It didn't work that way, because the University had powers greater than my own; they got to decide, not me.

My first quarter at MSU was in the summer. It was beautiful and fun. I had great roommates and within just a couple of weeks, I met the man I would marry, Joshua Black. I was introduced to him and his friends while they were painting the connecting dorms. Though they were all on the fencing team, they were also dope smoking, hippy types, barefoot while listening to The Moody Blues, painting one dorm room after another. This was their summer job, casual and friendly.

I met Joshua one evening when he came to visit Marta who was my suite mate and the Resident Assistant for our dorm. Joshua was nice. Like me, he played tennis. We began hanging out together, but to tell you the truth; we didn't have much in common. He was cute and he was a great fencer; I fell in love with him. That was the limit of my emotional intelligence.

The summer quarter at MSU was ending and the school would not let me enter. They were being true to their word. I had to find another option. I didn't want to return to Traverse City. I loved the environment in East Lansing.

Lansing Community College was close to the University. I applied, was accepted and began school in the fall quarter. I also got a job in a women's clothing store. I had no place to live so I manipulated Joshua into letting me move in with him and his three roommates. This was not a good arrangement as Joshua was already sharing the room with his friend Hank and now he was sharing a single bed with me. I never considered how awkward this was for Hank. I only knew I wanted to make myself indispensible to Josh.

Breast Cancer at Nineteen Years Old

It was a big deal in the 1970s for a girl to go on birth control pills. I was smart in that way, but it was something you wouldn't want your Catholic parents to know, even if your dad was a physician. But I found a lump in my breast. Damn! Nineteen years old with the potential of a life-threatening disease. I had to tell my parents.

Because they were both heavy drinkers (alcoholics) by now, it was necessary to be very strategic. I could only guess what it might look like. I chose to call them soon after I'd figured they had dinner. They would have had a couple of drinks by then, but not enough to be inebriated. When I told them I had a lump in my breast, it somehow became more about that I was sleeping with my boyfriend and on birth control pills. My dad then told me to get off the birth control pills and everything would be fine. I was scolded for being *that* kind of a girl; though at the same time my sister Mary Therese was having sex with her boyfriend on the coach in my parent's house.

Weren't parents supposed to be worried, frightened and concerned for their child's health? None of this appeared in that conversation. Shame, disappointment and dictates, "Get off the pill and stop screwing around." I hated my parents!

I went back to Dr. Beckett, who I had talked with a few years earlier about being homosexual. I told him about the lump and asked him for help, as my dad would not acknowledge a requirement for further concern other than to get off the birth control pills. Dr. Beckett was a little wary about going around my dad. They were neighbors and my dad already hated Dr. Beckett because he'd gone to Harvard Medical School, but he also knew my dad to be the man that he was, and so helped me find a doctor that would help me.

Going to another doctor and to a different hospital meant my dad's wrath. For my own health and well-being, I was willing to take those consequences. The surgeon who helped me said it was a good idea to take a biopsy and or remove what was in my breast. It was one of the few times my mom put aside her differences with me to take me to the hospital, be there for me and bring me home. No further discussions about it, but she did it. She supported me through it quietly, in that too much fuss would have upset my dad even more. The tumor was benign, which was a relief and good for me; however, because it was benign my dad was even angrier for not listening to him and because he was left paying for a surgical procedure and hospital stay with a doctor he didn't know and a hospital that wasn't *his* hospital. After a couple of days at home, I slunk back to East Lansing and into the warm, *caring* arms of my boyfriend.

Joshua hadn't come to the hospital either. This confused me a bit, since he *was* my boyfriend; shouldn't he care enough to drive the short hour to Detroit from East Lansing? I dismissed it as my own self-centeredness.

Twenty years after this occurrence, I was watching an episode of *Beverly Hills 90210*. The main character found a lump in her breast at the same age I had mine. Her parents were right there lovingly with her every step of the way; caring for her in the midst of her fears. Her boyfriend came to the hospital too, telling her how special and important she was. All her friends and family rallied. Every emotional and physical need was responded to with the utmost love and care. It triggered in me my complete sense of invisibility and isolation. My experience was juxtaposed to this character. I had no one to share with. My emotional needs were dismissed as selfish and self-centered. I minimized my sense of trauma and my fears, especially since it turned out to be benign. Big Deal! Watching this TV show allowed a moment of pure grief for that experience that I went through, for my aloneness, my fear, for my truth. I was able to own my pain and heartache. Living vicariously through TV actors can be extremely cathartic and healing sometimes. I was grateful in that moment for having been given a catalyst for release and an opportunity to own what was rightfully mine.

I'm Getting Tired

Joshua graduated that June from MSU, went back to Buffalo to make some money over the summer then off to Europe for three months. That was his gift to himself after finishing his degree.

I was finally accepted to MSU, moved into a dorm room of my own and had a wonderful, ten weeks. I was finally in my element studying psychology, biology and physical education, and riding my bike around this beautiful campus. I felt lighter and freer than I had ever. My depression diminished over the two years essentially away from my parents. My fears of being homosexual subsided, but were still haunting me from time to time. I developed a problem in that I couldn't pee. All of my plumbing worked fine, it just took a really long time to urinate. I knew it was related to anxiety or nerves, but I've never really understood why this particular symptom took hold and stayed with me for many years.

I'd been in school now for nine full quarters—back to back. I'd gotten what I wanted, but I was tired and wanted to take a break. In my limited thinking as a twenty-year-old woman, I saw that I had two options. One was to get married to Joshua; not that he was asking or anything, but that was an option. The second option was to get in my car and drive down to Guatemala to visit Daniel who was working with a Quaker organization, similar to the Peace Corp. Would I drive to Guatemala? I was hardly willing to drive out of Michigan!

Where did this come from—this adventurer willing to dream about something so unique, risky and undoable—driving to Guatemala? But, I felt the aliveness of this plan, that I could actually undertake such a venture. First, I'd go with plan A and see if Joshua wanted to marry me and take care of me for the rest of my life.

When Joshua came home from Europe, I approached him with my ultimatum; marry me or I'm heading down across the border. He said yes to marry me.

I felt how manipulative I was with him, yet at the same time, had he said no I would have probably done something else, probably not drive to Guatemala, as that was completely impossible. But I would have done something adventurous, I have no doubt.

Josh was approached with another ultimatum at the very same time. He had studied to be a physical education teacher. His plan was to find some place he'd like to live and find a school that would hire him where he could teach and coach. But when he returned from Europe he was presented an offer he couldn't refuse. A distant cousin, but dearly close to Joshua's mother, offered Josh and his parents the licensure to an A-1 Hamburger Restaurant in Niagara Falls, Ontario, Canada! Joshua didn't want to do it, but it wasn't an offer he was allowed to refuse. It wasn't an offer if he wasn't in. He decided he wanted to do this for his parents, so together we decided that we would do it for six years. In the mean time, he would think about what he wanted really to do with his life and I being the dutiful wife would follow behind.

I really didn't like the Niagara region. Though there was a great deal of beauty, there was also a great deal of toxic pollution and suburbia that just didn't work for me. I could do it for six years and in the mean time together, we'd dream of what would come next.

While I had the bull by the horns I figured that, I might as well get this whole wedding thing over with. I didn't want to wait. So, within six weeks it was a done deal.

I didn't want to get married in the Catholic Church and I didn't want the hassles my parents would have created had I planned the wedding in Detroit. Instead, I told them we would have the wedding in Buffalo with a Rabi, since Joshua was Jewish. He didn't really care one way or the other, but my parents bought the story and gave up control. Joshua's mom helped me plan the wedding at the Statler Hilton in Buffalo, February 23, 1973.

The weather in Buffalo in February was what it usually was in that part of the country, cold with a lot of snow. We'd had a major snowstorm, which could have caused a lot of people not to attend. All of Joshua's friends from Michigan attended as well as all of his relatives. From my side, all of my brothers and sisters came, so did my parents, my Aunt Laura from California and Vicki Siedlick, my dad's receptionist. Not one of my friends attended—not one. I made excuses that I'd really not known these girls for very long; at least the ones I'd become friends with at MSU, and the weather was challenging, yet Joshua's friends were able to make it. I didn't know what to make of it.

The wedding reception was an unforgettable rip-roaring event. We had so much fun. My dad created a very celebratory event. If nothing else, you could count on him for creating a lot of fun. It was one of those weddings that are talked about years after the marriage itself ends. We just had a fantastic time!

On the other hand, while all the fun was being had, I was suffering from cold feet. What if I'm not happy, I was already uncertain about the outcome. I remember sitting at the bride's table thinking, "Oh, well. If it doesn't work I can just get a divorce."

As long as I kept moving in the direction of the dream, it all would turn out dream-like. It had to … right?

Chapter Two

Marriage

I was one of those women who married a man with the intention of changing him. What potential! What power! What control! What manipulation! If I could find someone who loved me enough to marry me, I could do the rest. This would make up for any lack of love, acceptance and appreciation.

Getting married seemed the safe thing to do. I didn't want to risk not getting married, enduring more isolation in a self-loathing reality. My sisters *had* to wait until their mid to late twenties before they found the right guy to marry. My competitive nature, at that time, wanted to beat them to the altar. I loved Joshua and he loved me. He was willing to marry me; that's all I really knew and that's all that really mattered. I was about as unconscious as any young girl can get (anesthetized would be the better word for it).

1973: Marriage over Self-Exploration – Age Twenty

For the first three months, we lived in Buffalo, while Joshua and his dad went for training in Chicago to learn to be an A-1 Hamburger Restaurant owner. I found a job working in a department store selling women's clothing. When Joshua and I were alone in our apartment, I distanced myself from him. I used the restrained affection that I had picked up from my mom. I wouldn't let myself relax and enjoy this fresh new relationship; however, when we would visit his parents I was affectionate, playful and connecting. I don't know about Joshua, but I was confusing myself with this almost Jekyll and Hyde routine. I figured I had better figure this out; did I love him or not? I decided that I did and began being more consistently affectionate and connecting.

When the paperwork was accepted for our Canadian residency, we moved across the border to Niagara Falls. We found a two-bedroom apartment in a tall white building overlooking the Meyers High School football field. As independent as I had been for most of my life, I rarely went out of that apartment for the first few months. For some reason I was terrified to go out by myself. I remember being lonely, just waiting for Josh to come home. It took weeks to get myself out even for just a walk. Once I became acclimated, I started to get out on my own.

I took a job at A-1 Hamburger as a cashier. Here I was the wife of the owner of the A-1 Hamburger restaurant and I worked as a cashier. It gave me something to do and allowed me to be more connected to Josh, who was at the restaurant for twelve to fourteen hours per day on average. Working as a cashier didn't last long. My independent nature had me thinking how I could make things better around the store—a real no-no in such a corporate environment. The other thing was that someone was stealing money out of my till and it seemed like this whole idea of me working there wasn't such a good idea after all.

I decided it was time to finish my bachelor's degree at Brock University, which was only a short distance away in the neighboring city of St. Catherines. I was able to transfer the majority of my credits. Because we moved to a bilingual country it made sense for me to learn French; however, my language skills were horrible and I just about flunked that course. I was a horrible student back then. I felt like I was doing my best, yet I just wasn't able to make the grades. I finished all the requirements for my degree and ended up with a BA in Psychology after another year and a half of studies; it only took four different academic institutions to do so.

My parents came to Niagara Falls for my graduation. It was then that my mom shared with me that when I was a senior in high school, Mr. Parkhurst, my history teacher, told her that I wasn't college material and not to push me in that direction. I was somewhat shocked that my mom had been respectful with my desire to go to school and that she didn't share with me this tidbit of information until then. I was grateful for that. My dad, however, put the kibosh on the celebration by getting horribly drunk, enough so that he had to go back to their hotel. They left early the next morning.

Daniel Beckett Returns

I continually struggled to find peace and acceptance in my relationship with Joshua. I wasn't fulfilled in my role as a wife or even as a friend. We didn't really have a friendship, as I know a friendship could be. I fantasized about separating all the time and had actually threatened to leave twice within the first two years. I didn't really know any other way to be with my circumstance. There wasn't any change so what's a person to do, but to threaten to leave?

At twenty-two, while visiting my parents on Grosse Ile for a family reunion, Daniel was back from Guatemala to visit his folks. I gave him a call to see if he wanted to play some tennis. We sat on the bench after he won the first set and we began to talk; it was the first time ever that we had a real conversation. We talked about all of the years of me having a crush on him, and he admitted he had a crush on me too, but because I was younger, his sister's best friend and because I was quite naïve, he couldn't date me. It was one of those moments where the truth set me free. At the same time, I wondered how much pretending went on for Daniel in those high school years. I wondered what it would have been like if he had allowed himself to like me, to be friends and spend sweet, gentle time together.

That weekend Daniel and I spent a lot of time together—real time. We let ourselves enjoy the company of the other without any obstacles, pretense and aloofness. My dream came true to connect with Daniel after years of fantasizing. Yes, we slept together, but it wasn't the pinnacle of the weekend; the mad and passionate lovemaking kind of moment we see in movies. It was just really nice to fulfill that connection that both of us had for at least ten years. The day after day longing for him was satisfied. We were natural with each other; it felt as I always imagined it to be, comfortable and engaging.

This was the only time I committed an indiscretion during my marriage to Joshua. I never carried any guilt or remorse about this weekend with Daniel. I just didn't. It was as if Joshua and I had yet to seal our marriage in a way that I would have felt the deep devotion I hoped to have felt. From my experience, Joshua didn't treat me as if he were devoted to me either. I felt extremely lonely from the onset of our marriage and no matter how many conversations we'd have, that never changed.

I went back to Niagara Falls to be in my marriage and Daniel went to graduate school in California. A sense of completion occurred that weekend and my crush on Daniel vanished. It felt clean and done.

At night, much like the dreams I continually had of Outward Bound, my dreams of Daniel went on for another six years. When I left my marriage, the dreams of Daniel began to subside.

Cultivating Independence – Somewhat

After I graduated from University, I got a job working at the YWCA as a residential manager. My title was actually Housemother, but I was only twenty-two years old. The residents were women who couldn't live on their own. In addition, there were women who were using the space as a hostel. It was a good place to start my career in psychology. I knew nothing about real people. It's interesting how little a BA in psychology prepares you for being with people.

The first A-1 Hamburger of Niagara Falls was on Lundy's Lane. Three years later, Joshua opened up a second restaurant on the other side of town. He was working non-stop, always feeling he needed to be at one store or the other. When he wasn't working, he was playing basketball, baseball or watching sports on TV. I was busy with school, then my job, and then being a wife, but not a very good one. When Joshua was living with his parents, his mom would fix his breakfast, lunch and dinner. She washed and ironed his clothes. I was happy to do that for him if he was willing to do the same for me. He wasn't. So, his clothes were wrinkled and he made his own breakfast, which became easy once A-1 Hamburger began serving breakfast.

There was so much that we hadn't discussed before we got married. We had no idea what we were getting into. I had assumptions and he had assumptions and most of the time they were not in alignment.

I didn't know that I would want to talk with my husband about stuff; I didn't know that he wouldn't want to talk about stuff. I wanted to talk about feelings and emotions. He didn't. He liked reading the newspaper and watching or playing sports. I didn't. We played tennis sometimes, but other than that, we had very little in common.

Our communication styles didn't work well together either. We couldn't seem to grow our relationship. When we had problems or arguments, I ended up apologizing just to make things better. We both turned a blind eye to our lack of ability to work out the wrinkles in our relationship and continued with the business of building a business and building a family.

When I had threatened to leave Joshua a couple of times in those first few years, he promised to change and so did I. Slowly though we went back to the way that it was. The hope that things would get better spurred me on to keep trying and as unhappy as I was, I couldn't figure out how to leave. I figured too that perhaps once we had children things would change, and they did, sort of.

Home

Owning a home was the second step to creating a family. Months after moving to Niagara Falls, once I got myself out of the apartment, I began looking for a house. After our first year in Niagara Falls, we bought a wonderful three-bedroom, Tudor-style house on Dorchester Road. The house was just minutes from the restaurant. We had a wonderful back yard with a deck and many trees. It was the perfect size house for a budding family.

I spent a lot of my time painting and working around the home. Gardening and puttering made me happy. As long as I was busy making a home, things were fine enough. But really, I wasn't happy. I didn't have a partner who loved to be around me, who wanted to do what I wanted to do, who had a capacity to explore ideas and talk about feelings and emotions. And as much as I tried to make him that man, well, it just didn't work.

Children

I wanted children for as long as I could remember. Three years into the marriage, the stage was set and the nest was prepared; I was ready to get pregnant!

One of Joshua's basketball buddies, Les Pottersfield invited us over for dinner to meet his wife Pam. They had a darling little girl, Melanie, who was the catalyst for the whole baby thing in earnest for Josh and me. She was so cute and Les and Pam were enjoying parenthood so much. They inspired us to get started with making babies.

Babies over Marriage – Twenty-Three to Twenty-Five

At the A-1 Hamburger's Convention in Chicago, Joshua and I made a baby! I always knew this was the night that Hannah was conceived. Sometimes you just know these things. Finally, I was going to have what I dreamed. I was going to have a baby of my own.

I joined the La Leche league to learn all about breastfeeding, and later along in the pregnancy Josh and I went to Lamaze classes, as I wanted my children to be born naturally. I never got the feeling that Joshua was really into it. Like many husbands and fathers-to-be, it was a matter of dragging him along to the meetings. Again, we didn't talk about things. I just set about making things happen.

Something that was extremely important to me was doing whatever I needed to do to ensure my children wouldn't be subjected to the abuse of Catholicism or even Christianity as I had been. There are children and adults who'd experienced much worse than I had, and I just didn't want that for my own children. Joshua was ambivalent about this, his family was not practicing their faith of Judaism, but he was willing to go along with my choice. To me, it just seemed like a safer spiritual tradition in which to raise my children. Go figure!

I was five months pregnant when I was informed that the mother had to be Jewish in order for the baby to be born Jewish. I had to act quickly in order to ensure I was officially converted before Hannah was born. The process of converting to Reformed Judaism was the route I took and quite honestly, I found far greater connection with the Jewish faith than with Christianity. Though I rarely followed through with any spiritual practice in relation to Judaism, I've never regretted that decision. I believe it has given my children a very strong spiritual foundation from which to choose to explore their own beliefs and truth.

I loved every minute of my pregnancy, even through the morning sickness. I stayed active with walking and jogging and ate healthy foods. I kept my weight down, as I just couldn't face months of work to get the excess weight off after the baby was born. This was always important to me, to keep my girlish figure. And at the same time, I didn't starve myself in any way. I wanted my child to be healthy!

My water broke two weeks earlier than was expected though, according to my calculations, from that night in Chicago I was right on time. Hannah was born about ten hours later at 6:00 a.m. January 14. I was in labor only five hours. Though I'd hoped to go without any pain medication, I ended up with an epidural because my perineum was ripping, which meant Dr. Ainslie had to make an incision in order to make room for Hannah to come through.

She was a perfect little girl, with ten toes and ten fingers. What fun to bring this child into the world. All of the wishing, hoping and dreaming had come to fruition. My life was now complete.

After four days in the hospital, we took Hannah home; however, after just a couple of days, because her bilirubin count was significantly high and she looked quite jaundice, we had to admit her back into the hospital where she stayed in an incubator for another four days.

Hannah was a feisty one. She had to have patches on her eyes because of the constant light of the incubators. Hand mittens became necessary because she kept pulling off the patches. This made her frustrated and angry. The nurses tried swaddling her, wrapping her tightly to keep her arms and hands down, but she would have none of that. They constantly had to wrangle with her. She was a child that wanted her freedom from the get go!

While in the hospital, she was cared for during the night by the nurses. This allowed me sleep, for which I was very grateful. I knew what a gift this was for a new mother to be able to sleep through the night. I took advantage of it, believe me, but I was also back at the hospital again at 6:00 a.m. ready for Hannah's first feeding of the day. I couldn't wait to be with her. She gave me a reason to be alive.

One of the most wonderful experiences in the world is breast-feeding. I wish every woman could have a successful breastfeeding relationship with her child, as I did with Hannah. I felt important and needed. I felt complete in that I was fulfilling what I came here to do. I loved the connection, the bonding, the nurturing of both of us. It didn't matter if it was day or night. And on the rare occasion when I'd feel a little lonely, I'd wake her up to nurse; this gave me great comfort too. I was happy!

She liked activity and wasn't interested in being put down in her crib to sleep. As long as she was being held and around people she'd be asleep, but as soon as we'd put her down in her crib she'd begin to cry and wouldn't stop until we picked her up again. My experience is that there is no right way for new parents to handle this situation. Too many experts had conflicting opinions about whether to let babies cry themselves to sleep or whether to soothe them. We decided to soothe her and were happy to do so.

When he was around, Joshua was wonderful with Hannah. If I couldn't get her settled down by nursing or cuddling he would take her and patiently walk with her around the house until she fell asleep. He's always had a way with her.

I was excited to create activity with Hannah. I couldn't wait to do all of those fun things a parent can to do with their children. I registered us for swimming classes at the YMCA when she was just three months old. My understanding was that the earlier you start children swimming the less fear they experience when going underwater. She was a natural. Even with a nose full of water, she didn't seem to mind.

At these Gym and Swim classes, I met Margaret Dunker and her daughter Alison, who was born just three days before Hannah. We became best of friends. Margaret wasn't breastfeeding Alison, but aside from that, we were both on schedule for having babies. We were also going to the same pediatrician, Dr. Ainslie. Margaret and I have had a lasting friendship from then on.

Willing and Ready for Baby Number Two

I wanted to get pregnant again as soon as I could. I wanted my children close together. Joshua didn't have much to say about any of this, as I recall. I had my own timeline for things to unfold. I was on a mission to build myself a life that would be fulfilling and satisfying. To me, Joshua and I were more like roommates than what I imagined to be like as a married couple; he was on his schedule with his priorities—the restaurants, his parents and his own activities—I came after all of that. I had my own schedule—the kids came first, then Joshua and then me.

When nursing, a woman's menstruation generally doesn't occur, and there is less likelihood of getting pregnant. When Hannah was about eight months old, I thought I was pregnant again; I thought I could feel a baby moving inside of me already, which meant I would have been about four months pregnant. When I went to the doctor, (Dr. Ainslie was away) to confirm the good news, he told me I wasn't pregnant. He called it a hysterical pregnancy. He didn't say anything else. He didn't suggest I see a shrink nor do anything about the fact that I fabricated a psychosomatic pregnancy. I was somewhat embarrassed and felt there was really no need in telling anyone about it, aside from Joshua and I don't remember us talking about what it was that would have me construct this pregnancy. I just pretty well kept it to myself and continued to try to get pregnant. It was another eight months before I was officially pregnant with baby number two, Noah.

As much as I loved the house in which we lived, it became obvious that the street it was on was a very busy thoroughfare and there were rumors that they were going to be widening the streets in the next year or so. I was concerned about raising children on a busy street. Coming from my home on Grosse Ile, where very few cars would pass by our house on any given day I wanted to recreate that sense of country and safety for my children and myself.

I began working with a realtor. I told her I was looking for a house that was unique, that I hated subdivisions. More often than not, when driving through subdivisions I'd get lost, going around and around and not being able to get out! Because of the restaurant, Joshua wanted to stay in town as opposed to the more rural areas toward which I tended to gravitate.

The realtor told me about a house that had an acre and a half of land. It was one hundred years old and was the original farmhouse of the acreage that now was a subdivision. When we drove up in front of it, I was certain she had made a mistake and that we should be pulling up in front of the next house. No. This was the one!

The driveway was about five hundred feet long and the landscaping was beautiful. The house was white stucco with a beautiful closed in porch and a balcony above it. The house sat in the middle of the property surrounded by subdivision, but I felt like I could live here with all of the trees and space. It was the closest thing to Grosse Ile I could find in the middle of Niagara Falls.

It was only $100,000 (this was in 1977) and for a person who owned A-1 Hamburger Restaurant—soon to be two A-1 Hamburger Restaurants—it was perfect. It was the kind of house someone of Joshua's stature should be living in. I convinced him of the value and what a wonderful place it would be to raise children. He had to talk with his parents to see what they thought. Since they were partners in the business, they were partners in almost every aspect of our lives. We all figured out how to make it happen. The house was ours!

For the next few years, I worked at peeling off layer upon layer of wallpaper. It was curious to see all of the different manifestations this house had gone through over the years. Now I was putting my own imprint on it too. I was making a home and that seemed to be all that mattered.

While married to Joshua, there were times I'd thought about going back to school, but Joshua would remind me that we agreed I would raise the children for six years and then I could go back to school or work. As I said, we didn't have the kind of marriage where we talked things out. I did the things I did, controlled the things I could control. Much like my parents, I'd say what I wanted, then he would say what he wanted, and that was the end of the conversation.

Quite often though, I would find a way to do what I wanted to do, hoping it wouldn't stir the pot too much and upset Joshua. His response could not be anticipated. His frustrations and anger came out in subtle, passive ways. He never yelled or even acknowledged that he was angry. Instead, as he'd walk out the door to go to work he would say something that left a upsetting, stinging feeling, almost imperceptible, but boy, did it hurt! It was his way of avoiding open, honest expression of his own truth. I'm sure this was a required survival strategy for him while growing up in his own family.

Me? I collected enough emotional baggage that when I just couldn't stand it any longer I'd dump it on him all at once. I'd tell him I could no longer be with the lack of communication, lack of affection and connection, the isolation, the boredom and the loneliness. I'd go visit my parents in Grosse Ile, which would inevitably make me glad I was returning to my home in Niagara Falls.

During my pregnancy with Noah, I again got very close to leaving Joshua—the closest yet. His lack of presence and partnership and my loneliness became unbearable. I remember being in Hannah's closet, stealthily pulling out infant clothing while Joshua was asleep. My plan was to leave the next morning. I called my parents and told them I was coming home. When Joshua woke up, I told him that I was leaving to go to my parent's home. As you can imagine, he was surprised and sad.

I remember that day, watching Joshua through the window, pushing Hannah in the carriage one last time before we'd leave for Detroit the next day. He was so unhappy. This was my fourth and most serious attempt at leaving in four years. With a two-year-old and second child just months away, I must have been desperate to consider such an act.

I don't remember the details of the switcho-chango. I just remember hanging up the phone after talking with my parents and sobbing uncontrollably. They convinced me to try one more time. They had talked with Joshua and were sure he was serious about being more available and present to the relationship. I was exhausted and I was devastated.

I don't ever remember being in such despair. I felt lost and trapped in a relationship with someone who didn't have any idea what marriage and partnerships were about. He was twenty-six and I was twenty-four. Neither of us had the tools to talk deeply enough to truly understand what was required to make this marriage work. I could only hope that something would change.

It takes an incredible amount of energy to raise oneself up in order to make such a declaration—I'm leaving. The months or years of that inner dialog of what's true and not true; what's real and what am I making up; how do I be with things as they are or make changes so things are better for us all? Endless hours trying to work things out in my head, since I couldn't seem to work them out with Joshua. How could I change, what did I need to do differently—on and on and on.

I don't know that I had any other choice but to try again. I went back to focusing on motherhood and our home life and trying to be happy in my marriage.

Four months later, Noah was born. His birth was even easier, only four hours of labor. Dr. Anslie knew I'd been involved with La Leche League and Lamaze and that I wanted the least amount of intervention. He asked if I minded if some nurses came in to witness a natural childbirth process. Again, I had to have an episiotomy and an epidural. In addition, Noah had high a bilirubin count, but stayed in the hospital just one extra day.

Noah was a very different individual than his sister Hannah. His nature was more subdued and quiet. Even now as grown adults, their ways of being in the world truly contrast each other. Hannah is a headstrong Capricorn. She's independent, tenacious and a social extravert. She always had friends—even today, she is connected to her high school friends as if they were sisters. Where Hannah goes out, Noah goes in and isolates into TV, music and books. He played rugby and football in high school. Both were in drama, music and dance class, but this was and is Noah's true calling. Noah is a laid-back Aquarian. His aloof nature makes him seem unreachable, yet when he's willing, he is social and fun loving. He's deep and spiritual in his laid-back way. I trust him in many ways I've never trusted any other human being.

In anticipating Noah's birth, we told Hannah early about how she would be having a new baby to play with. She was so excited! Once he was born though, an evilness showed up that was phenomenal to watch. She would scrunch Noah's face with her little two-year-old fingers, her face looking as if she wished she could rip him off the face of the Earth. Once I caught her trying to push him out of the car. I'd read about this sort of thing happening between the first and second child. Punishment didn't work, but reason did. A book called *Children the Challenge* by Rudolph Dreikurs, was the best book I ever found for raising children; even infants.

The premise of Dreikurs book was built upon the natural consequences of people's actions and inaction. It gave children more responsibility for choices they make—even at two years old. Using this method shifted the level of frustration Hannah was demonstrating and the level of frustration I was feeling with her defiance. We all calmed down and had a lot more fun. Thank God, for the wisdom that comes through books.

My Life was Perfect, but I was Depressed

Depression set in slowly as I realized at age twenty-five that I had the whole dream package together. I had my house, my children, my dog and all of the security and stability I had dreamed of. I realized I had nothing to look forward to until Hannah's wedding. She was only two years old. What would I do with my life for the next twenty or thirty years? I scared myself in that moment. I really didn't know what the rest of my life would look like.

I should have been happy. I'd worked so hard to make things happy. I was really happy as a mom, but there was no life force, no stimulation or fulfillment in my marriage with Joshua. There was no connection or real partnership, no real communication or respect. Neither of us knew how to listen to each other, respect each other's points of views, needs or wants. We were in our mid-twenties, acting like grownups, but being children. I never knew if he felt any less lonely than I did. He must have.

Joshua was really a pawn in my game to set up house. Though I did love him, I didn't know how to love him, accepting him for who he was, how he was. Instead, I focused on what annoyed and aggravated me, what needed to be changed or fixed in order to make me happy.

Being so controlling of Joshua, trying to force him to be what I wanted him to be, only made him more resistant and uninterested. Go figure!

Self over Marriage

Imagine attempting to leave a marriage five times in five years, from a really nice guy that everyone likes, who isn't abusive and isn't addicted to anything. I just could not find a way of relating that filled my heart and soul or that nourished a quality of being that I required. Joshua was a good husband in that his intention was to provide for his family, but he worked seven days a week, came home late regularly, read the newspaper and watched sports. This may sound somewhat normal for some marriages and if it works, don't fix it. It just didn't work for me.

In my experience, there is nothing lonelier than being in a disconnected marriage or partnership. It was very much like being enmeshed in my family all over again. I had no one to talk with, to hear me or care or to listen. The words "I love you" were thrown about daily, like bones to a dog, with no meat on them; there was little substance. It wasn't followed up with meaningful sharing or acts of kindness. I had found a husband who related in the same way my parents related. My lenses were perfect for finding the perfect picture, yet it disguised the dysfunction with which both Joshua and I were living. Each of us

carried symptoms of unloved childhoods, seeking love from people who were not any more capable to create a healing, loving environment. Both Joshua and I entrenched ourselves in this marriage as a way of hiding from the pain of healing.

Joshua Commits an Indiscretion

In our fifth year of marriage, I was informed by Joshua's sister and brother-in-law that they discovered Joshua with another woman in a broom closet at the restaurant. Joshua denied it at the time; however, too much evidence added up to another woman.

What do you do when your husband flat out denies something that was witnessed by someone who would have no reason to fabricate such a story? I pretended to believe Joshua, to the point that I went numb or perhaps into denial, though in my body I knew something wasn't right. What else could I do? The human mind and heart has such an incredible capacity to reorient itself to the given circumstance. The mind has the capacity to make believe based on whatever we tell ourselves is real. I shut down in so many ways, especially to my own truth in order to live in a world that aside from my children was empty and unfulfilling.

As it turned out, he was having an affair and when he admitted it, he said it was only sexual and that it was only one weekend. I knew the flirtations and broom closet events were occurring over more than a weekend, but what good does it do to try to be right. Pointing the finger, blaming or shaming really adds up to very little. In the end, it didn't matter. He wasn't any happier than I was and where I sought comfort with my children, he sought comfort from another woman. I totally got it! One way is okay; the other is not.

For whatever time this affair existed, Joshua found himself with someone who could see him for who he was. She was able to relate to him for all of his intelligence, charm and kindness. She could see what I couldn't see. He and I were both lost and alone in our marriage. We were both attempting to be seen and heard, witnessed and loved. No matter how much we wanted it to work out it wasn't working out.

I was so afraid of losing what I didn't want, without losing the stability and security I did want. As I said, I went into denial about what was really true.

From a spiritual perspective, the setup was more perfect than I could imagine. I entered into this relationship thinking Joshua was going to be a gym teacher. And, here it turns out he owns two A-1 Hamburger restaurants. The *potential* for wealth was tremendous. I say potential because though the image of success was there, we weren't allowed to live as though we actually were wealthy. We always had to pinch and save where we could. There was no extravagance or luxury. We were comfortable enough, yet quite often, I felt guilty for wanting what I wanted, in terms of buying things for the house or for the children.

A Catalyst for Leaving

In December of my twenty-sixth year, life began to get really messy, which is a requirement for transfiguration and transformation to occur. Who knew?

Joshua and I attended a large Christmas gathering that was hosted by the culinary school in Niagara Falls. Our friend, Cindy was one of the student chefs. We went to support her and enjoy a night out on the town. We were dressed in gowns and suits. Joshua wasn't the type that liked to dress up; he was uncomfortable in a suit. So, this was a rare occasion for me to put on a long slinky dress and be treated to a fancy meal, dancing and a beautiful view of the Falls.

In one quick flash of a moment, life as I'd known it was over. A shiny Prince Charming-type man walked into the room and as I looked at him I said inside my head "That's the kind of man I've been looking for all my life!" I truly believe I fell in love with the *suit* as opposed to the fellow in the suit. I couldn't have known the quality of the individual since we'd never met, but I certainly liked the way he dressed. I'd never heard our mutual friend Cindy speak about him. All I knew was what I created in my mind—that he was very shiny and clean and had a smile that woke me up.

"You look beautiful," he whispered in my ear. It wasn't Joshua who spoke these words. It was this strange new shiny individual, Sam. Flirtation! Wow! It made my head spin. My husband hadn't told me I looked beautiful, not like that, anyway; nor was there much flirtation in our relationship. Those words in my ears did something to me. They allowed me to remember that I was a woman; a beautiful woman, who wanted to feel adored and cherished.

Sam didn't smell like French fries and hamburgers. He didn't have on the blue A-1 Hamburger uniform. He represented everything that I tried to make Joshua into charming, sophisticated and playful. Joshua, now at sixty years old, is still a very handsome man and is charming when he wants to be, but when we were married, he wasn't interested in being the spit, polish and sophisticated type that seemed undistinguishable from Sam. I worked very hard to change Joshua into a Sam-looking man and it wasn't working.

During the next few months, Sam visited his friend Cindy and me. It then became very clear; for the past six years, I'd been manipulating and strategizing to get Joshua to be someone other than Joshua. All my hoping and wishing, my frustration and expectations created so much suffering for both of us. It's a horrible thing to do to any individual—not accept him as he was. He would never be anything, but who he was, at least with me as his wife. This was probably the moment I stepped out of the fantasy of how the dream was suppose to go, and stepped into a mature reality and decided to end the marriage.

I wanted to stop punishing Joshua for being Joshua. It wasn't fair to him, nor to me. I realized I didn't love him enough; enough to keep trying to accept him as he was. There was so much that was missing for both of us. We didn't have the glue to hold us together. Though many couples hope that children will be the glue, rarely is it enough, especially when they don't have the internal resources to relate with each other in a way that is nurturing and fulfilling. I certainly didn't have it and at that point, my experience was that Joshua didn't have it either.

Sam was the catalyst for the separation. He was the serpent who offered me the apple of truth. Eden's gates opened to me—I was walking out alone.

When I told Sam in essence, I was leaving Joshua; he wasn't ready for that news. In actuality, he had been playing a game of seduction with a married woman. Fun for him, fun for her, until it became something else. He was twenty-three; I was twenty-six with two children. He had no real interest in developing something deeper with me. For me though, he seemed to be what I'd been seeking all along. Whether he liked it or not I was leaving my marriage and he was my fantasy man *incarnate*.

In the Present Moment

As I write this, in the autumn of 2010, thirty-two years after the fact, feelings begin to surface. I thought I was done with all of this. The experience of not knowing the truth, the confusion and the disorientation on the surface imbued with sadness, vulnerability, not being able to trust, not being happy, wanting the happily ever after, and struggling to keep my head above water emotionally, with the potential drowning in the betrayal.

You can't write about the circumstances of your past without bursting bubbles of emotions that for decades have been out of sight and out of mind. The residuals of those past events spill out all over today. I see the elements that repeat themselves, relationship after relationship, decade after decade. It becomes apparent that I'm only a victim to my own resistance, to my own patterns of thoughts and to my beliefs. I'm also a victim to all of the emotions embedded in my cellular structure that have me continually pulled by the undertow toward the dark, rich qualities of being that I've neglected, avoided and denied forever. Emotions begin to release and press their way out of hiding in order to be witnessed, acknowledged and released.

This story telling reveals a great deal to me as the author and the teller of this story. I gain awareness. The process of purging old energy patterns that have been the catalyst for all of the thoughts and body sensations I've been living with this lifetime and believed to be real reveals something else. It's as though I'm seeing for the first time the extremely fine print found at the bottom of a contract that says, "In order to really and truly have the life you want you must abandon hope that the way you are going about your life will actually bring you to your dreams."

I didn't see it. I didn't see that paragraph when I signed on for this life. And now it's too late to renege. I've come too far in this process of writing this autobiographical piece to turn back. The writing and the writer are now one and the same.

It is becoming a time for introspection and far more solitude than I anticipated as I begin to be the partner to myself I've always wanted. I listen beyond my comfort level and I realize that within this activity of writing is an emergence process. I'm coming out from beneath the cloak of illusions I've clutched to forever. Do I really have to abandon hope?

Leaving the Last Time

It wasn't as though I walked out of the house without my children, never to see them again. And it wasn't as though I moved out of our house and into Sam's house. There were months of unfolding events and time for discernment that brought about my decision to leave the children with Joshua. Once I realized that my way of being in this marriage was actually destroying any love that was there and realizing how much energy I was putting toward changing Joshua because there wasn't enough fulfillment within the partnership between us, I decided it was over. This moment came after long sleepless nights—in the silent, quiet, uninterrupted space of aloneness. I had time to think and truly be with what was true. It was a time to weigh my own feelings and discern all of the pieces of the relationship I'd been in. After years of unfulfilled, self-deprecating practices it took three weeks before that moment came when the complete truth revealed itself to me. After six years of struggling I knew this time, I was going to leave.

There is never a right time to tell someone it's over. There is only that moment when somehow the courage rises up and sustains itself long enough to meet the challenge.

After the decision was made, it took another three weeks before I told Joshua I was leaving with the children. The words came out of my mouth awkwardly. Though I'd told him five times before that I was unhappy and wanted to leave, he never took me seriously. It was though he had never understood that I'd been so unhappy. It was as though he'd never heard me say how unhappy I was; it was as though I had never attempted to leave so many times. It was as though it couldn't be true.

I told him about my plan to take Hannah and Noah back to Michigan. We'd stay with my parents until I was registered at Michigan State where I'd go back for my master's degree and the children could go to the day care there. It felt like a solid plan that I was happy with. I'd yet to tell my parents this plan or their part in it. My brother Michael with his two daughters had been living with them for four years. He'd just moved out months before into his own home. It's one thing to tell my husband I'm leaving and another to tell my parents I'm moving in.

It was interesting to watch the process unfold. I remember thinking that making the decision to leave was the hardest part of the process. Then telling Joshua became the hardest part; then packing the children's things became the hardest part; then loading the car and finally, pulling out of the driveway. Each step in the process was the hardest. None of it was easy. The process didn't let up until I drove out of the driveway, children in tow, feeling finished and complete.

We moved into my parents' large home while they were off at the Kentucky Derby, an annual event for them. My siblings weren't glad to see me. They didn't support me in leaving, even though they all knew for all those years I wasn't happy. Michael, who just moved out was most against me moving into Mom and Dad's house. "You're going to kill them!" He yelled at me. How could he be so against the very thing that he'd been allowed to do? He had the love and support of his parents. Couldn't I be allowed the same level of support from mine?

The piece that I didn't get was the Sam element. I saw him as the catalyst, a friend that allowed me to get clarity. Everyone else saw him as the villain who had murdered my marriage. They saw me as irresponsible and negligent as a wife.

The fact is, when I chose to move to Michigan I had no real thoughts of including Sam in my life anymore. I had to make a life for my children and me. I didn't see him as part of the picture from here on.

I began to wake up to the level to which they were all asleep; they had never really heard me or taken me seriously that I was as unhappy as I was. It didn't seem to matter how unhappy I'd been and how I'd struggled to find a reality that would make this marriage good and healthy. It didn't matter. They judged my actions as wrong and bad. They couldn't listen and they couldn't hear. I felt alone in the midst of this group of individuals, my brothers and sisters.

Because I wasn't getting support from anyone at home, I called the only individual who seemed to care. I called Sam. He drove four hours to comfort me. He came down, arriving late in the evening. Already I could hear my controlling nature. My expectation was that he would arrive around 6:00 p.m., but instead he showed up around 10:00 p.m. These were the days before cell phones, so there was no way to communicate unless he called by pay phone.

Having someone to hear me was wonderful, someone who really seemed to care and listen. It was the first time Sam and I slept together. There was no intercourse due to an inability to create an erection on Sam's part. That was truly fine with me.

I allowed myself to feel complete in his arms. I remember feeling that I could die now, having felt whole with the level of connection I experienced that night. He left the next day; however, as I experienced the essence of Sam as this loving caring individual the other side of Sam also started to appear. Before he left, I asked if he would watch Hannah and Noah, while I took a shower. He looked at me as if he didn't understand. I was asking something of him and he didn't take me seriously, and the kids kept trying to get into the bathroom. I just wanted a few moments to shower. He didn't get it. No one was getting it!

After Sam left, out of the blue, Joshua and Cindy turned up with our dog, Winston. They had concocted a plan that Cindy would stay with the kids while Joshua swept me off to some hotel with hopes of working things out. With my parents arriving the next day there's no way I'd let Cindy be here when they arrived. And, hadn't I made myself clear with Joshua that it was over? Wasn't anyone *listening* to me?

So, instead, Joshua and I went upstairs and had a heart to heart. I told him in more detail than ever before everything that wasn't working in the marriage. He seemed to hear me and take it all really well. I told him about all of the little idiosyncrasies that bugged me, his parents always around, his hating my cooking, always being late, his loss of hearing, never being home and when he was home he was reading the newspaper, watching TV or unavailable in the bathroom. I said it all and felt he had heard me and understood I was done.

As an attempt to create reconciliation, Joshua confessed his affair with Cindy. By then I really didn't care anymore and I totally understood what he was needing, but couldn't give to him. I didn't have any need to make him wrong or to shame or blame him for the end of our marriage. And, though we loved each other, in my mind we just weren't compatible.

After hours of talking, he agreed to let me go, but suggested I come back to Niagara Falls until we worked things out. He didn't want me at Michigan State University, so far away with the children. He said we would work things out in a good way. I agreed to come back to Niagara Falls, but not to reconcile the marriage. He understood. With all of that said and done, Josh, Cindy and Winston left. I was relieved to have had that conversation, to feel understood and accepted. It felt mature on both our parts to look at ways to collaborate in this separation. It felt clean and healthy.

My parents' arrival the next day was not full of care and concern for their daughter and grandchildren. They were angry. They didn't remember how hard I tried to stay in this marriage after they convinced me to stay the last time. Again, the Sam factor disturbed them. They didn't get that no one was listening to me, and that I had to create this strange man to facilitate a change in my life for the better! All they could see was that I was having an affair and was being self-centered. I left the next day with Noah and Hannah and headed back to Niagara Falls, back to their home and their own little beds.

Come into My Web, said the Spider to the Fly

Once home, Joshua suggested we see a marriage counselor. While I was away, he had spoken with some friends of ours who were counselors, and they recommended a particular therapist they respected. I felt trapped into saying yes to seeing a therapist. This was his way of trying to get me to stay in the marriage. I was angry. I felt manipulated and so frustrated. I thought he understood that there was no more room for possibility.

Because I felt trapped, since we hadn't tried everything yet, I said I would go to therapy, but I was extremely clear that I wasn't going to work on the marriage. I agreed to go to work on myself and if in the process I wanted to come back into the marriage, I would do that.

In the therapy session, I was adamant about my position. I was so clear that I no longer wanted to be in this marriage, the therapist was clear that couple's therapy wasn't what was needed. So, I began going by myself to work on me. Joshua stopped going as he thought it was I who had the problems. I really, really hoped that what would unfold would allow me to want to stay married to Joshua, but by this time I was so done, it would take a miracle to turn things around.

Somewhere in the mess, Joshua offered me a deal; if I stayed for six months and tried working things out in the marriage, then chose to leave, I could leave with the children and all the money I would need to support myself and the children. If I left now I'd go without children and support.

I cannot tell you where this switcho-changeo maneuver came from. That wasn't in the conversation we had at my parent's home. And I can't tell you why I bought into it. I don't know why I didn't tell him to … well you know. I just can't tell you. All I know is that in that moment I couldn't and wouldn't leave my children. I figured I could endure another six months, couldn't I?

The next day, Joshua arrived from work with expensive perfume and some beautiful opal earrings. A dream come true, to be lavished with gifts from my husband. And I was devastated. These were not gifts. They were bribes. Perhaps he really meant love and adoration, but to me it felt like manipulation. I can't tell you what it was like to be me in that moment. Throughout the marriage I wanted to be seen and wasn't; I'd wanted flowers, but didn't get them; Joshua would yell at me that I'm already angry because he is late every night; he certainly wasn't going to stop for flowers and risk further wrath.

I was crushed by the weight of Joshua's gifts. I couldn't carry the burden of the lie I was once again trying to live into—just for another six months—a six-month life sentence.

Invisibility is what we all experience, even endure to some extent. I believe what we are trying to gain or to experience is to be seen for who we are inside our skins, beyond what we do. Many affairs are founded on those moments when a stranger acknowledges us; they see us in our essence. They understand us as our spouse hasn't or couldn't. I know that I wanted children so they would love me forever for being the source of life and love for them. That was one of my ploys; to use my children to maintain visibility; to be seen by them and loved by them, no matter what! It was far safer than expecting a man to provide that for me.

The Compassion of a Child

There was a moment—*there are always those moments that I'll never forget*—I'd been in the house and on the phone with Joshua. I don't remember what we were talking about, but when we hung up, I burst into deep, deep sobbing. Hannah, who was only three, came over, threw her arms around my neck and hugged me with such love. She was such a comfort to me, always had been and yet I wondered how she knew to be so caring. How did she know to give herself so freely in that moment? I felt guilt that a child should have to console the mother. On the other hand, I believe it was her natural capacity for compassion and love that allowed her to comfort me so spontaneously. Why not allow her the full expression of who she is? She consoled me for just a few moments before I let her know I was okay. I blew my nose and shifted our focus to what we would have for lunch.

Nancy Bethune

The next day, once again I struggled with what I'd gotten myself into. On my walk back from the park with Hannah and Noah, my neighbor Nancy Bethune was in her driveway with her two little ones. Nancy was probably ten years older than I was. She had known for a long time that I wasn't happy and had been struggling in this marriage to Joshua.

I told her of my decision to stay six months more. Perhaps she was tired of my complaining, but she had a wisdom I lacked. And so when she spoke I listened. She encouraged me to leave the children with Joshua. She was really clear that I needed to grow myself up and that Joshua needed to grow up too, through being a father. She was clear that the children would have stability, grandparents, neighborhood friends, daycare, all of the things they needed. She emphasized that I needed to find myself. I needed to follow my heart and make a life for me and inevitably for the children. When the time was right, she said, they *would* come and live with me. This all happened in the driveway of a neighbor.

What Nancy said made sense to me. Her wisdom focused primarily on what was best for the children. Hannah and Noah would continue to have the stability of the home they knew with all of the people and the places they knew, and they would be with a good dad. Joshua *was* a good dad. I would take the time I needed to create a life and hopefully a home for them.

As much as I knew that this was in the best interest of Hannah and Noah, I also figured that Joshua wouldn't last a month with the kids. He rarely took a day off from work or spent a whole day with them on his own. It made total sense to me, even though it meant taking them away from their primary caregiver, me; I was still breast-feeding them both and up until that moment we had been inseparable. It meant putting their needs before mine, my need to be loved, my need to have an identity as a supermom, my need to be needed by them.

Regardless of my attachment to my children and to my role as mom, Nancy's advice rang true. Rather than seeing the children as pawns, and rather than ignoring their needs for stability and security, I believe I was seeing them in the way I'd wanted to be seen by my own parents when I was a child; to see me and my needs and act in my best interest. With nine children, it would take a hell of a lot of presence to discover, recognize and acknowledge each of our unique needs and act accordingly. My parents did the best they could. I wanted to do the best I could, and hopefully that would be a whole lot better.

From the first time I read Kahlil Gibran's poem, *On Children,* I took it as guidance to my parenting. It gave me the courage to make the choice I made.

On Children
~ Kahlil Gibran

Your children are not your children.
They are the sons and daughters of Life's longing for itself.
They come through you, but not from you,
And though they are with you yet they belong not to you.

You may give them your love, but not your thoughts,
For they have their own thoughts.
You may house their bodies, but not their souls,
For their souls dwell in the house of tomorrow,
Which you cannot visit, not even in your dreams.

You may strive to be like them,
But seek not to make them like you.
For life goes not backward nor tarries with yesterday.

You are the bows from which your children
As living arrows are sent forth.
The archer sees the mark upon the path of the infinite,
And He bends you with His might
That His arrows may go swift and far.
Let your bending in the archer's hand be for gladness,
For even as He loves the arrow that flies,
So He loves also the bow that is stable.

As an extremely reluctant adventurer, I had no idea what steps I'd be taking once I walked out of the house without my beloved children. I only knew that it was essential for my well-being, and hopefully for my children's well-being, that I do so.

Chapter Three

No Regrets, No Hard Feelings, It's Over

I felt not so much like I was undeserving (in the bent head, tail between my legs kind of way), but that I put what I put into the marriage and I would walk away with that and no more.

Like other A-1 Hamburger's widows—as we were called because our husbands were at the restaurant essentially 24/7—who divorced their spouse, I could have walked away with money, the house and the kids. It didn't feel right doing that to everyone involved. Joshua would be supporting the children, so as long as he had them, I wouldn't be receiving alimony. How long he would be able to manage as the primary parent was the main question. My hope was that he wouldn't and the children would return to me.

You can see that I had mixed feelings. I wanted what was best for Hannah and Noah and at the same time, I wanted them with me. Of course, I would!

It felt as if Joshua was using the children as pawns. He seemed to be hoping that because I'd been so attached to the children, there would be no way I would leave them. Why else would he say, "If you stay for six months, you can have the children? If you go now, you go alone."

If I had taken the children with me while I was trying to go to school, they would have had it worse than staying in their own home, their own nursery school, with their doting grandparents who lived around the corner. My children meant the world to me. They had been the center of my life. It was important to me that I chose what was best for them and trusted that everything would work out for all in the end. The identity I'd always been attached to as the best mom in the world would mean letting go of my role as Hannah and Noah's main support. Their best interests had to come first. My hope was that Joshua would see that too, and one day encourage them to come live with me when the time was right.

Joseph Campbell wrote about the process of the hero's journey in *Hero with a Thousand Faces.* Initially, he (or in this case *she*) experiences a compelling pull to leave everything behind for something that is yet known. Sometimes there is a searching, but often it is just a knowing that leaving is required for a returning to occur. I wanted to leave my marriage behind, sensing that there was a better way to feel about my life and myself. My plan was to create a stable environment for my children and me within which we could thoroughly revel in the glorious God-given beauty that abounds, but first I had to create my own stability.

Stability

Stability, what's that? What does it look like? How would I know when I have found it? I thought I had found it with Joshua and the children. Okay, that was stable, but not the kind of stability that comes from within. How would I create stability for my children when I've just created the biggest upheaval possible in my own life? On top of that, I was breaking the prime taboo regarding a mother's role in a child's life. I challenge you to go find inner peace after taking that on!

I'd left the stability of my parent's home for a home with Joshua. Physically, we had created a comfortable and secure home. Emotionally, well, it would be truthful to say that I was to some degree emotionally unstable; it couldn't be any other way. I'd grown up in a dysfunctional family, created a dysfunctional home life, and now I was only twenty-six years old. Up until this moment, I knew myself only in relation to people and things I'd made significant. Now, I couldn't except that this was as good as it gets, though it was everything I thought I wanted. That sounds crazy, I know, yet how can we know that we want what we want until we have it? I mean, we can want what we want, but once it's in tangible form, we have an experience in response to having it. Too often, once we have what we want, we are on to the next thing we think.

Once I had my children, I couldn't have felt more fulfilled in my role as a mom. I never imagined myself without my children; it would mean death to me, or so I thought. It was in the role of wife that I was unfulfilled. It was my relationship to Joshua as a partner that I couldn't get right for myself or for him. As effortless as it was to be me as a mom, it was the complete opposite to be me as a wife.

The calling that required me to leap out over the abyss, leaving behind the stability of my life as a wife of a soon to be wealthy man and my heart and soul love for my children and my role as a mom, well …

The circumstances were extraordinary; this was just another event in a life-long struggle to find my true north. It ripped a huge tear in the fabric of my world, fraying my connections to many people. I alienated myself from anyone who would offer an opinion on my choice to leave my children. And it undoubtedly created irrevocable damage to my relationship with my mom. As much as I wanted to have an honest rapport with her, our ways in the world were too different. We could not find a place beyond right and wrong, shame and guilt, or good and bad. I had to choose. My primary intention was to act in my highest truth and in the best interest of my children. As with so many of my connections, my relationship with my mom had to be sacrificed in order to save my own life.

When I left Niagara Falls, I left behind all my friends. I didn't want anyone to tell me that what I was doing was a mistake. It didn't matter what other people thought. Up to this point, I had listened to what others thought and it just didn't align with my own knowing. I knew I had to listen to my intuition and follow my path, regardless of the outcome.

Disorienting Reality

I felt I didn't have a support system, except for Sam and he was marginal at best. Because I wanted to go back to school to further my education, I felt that Kitchener, Ontario was the best place for me to go.

It was where Sam lived and there were two universities close by, Wilfred Laurier University and University of Waterloo.

I left a stable, but unfulfilling support system for an unstable one that seemed at the time more fulfilling—Sam. I began to carve out a reality that supported health and well-being while at the same time creating an enmeshed relationship dynamic far worse than with Joshua. With Joshua, there was minimal amount of intimate conversation and emotional availability. With Sam, there was fun and playfulness, but he was also emotionally unavailable and sometimes emotionally abusive. I stepped deeper into the practice of self-deprecation while at the same time attempting to create a life of self-fulfillment. I was stretched in both directions; toward growth and self-realization; toward developing self-respect as I saw myself grow, and at the same time I saw that I was addicted to a pattern of being in a relationship that encouraged self-abuse and crazy-making behavior.

Finding Work

Since I left my marriage relatively penniless, I had to get a job. I was acquainted with the owners of the A-1 Hamburger Restaurant in Cambridge, Ontario, close to Kitchener. I asked if they'd be willing to hire me. I went from being the wife of the owner of the A-1 Hamburger Restaurant in Niagara Falls, Ontario to making minimum wage as a cashier and I didn't even blink an eye. I didn't think it was below me; I didn't blame Joshua or feel any anger towards him. I was grateful for the job, and mostly I was grateful for my freedom. Getting clear that this separation wasn't his fault or my fault, but essential for the well-being of both of us, I could move on to what needed to be done next.

The Fear of Not Surviving

Essentially, I'd never lived alone until I moved out of my home with Joshua. I was actually terrified of being on my own. It took nearly a year for me to wean myself slowly off constant contact with people, especially Sam. I was so afraid to be alone in my own little apartment. I had no idea I was as dependent on other people as I was. It hadn't occurred to me that I might someday have to live on my own.

My neighbors across the hall, Jenny and Tom understood my challenges. They were sensitive and compassionate people who'd had enough wisdom and life experience to see that I was up against an enormous bout of personal challenges. They became guardians in a good sense. I knew they were there, but I didn't need to call on them for much. Knowing they were sincere in their care for me, I could practice learning to live on my own.

Weaning myself off my dependency to people in general and men in particular took an incredible amount of time, courage and discipline. Like every addict, I avoided being with my underlying issues of self-worth, which on an ongoing basis created restlessness, irritability and discontent. Focusing outside myself, whether on my husband, my children or now on Sam, provided relief from the inner mayhem that at some point would need to be sorted out. In the moment, though it was imperative that I pay the rent and keep Sam in tow, regardless of how bad I felt about myself. If the truth were known, what I really wanted was to find another man to marry and take care of me. I really believed I'd remarry within a year of my separation from Joshua. My eyes were set on Sam.

To this day, my children still don't understand how emotionally crippled and handicapped I was.

Abandoning Motherhood

This is an unending process of grappling with right wrong, good, bad mother, woman, human.

How do I honor my wisdom in support of my highest truth, my highest knowing and for my highest good and then consequently hurt those that are most dear to me?

As a child, my dream was to give to my children everything I could, essentially all of myself, to comfort, nurture and nourish them; to keep them feeling safe, protected; that whatever happened, they could count on their mom to do everything in her power to make things right. I wanted them to feel loved unconditionally and protected, comforted through every storm of growing up.

I didn't do that. I didn't comfort them or protect them as I imagined. In fact, I may have created some of the most significant storms in their life.

I know I followed my wisdom in the long run becoming a far more effective parent that loved them more than I could have dreamed.

This has been haunting me for a very long time; this dilemma of my will over the will of my husband, my children, my parents or even God's will. That's what this struggle feels like and probably feels like from Joshua's point of view. Either I abandon my truth or I abandon my concern for causing people pain and hardship. One way or the other, someone suffers. My suffering, when not heeding the call of my higher wisdom would only fester and not allow healing, and I believe would actually cause long term disease. I've watched this in my own family of origin and I've seen it in clients. Though I was not sick, I knew that if I didn't leave my marriage to Joshua I was going to die. That may sound dramatic, but some things you just know.

Finding Interfaith

While searching for a job that paid more than minimum wage, I found Interfaith Pastoral Counseling Center in Kitchener. Since I'd earned my B.A. in Psychology, I assumed I could put it to use. I walked over to their center to see if they were hiring. Gloria Taylor, the woman I spoke to said, "No, you don't understand. We don't pay you; you pay us to work here." At first, my heart sank as I thought I'd found a good place to work. Then I realized that with synchronistical timing, I had found my home.

Interfaith was a training program for people who wanted to enhance their capacity to be effective pastoral counselors and Marriage and Family Therapists. Originally, this was a program to provide training for ministers in pastoral counseling to support their parishioners. Soon they allowed lay people to train there as well. For many years, it was the only training center in Canada for Marriage and Family Therapy. Eventually it became a program associated with a graduate school in southern California called Azusa Pacific College with the California Family Study Center known now as the Phillips Graduate Institute.

You know You are Home When ...

What I learned that day from Gloria Taylor, who became one of the most influential people in my life, was that to get into the internship program I'd have to take three prerequisite classes in counseling skills, and then I could apply to the internship program. There was no hesitation on my part. I signed up for the classes and felt like I'd found my ground of being. I could take the classes that year then apply for the internship the following year.

Another piece to this puzzle was that to be an intern, I'd also have to apply and be accepted to Azusa; it was a two-for-one deal. I was very confident that I could pull this off effortlessly.

I was only months out of my marriage and away from my children. Though my bachelor's degree was foundational, I realized I knew nothing about real life or people and how we operate as humans. I had no real basis at all for being helpful, except that I felt called to do this work. I didn't know how little I knew until I came to know what I came to know.

Dixie Gauldner, one of the founders of the internship program, taught the introduction classes to Marriage and Family Therapy. As I was developing skills to be a therapist, it was also the best therapy imaginable for me. The people were loving, open, caring, wise, compassionate, present and available, all of the things that make one a good therapist, but more importantly a good human being. This training was so different from any academic course work I'd done in the past. This was hands on, experiential learning. We practiced what we expected our clients to practice. We pushed our own edges, revealing patterns and processes that in the past allowed dysfunctional systems to stay in place. We learned to discover, recognize and acknowledge ways of being in the world that were chosen in order to support the systems of our families whether they were dysfunctional or not. We were learning that *we* could choose differently, and if *we* could choose differently, we could support our *clients* in choosing differently.

We cultivated the skill of listening with empathy and compassion; how to be present without enabling our clients to continue ways of being that weren't in alignment with their best interests. In essence, we learned to empower our clients to find and follow their unique course to their own true north.

Through practice sessions, we learned how our own dysfunctions operate in relation to our clients dysfunctions, often interfering with their own growth process. It was all extremely fascinating to me. The more conscious I became about how we *be* as humans the more I wanted to learn. There was a moment when I knew that it wouldn't be enough just to be a therapist; I'd want to train others to do this work. I hardly knew what I was doing myself, but I knew I loved what was happening to me as I awakened to myself.

While taking these classes at Interfaith I worked as a waitress and I worked for a small company that taught CPR classes and provided tutoring to children. I barely made enough to live on, scraping through month after month. Interestingly enough it wasn't that different from living with Joshua. Even though he was the owner of two A-1 Hamburger restaurants, it never felt as though we could enjoy the financial benefits. We never allowed ourselves vacations or any real lavishness. The angst of *not enough* in my life was perpetual. The only difference now was that I didn't have anyone with which to share the anxiety of how I was going to pay the rent.

A Split Second of Reality

One particular afternoon as I was walking into the building where I tutored a young boy; there was an inexplicable instant that momentarily disoriented me. I had paused for only a moment to look at the façade of the building to observe the intricate carvings above the doorway. As I did so, for one, brief, split-second, I felt whole and complete, a feeling that I'd never experienced before. It was like experiencing how it would feel to be me later in my life. I had no doubt that this was a future me, one I'd come to live into. The experience was so brief there was nothing that could be considered describable, no indicators to say when, where or how. It was just an occurrence that wasn't life changing, but allowed me to experience another dimensional process—what I would later come to call *transpersonal in nature*. I had a knowing that the suffering I was creating in my current life was not what was real or necessary. Somehow, I would find myself beyond the reality that I'd been living from birth. This fraction of time took me beyond hope into a knowing that my life would far surpass all my expectations. I would know when I had arrived and not a moment sooner.

Interfaith Internship

The year passed. I finished my course work at Interfaith. The CPR and tutoring business wasn't supporting me so I had to go back to waitressing full time. And, I handed in my applications for both the internship and graduate school.

The day came when I was to hear whether I was accepted or not. It was after dinner when the phone rang and I answered it anxiously, confident that I'd be accepted. Gloria shared that neither program accepted me. My grades in my undergraduate work were very poor, so Azusa said no. And Interfaith felt I needed another year of healing from my marriage before I was ready to enter the program. I needed to do a make-up year at a college or university to get into Azusa and I needed to work somewhere else for a year where I could practice my counseling skills. Interfaith also offered practicum courses that would support my learning process prior to entering the internship program. It was suggested to me that I take these practicum courses over the next year.

Though I was disappointed, I realized that my expectations were unrealistic. Given the relationship I'd developed with Interfaith and the way they shared their concerns for me I took the news well and anticipated entering the following year. I was dedicated and committed in a way that I'd not been for anything other than to my children. I loved the feeling of clarity and intention that continually drove me past hope into knowing that this was my path and Interfaith was my home.

DENIAL: Don't Even Know I Am Lying

Every time I would go back to Niagara Falls to pick up or drop off the kids, I would *almost* cry and then instantaneously cut it off. A welling up of emotion surfaced that would suspend itself like water brimming over the edge of a glass. Then the feeling would subside, disappearing into the shadows of my unknown self again. My years in the Kuhn Family had taught me how not to feel what I felt, so as huge as it was to have given up my children I could numb myself when leaving them time after time. If I allowed myself to feel the truth within, my heart would not have withstood the shattering. I created circumstantial distractions that caused me to focus elsewhere.

Moments after leaving Hannah and Noah and backing out of the driveway my attention would quickly shift away from them and onto Sam. I worried that he was in the midst of some sexual affair while I was away for four hours. He talked about his old girlfriend a lot and he loved strip clubs and porn magazines. I didn't trust him.

When one uses denial as a survival mechanism, it's as if something or someone else actually flips the switch, turning off the ability to feel or to know what you don't want to know or feel. I felt a lot of pain around Sam. I felt scared about how I was going to make a living. I felt a lot of anxiety when left alone on my own. So it wasn't as though I'd become numb and unfeeling. It was if I was required to focus on survival as a way of turning off that part of me that had been so connected to my children and to my role as Mom. I knew the children were safe, secure and in a stable environment and they would be receiving all the love they could from their dad, their grandparents and everyone else, except me. I didn't have to worry about them, but I did have to worry about my livelihood.

I'm challenged to describe the experience of denial because obviously I didn't know I was denying anything. I thought I was just getting on with my life. I thought I was acting in the best interest of my children. Nothing else mattered.

New friends would ask me how I was doing. It never occurred to me that I was doing anything, but fine enough, since I was more focused on working as a waitress, making enough money to pay my rent, looking for work other than waitressing and being in relationship with a man as dysfunctional as myself, if not more so. My obsession with being loved by Sam took up any extra emotional energy, which is how I coped with not living with my children. My responses to, "How are you doing?" came out as, "I'm doing fine, since I know the kids are good—they are doing great!" It never occurred to me that I might

need to process my reality, the trauma of letting go of the most significant relationships of my life. Denial is a very powerful medicine.

Self-Realization Takes Hold

I was blessed because Kitchener and Waterloo had two universities, both of which were wonderful assets to my education. Wilfred Laurier University was in Kitchener and summer sessions had yet to begin. I was able to sign up for one class, which was a great start. I remember one particular day walking towards the classroom. We were going to have a quiz that day and I remember saying to myself, "Okay, you can do well on this and move towards what you say you want, or you can flunk this and become a secretary for the rest of your life. It's up to you!" Well, I aced the exam. I believe that this was one specific choice-point set me on my path of self-empowerment and self-determination to find myself and to discover my fullest potential.

From then on, the grades I received were the highest I'd ever received in my life as a student. Primarily, it was because I was studying subjects that were of interest to me. They weren't just theoretical courses that were part of my Bachelor's Degree; these had to do with real life processes; aging and change, death and dying, problems with self. These courses were pivotal in exploring the dilemma of being a *spiritual being* having a human experience. They challenged me to think for myself, to feel inside myself. Each course stretched me and I was happy.

I'd found a job working as a teacher's assistant at an elementary school. The class was for third and fourth grade boys who had emotional problems and were acting out at school. It was a perfect job for me. It was low pressure and fun. I was being helpful and enjoyed the camaraderie of the teachers at the school. This was a real job that paid real money. I had a very good year!

Two More Years at Interfaith

The following year I was accepted into Interfaith and to Azusa Pacific College in Southern California. Azusa in conjunction with Cal Fam, as we came to call it, had a program set up for individuals who worked full time or lived some place other than the Los Angeles area. People like me could study at the center for six weeks during the summer for four years. The rest of the year we would go back to their full time jobs or families and complete reading and writing requirements. For us at Interfaith we'd be in Burbank for six weeks then return to fulfill internship requirements. Our internship fulfilled the requirements for the Cal Fam requirements for internship. What this did for us specifically was made this a three semester program instead of four.

These two programs together created an incredibly in-depth, rich and qualified training. The theoretical component balanced nicely with the experiential element, plus there was the spiritual component too, given that Interfaith was in the business of training pastors and ministers in supporting their parishioners. My heart was fulfilled. I found authentic friendships and a sense of belonging.

My experience of training through experiential programs was that it was challenging to know what I actually learned. Yes, there were exams and papers to write, but I couldn't measure the value of the learning I'd been doing. At the end of the first year I felt that I hadn't really changed that much or knew more than when I started.

The first day of the second year of the internship was a fascinating moment. I realized just how much I had learned. While sitting with the new interns who were just beginning their new adventure in Marriage and Family Therapy, I listened to their questions and thoughts, their worries and concerns and was able to reply effortlessly with far more wisdom, clarity and knowing then I ever could imagine. I was shocked with what flowed out of my mouth, the answers, and the empathy I experienced for their new journey. I was amazed with myself and it felt *so* good! I came to feel a level of true competence, which felt grounding and stable. No one could take that away from me. Let them just try!

Because I had to continue to work throughout my internship and had my children to visit down in Niagara Falls, I put in fewer hours with clients than other interns. The faculty wasn't happy with my level of participation at the center, but I also remembered my time at Outward Bound where my level of involvement was unsatisfying. I knew I was slacking, but wasn't willing to give up the work, the pay or the little time I spent with my kids for a few more client hours. I could have given up my time with Sam, but the addict in me wasn't going to allow that to happen. He was my drug of choice.

Mother over Self/Girlfriend over Mother

As is currently obvious to you by now, I wanted to be loved by a man. Someone to adore me, give me a sense of value and self-worth; someone who was able to see into my soul and tell me what was there.

The moment I met Sam he looked and talked as if he was the kind of man who could fulfill that need. I was able to see the essence of his being, but the truth was that his survival mechanisms wouldn't allow him to be that except for sheer moments in time.

While married, my children took precedence over my husband. I knew who I was as a mother, my identity as a good mom didn't falter at all. My identity beyond motherhood was not yet known. Like most women, at least thirty years ago, I tried to find myself through a man. I believed a man would give me something to live for, to be for, to grow and change for. If only he could see how important he was to me, how valuable I was to him as a sex partner and friend; however, once I partnered up with someone my self-development took a backseat.

I projected onto Sam that he was looking for a woman who could meet him in all capacities of life. I wanted to meet the mark, though that wasn't necessarily who I was. I wanted to prove myself worthy as a woman. How silly I was to create the illusion that this man was worthy of sacrificing my essential self for an identity as a sex partner to a sexual addict (for a few more years, I didn't understand that he was addicted to sex). At one point in my relationship with Sam, I felt suicidal. I'd come to feel unworthy as a human being because he didn't find me worthy as a partner. I'm grateful that I had friends and a therapist that let me see how ridiculous I was to give myself so little value and give him so much power.

Each moment in this relationship with Sam was a moment of choice as to my self-worth or lack of self-worth. I eked my way out of that relationship, inch by inch, to a point where my time alone was valued more than being with him. Though I broke it off with Sam probably over three hundred times in seven years, I had years of wounding to heal. And he was just one man of many through which my healing came.

There is a lot of talk here about what I was doing in this life void of motherhood. Again, denial was a factor. It created a capacity to numb out what was too fragile or maybe too horrific to deal with. Many women *who relinquish custody of their children end up with substance abuse or mental health issues. I probably would have been considered good candidates for both camps. My substance of abuse was my fixation on relationships—being loved by a man. It's what allowed me to let time heal everything else while I took care of what seemed to be needs of physical and emotional survival.*

My mental health issue would be considered the denial with which I was living. Even after thirty years, I'm still unfolding and awakening in the fullest expression of my sorrow and grief for not raising my children. And as unhelpful as denial can be, I know it to be a lifesaver. It protected me from what I could not be with. If given the time, the space, and the people that could provide a safe, loving space within which to speak and feel the reality of life, many of us could begin to be present to those life-choices that go beyond belief. I've come to believe that again, with an understanding and compassionate environment, all of us can come to accept the choices we make.

The killing of human life is one of the ravages of war. I believe that this can feel irreconcilable in our soul. The killing of the human soul and the human spirit is the ravages of heartless choices as well as choices made from the heart. The individual who is required to endure the pain of other people's choices may never know the difference. Theirs may be to forgive regardless of the intention coming from hate or love. This cycle perpetuates itself in giving and receiving.

I inevitably have to forgive my parents if I'm to heal myself fully and to know my true north. My children will have to do the same, so will their children and their children. The practice of forgiveness is required for those adventurers committed to finding their true north. Without it, we will be pulled off course by the fragments of emotional debris – the flotsam and jetsam on the ocean's surface that too often causes boats to falter or to sink altogether. No survivors found.

Children

Sometimes we take for granted that the resiliency of our children will undo any neglect or absence over time.

I believe this is my biggest regret; that my need for personal survival took precedence over my commitment to my children. It's one thing to leave them in the custody of their father; weighing all of the variables, he had a better environment for them than I did. It's another thing not to have the consciousness to focus on what time I did have with my children. I regret mostly the time in Kitchener when my focus was on Sam. I want to say that I was crazy and dysfunctional; in the I didn't know any better, kind of crazy, but I also have to be compassionate for this young me who just couldn't do anything else. Forgiveness is an ongoing multifaceted process. I believe regrets aren't meant to be endured, but are learning opportunities; not so much about what I could have done differently to alleviate the regret, but what is it I need to realize in this present moment, looking back at that regret. Through this process, I've come to forgive others and overtime myself, releasing the regret and all that it holds.

I've come to accept that I was immature and dysfunctional in so many ways, and that my priorities and my actions were indications of that immaturity and dysfunction. I took it upon myself to focus, as best I could, on growing up, which would mean less regrets and more self-fulfillment.

Can I Get a Witness?

My parents had shunned me—my whole family shunned me. Though my brother Michael took custody of his two very young daughters for a number of years, in my parent's home, and they accepted this as a good thing, when I chose to do the same thing; first by bringing my children home to live with my parents, then later deciding it was best for the children to be with their father, they would have nothing to do with me, especially my mom. I think my dad had more understanding, but to protect his relationship with mom he had to act as if I was a scorned woman.

It was so confusing that what was good for Michael and in the best interest of his children was totally the opposite for me. He was the hero in rescuing his children. In so many ways, I rescued my children by having them stay in their own home. They didn't have to deal with the inconsistent, crazy-making world I continually created for myself through my relationship with Sam. There was no arguing or sharing points of view with my parents. It was their way or the highway. I took the highway, obviously. I was grateful that I had Interfaith and the support through which I could make my way through the maze of relationships—functional and dysfunctional.

Mrs. Powers

In 1980, my sister Annie, the youngest sibling, was getting married. She'd come home from Flagstaff to attempt to rally the family into celebrating her and her engagement as we had done for every other member of the family. From my point of view, Annie had alienated herself in so many ways from her siblings. Primarily, because she was so much younger than the majority of her siblings, there wasn't the same connection as there had been for the others. But Annie was also very angry and rebellious. She had a *Fuck You* attitude toward … well it seemed to be towards the world. In my mind, this was her way of empowering herself, bringing focus to her value and worthiness in a world that would not acknowledge her or her beautiful essence.

My mom had a wedding shower for her inviting cousins, sisters and close friends of the family. It was rather a sad turnout.

I came home for the weekend wanting to support Annie and also continue working towards reconciliation with my mom. I'd been murdered many times by her contemptuous looks. This weekend was no different. Even after years of separation from my children, my mom would scarcely speak to me.

At the wedding shower, I made myself as inconspicuous as I could—no use putting myself in the line of fire. At one moment, one of my mom's dearest friends, Mrs. Powers, in her late sixties, circled around the group of younger women. I hardly noticed her presence until she bent down and whispered in my ear "You did what many of us wish we could have done." Just as quickly as she came, she left my side, never to speak of this or anything else to me again. I'm sure she never spoke to my mom about this, as it was not one of those things good Catholic women would reveal to another.

I'd always loved Mrs. Powers, though we were never close. My mom's friends were much older and didn't relate to us the way that my children relate to my friends. Mrs. Powers lost her sixteen-year-old daughter in a car crash about twenty years before her exchange with me. I wondered if her loss gave her a perspective that allowed her to share what she had with me. I only know that it was a whisper from an angel that guided me to stay the course, regardless of my mom's inability to see things from another perspective.

Cal Fam and the End of the Internship

Those three summers in southern California were exceptional. They were eye opening for someone who'd hardly been out of the Midwest. The contingency of Interfaith interns who traveled with me for our summer stints at Cal Fam lived in an apartment complex in Burbank with a pool and hot tub. The courses were intense and jam-packed, profound and full of opportunities to gain self-realization. I was stretched and grew far more than I ever anticipated.

My ex-boyfriend from high school (Peter) lived in Los Angeles. At our ten-year high school reunion, I told him I was coming down to Los Angeles to go to school. He encouraged me to call when I got down there. When I arrived, he graciously loaned me a car for six weeks. He showed me around and introduced me to his new wife. He had arrived in Los Angeles with $40.00 in his pocket ten years earlier and began working as an auto mechanic. Now he owned his own shop and had created an enormous amount of success for himself. I was so happy for him and really appreciated his kind and open heart.

Venice beach, Rodeo Drive; all the fabulous and outrageous aspects of Los Angeles were tremendously entertaining. I felt guilty for leaving the children for six weeks. Was I worthy of all of this? Was I having a wonderful time at the expense of my children? These questions plagued my existence.

Codependency Recognized

In the third year at Cal Fam, we had a course in addictions taught by Craig and Samantha, who were both recovering alcoholics. As they described certain behaviors that indicated addiction, I spoke up because what they were describing was what I'd dealt with while living with my parents. I shared that my parents couldn't be alcoholics because they didn't drink until after 5:00 p.m. Many of the things they shared brought me to the realization that my parents *were* alcoholics and not only had I been in denial about it, but my whole family was in denial about it too.

I felt relief in this realization. It made sense out of so much of the craziness. The conversations with Craig and Samantha also shed light on my own process as a child of alcoholics and all of the coping strategies I developed in order survive the crazy-making reality of the my family. I could see how I continued to carry these same strategies into my relationships with men. I couldn't at this point stop myself, but it became more obvious that I needed to.

Master's Thesis Short and to the Point

A thesis is one of many requirements for a master's degree. I had to write a literature review on some specific topic of interest related to my work as a Marriage and Family Therapist. I couldn't seem to find the underlying cause of my emotional issues in relation to being a non-custodial parent, so I decided that perhaps by doing research around the subject I'd open up the floodgates to those hidden emotions.

My thesis for my master's degree: *Mothers without Custody: In Search of Authenticity* was probably one of the shortest theses ever written—thirty-two pages in length. In the early 1980s, there were only two books in print on the subject and very little research had been done. The faculty was not impressed with the overall length of the paper, but accepted it nonetheless.

I didn't reveal or uncover anything that would make sense of my choice to give up custody of my children, nor did it open those floodgates of emotions. I found out that most women *lose* custody of their children as opposed to choose it. And that most will either experience a mental breakdown or end up with substance abuse. I counted myself lucky that I had pulled through the first five years mentally stable—relatively speaking.

Finding Home in Nova Scotia

As I was nearing the end of my training and graduate school, it was time to consider what was next. Where would I go to begin my new life as a therapist?

As much as I wanted to be with the children, I could not allow myself to move back to the Falls. It had been challenging enough for me to live there for the six years I was married to Joshua. I was never happy there and worried about the toxicity of the environment for the children. My hope was that if I could create a home somewhere else that was cleaner, more beautiful and fun, Noah and Hannah would want to come live with me.

I thought about moving north, to Collingwood, Ontario, a town on beautiful Georgian Bay. It had many outdoor activities, including sailing. It would be a great place to raise the children. The downside was that Georgian Bay was five hours north of the Falls. That would be an extremely long commute to visit the children if they chose to remain with their father.

The other possibility was the east coast of Canada, Nova Scotia in particular. Now that made no sense to anyone, but me.

I'd visited the Province of Nova Scotia a couple of times with Sam. His cousins had moved there from Newfoundland. He loved to take road trips to see them every summer.

Nova Scotia was incredibly green, unpolluted, unpopulated and breathtakingly beautiful, but I didn't feel compelled to make it my home; not until Holder, a friend from Interfaith, who did some research around the best places to live in Canada, remarked that Nova Scotia had the highest divorce rate and the lowest price per acre of land in the Country. In that moment, I assessed my values and priorities and decided that Nova Scotia would be my home.

As a Marriage and Family Therapist, divorces and family breakdowns would be my bread and butter. From what Holder shared, there was indeed a great deal of potential for developing a successful therapy practice in Nova Scotia. And because land was so inexpensive there, I could most likely purchase land on the beach with an ocean view. This would allow me to create the lifestyle I so wanted for my children and me. I loved lobsters, mussels and clams, which were there at your fingertips if you were willing to do just a little digging.

Nova Scotia is a playground with beautiful long beaches, miles of trails to hike and of course a wonderful place to sail. It was the clean and safe environment I wanted for my children to experience and perhaps live in, if they chose. I hoped they would fall in love with the adventure that nature always provided for me. It would be much further away than Collingwood, but from my point of view, the advantages would far outweigh the disadvantages. Though my hope was that the children would want to come and live with me it certainly wasn't a slam-dunk conclusion. I prayed a great deal for direction and Nova Scotia was where I was led.

It was a choice I was making on my own, one about which no one was happy. I'd be moving out all by myself. It was the call to a simpler life connected to nature. Getting my master's degree and the five years of settling into Kitchener helped calm my relationship with my parents. They could see that I was creating stability and a future for myself. Of course, my decision to move to Nova Scotia created another new rift. Now I was a noncustodial mom who was choosing to live fifteen hundred miles from my children. My mom could not find room in her life for such a daughter. It was outside her capacity for empathy, understanding or compassion.

My upbringing on an island gave me a perspective that was different from Noah and Hannah's. Niagara Falls was their home and they were settled, content, even happy. They had acting and dancing school and all of their friends. They also traveled a great deal. Their lifestyle was far more urban and citified. What I offered them would take them away from all of that. Long, sandy beaches, woods and forests to explore, rivers, lakes and the ocean right outside their front door; it was compelling enough for me, but again, nature and beauty always were some of the most compelling elements of life for me. I hoped that they would be for my children too. If not, at least during vacations, they would be exposed to the ruggedness and rawness of nature and it would perhaps seed itself in their souls.

Was this choice made from a selfish self-serving place in me or was it made with my children in mind? Was it in their best interest that I create a home so far away from their home? Would they be compelled to choose to live with me perhaps for just a little while? And, though I questioned my motives endlessly, I followed my calling to the furthest reaches of the world as I knew it to be.

Chapter Four

Anguish of the Undertow

The first two years in Nova Scotia were full of upheaval. I landed in Halifax, found a psychologist who brought me into his practice as an associate and from there I attempted to build a life.

I thought I was free from Sam. He originally decided to go to law school at the University of Windsor in Ontario, but when I decided to move to Nova Scotia, he decided to go to law school at Dalhousie University in Halifax. There was something so compelling about the pull of this relationship that, like an undertow, I could not help, but be swept back into life with him. He moved in with me, but within a matter of weeks, I knew I needed to get out. In order to separate from him, I had to give up my apartment because he was emphatic that he wasn't going to be the one leaving. I had to find somewhere else to live.

I remember my friend, Missie, from Interfaith, who also grew up in a large chaotic family. She put words to my predicament with Sam that made sense. She explained that my life experience in my family of origin was such that confusion, chaos and disappointment were normal. The crazy-making that I continually found myself in with Sam was an automatic, unconscious process. I was addicted to chaos. It was a pattern that was painful, but comfortable in that I knew how to function well in chaos. And like any self-abuse process, it continually pulled me off course. From inside me it looked as though I was steering a direct course for my true north, yet at the same time, undercurrents were creating rifts and turbulence.

For most of us, this is part of sailing our own course. And as conscious as we are of currents, storms and unforeseen obstacles, we are still pulled off course. The question is, what do we want to do about it.

Though there was a longing for something peaceful and serene, the threshold of anxiety created by being outside the confused, chaotic suffering was too great and I'd be pulled back into the maelstrom. Time and again, I reached further and further up the shore of serenity until I could no longer be reached by the tide of the crazy-making that was part and parcel to being with Sam.

Though I wanted stability, I was continually feeling the pull to move in a direction that was unknowable. I couldn't know what was in store for me. I could only get glimpses of freedom. I knew what didn't feel right and so my task was to move away from *that* reluctantly, yet tenaciously. This took me towards what, I didn't not want. I know that sounds crazy, but sometimes the only way we can find what we do want is to move away from that which we don't want.

I moved out from the apartment with Sam into a flat with my wonderful and generous friends Pam and Grant. I lived with them for just a few months before I found an affordable basement apartment in downtown Halifax. What a wonderful city! Halifax was intimate, very hilly and of course very green. I loved walking to just about any destination, especially the waterfront, where the Bluenose Schooner was birthed.

Duplicity and Disloyalty

Pictou Island, Nova Scotia - Wounded, dysfunctional and inappropriate with my priorities, still; too often I stupidly chose boyfriends over my children. One night when visiting, Frank on Pictou Island, Hannah couldn't sleep. She was afraid in this new environment and so she kept coming into the room where I was sleeping with Frank. I'd take her back to her bedroom and lay down with her for awhile then go back to Frank's room. Hannah would wake and return to find me. I was angry and frustrated with her enough that I felt like I could break her little arm. I didn't.

I have never forgotten that feeling or the betrayal of my daughter. I think that moment was the low point for me regarding my children. It could not have gotten any worse than that, not in my mind and heart. I carry that moment with me even now, as I attempt to resolve the guilt of that betrayal. At that time in my life, I did not have the wherewithal to be any other way. Call me an idiot, abusive, irresponsible and neglectful. I was wounded; continually seeking the salve that I hoped would heal my heart. Where did I learn that a man's love is an overriding requirement for a woman's fulfillment and how come while being married to Joshua, my love for my children was overriding to my husband?

I do believe that to experience real love from someone *is* a salve that supports self-love, which in the case of a mother only supports the potential to give a deeper and more authentic unconditional love to her children. I was trying the best way I knew how. It wasn't working. It has taken me a very long time to acknowledge myself for loving my children the best way I knew how and to continue to find ways of loving my children that truly honors them as unique human beings.

Hannah and I have talked about this moment in our relationship. I acknowledged to her that I was wrong in not putting her first. I've apologized more times then she cares to hear. The forgiveness needs to come from me now and not her.

It Was the Best of Times-It was the Worst of Times

"That will never happen to me." I've said that more times in my life than I care to remember. And I've regretted it every time I uttered those words.

The experience came when I could not support myself on the money I was making as a new therapist. The psychologist with whom I was associated was giving me money towards the clients I should have been seeing; however, I didn't have the wherewithal to bring new clients into my practice. I was new. I was green. I hadn't a clue what I was supposed to do to create a clientele. Jason, the psychologist referred clients to me, but that wasn't enough. As well, he and I began to have challenges in what we considered ethical practices. After about six months, it was time for me to leave his office and I was in debt for the majority of the $1,500 a month he had given me.

I began to look for a job, but because my master's degree was in Marriage and Family Therapy, and in Canada, in the 1980s Marriage and Family Therapy was relatively unheard of, I couldn't find anyone to hire me. Much of the mental health work was done by the Province and one needed a degree in social work or in psychology.

My relationship with Sam continued to be on and off, though the dynamics never changed for the good.

I had to take a really close look at my life. I kept seeing myself as the victim of my circumstances. Waves of bad things washed over me, repeatedly. I would get my head up and another wave would send me down under.

The month of April could not have been more demoralizing. Muffin, this really cute puppy I bought at the pound on Sunday died the following Friday of Parvo. My birthday gifted me with a call from my parents who were drunk and almost incoherent, and Sam showed up close to midnight, having no recall at all that it was my birthday. There were other bad circumstances I had to deal with all on my own. All of this led me to wonder what the heck was going on that created such hardship.

I called Gloria Taylor, the only person I knew who would have a clue about what was going on; she had a deep understanding of how Universal wisdom works. What she said was this, "You better start waking up before you get a two-by-four-upside the head. Find someone out there who can give you some sort of spiritual guidance. You'll be fine." That was it! I loved her for her clarity and that I couldn't manipulate her in being maudlin with me. Our relationship always required me to grow up.

The Seth Book

In one of my lowest points ever, Sam introduced me to Bryan, a young law student who practiced Buddhism. I told him what was happening to me. I kept saying, "It can't get any worse." In response, he would say, "It's not worse, it's just different." I hadn't a clue what he meant, but did take his advice and purchased a book called *Seth: The Nature of Personal Reality*. The book was fascinating. It focused on two questions: What do you believe, and what do you do in service to those beliefs?

I learned that through the beliefs I'd chosen over time I created the reality that was showing up in front of me. I did an exercise that brought me back on course aligning me once again with my true north. I listed all the beliefs I held about my family, my children, work, money and relationships. I was horrified and at the same time astonished, and greatly empowered through this practice.

For instance, one of the beliefs I wrote down was that my parents were crummy parents, and that I wanted to punish them for not being the parents I had wanted them to be. I punished them by getting into relationships with men that didn't take care with me. That would show them; however, the reality was that they had a life down in Florida where they were sheltered from their children's problems. They didn't even care about what I was doing to punish them. They didn't have a clue. I had to choose whether I was going to keep trying to punish these people or start living a life that was fulfilling and fun for me.

The other major belief that was affecting me was that if I became fulfilled and successful financially, in my career and in relationships, it would be at the expense of my children. I would be guilty of selfish motives if I became successful at anything. Again, I realized that because of this belief, I created the reality of being on welfare. I could not afford to have my children live with me or even visit me. I couldn't even send presents with the little money I was making.

It was a profound moment of revelation. I realized that I was making the choices I made to punish my parents and avoid any guilt for leaving my children. That was basically it! The irony, my parents could care less, and the consequences to my children far outweighed the guilt I was attemping to avoid. Without taking responsibility for the beliefs I had created and held onto, there would be no hope for reconciliation with my soul or my children. They would continue to be the victims of my desire to avoid guilt and accountability for my beliefs and for my actions.

Boy, I was in a ridiculous situation and I could see how I had created it all by myself. From this moment on, I began shifting my thinking, creating new beliefs and acting in ways that would support a better way to live that was more fulfilling and a whole bunch more fun.

Within three months after doing this exercise, I had a part time job working in a transition house for women; I was off welfare and was being interviewed for another position with The Nova Scotia Commission on Drug Dependency. I had freed myself from the constraints of beliefs that no longer served me. My life as I knew it had to disintegrate so that I could find my way clear to a more real and loving way to be with myself, my children and hopefully with a partner who could be up for a healthy relationship.

This process of transfiguration, the spiritual dismantling of my whole world, created an opportunity to look at the world of my creation and myself. Little by little, I gained the wisdom to know the difference of what was good for me and what wasn't. I began to listen to myself, feel my authentic feelings, and know what I wanted for me. This process allowed me to create a life that has been more and more fulfilling as I inch myself away from interpretations I made about my life based on my childhood years. I practiced letting go of all of the beliefs I had held onto that created the same dysfunction in which I was raised. I created different ways of thinking about money, success, relationship and family just for the practice. If it didn't work, I could create different thoughts that might work better. Why not? What did I have to lose?

This process freed me from a way of being that over decades, created remorse and despair. It gave me an opportunity to align myself with my spiritual self, though at the time, I had no idea what that meant. All my barriers were broken down. I was free to explore and be curious about what was possible. Step by step, inch by inch, I unraveled the tapestry of the life I created as a child. I continued to weave old threads of the past that had been good, healing and fun with new strands that I picked up along the path that I walked.

A Never-Ending Practice

One of the miracles born from the work I did with the *Seth Book* was that I received a phone call from David Cassidy, the director of the South Shore Region of the Nova Scotia Commission on Drug Dependency. "Why haven't we heard from you?" he asked.

Over the previous months, I'd sent numerous applications to the Province of Nova Scotia in regards to a particular position in the Nova Scotia Commission on Drug Dependency. The position was Clinical Therapist for the satellite office in Liverpool, Nova Scotia. Everything they required in experience I had, except that they were looking for someone with an MSW or a MA in Psychology. My application was bypassed time and again. I'd finally sent an application directly to David, which precipitated the phone call that quickly led to a job and a new life in rural Nova Scotia.

You Can Take the Children Out of the City, but You Can't Take the City Out of the Children

What better place in the whole world than Nova Scotia to create a home for my children and me. After nearly six years of struggling financially and otherwise, I finally saw the possibility to create an environment I could share with my kids. Overall, it seemed like a perfect place.

I imagined a home with my children in this beautiful province; a house on the water, beaches to walk and many adventures to be had.

There was incredible magic and wonder with so many opportunities for playful imagination. This was the dream I had for us. I imagined them having a sense of place, a connection to the land and to nature that I'd realized for myself during my youth.

I had no idea that for Hannah this dream life I was creating for my little family, this move fifteen hundred miles away to this *ideal* environment was a huge violation of my role as a mom in her life. I had no idea that she saw this move, not as one that would finally create a home for us, but as a further betrayal as a mother. Traveling back and forth on the plane from Toronto to Halifax as unaccompanied minors was also a violation. I didn't know any of this until much later when she felt strong enough to confront me with her truth.

Niagara Falls, though not a big city gave them access to a lot of activities, sports, dancing, acting, and singing classes and friends. Hundreds of TV stations; restaurants, especially pizza parlors. Their dad would take them to Toronto and New York City to see plays and musicals. They took vacations to exotic places: China, Norway, Peru, Mexico, and the Caribbean. I, on the other hand was giving them rural, isolated, create-your-own-fun Nova Scotia and they didn't seem to get what a wonderful world this was. In retrospect, it wasn't much different for me growing up on Grosse Ile, where I too struggled to create fun as a kid.

I became clear, a long time ago, that my children had a life without me. In many ways, I told myself that I was nothing more than a distant aunt who they called Mom. They had a whole life: school, friends, everything, without me. My short visits and their short visits added up to a hill of beans in relation to their everyday life. I didn't have a right to expect them to drop their world when I telephoned, or for them to rush with excitement to their visits with me. I was taking them away from friends and their routines. From their perspective, I wasn't offering them anything, really. As infants, I was an exceptional mom, but now that I had work and other interests, I wasn't focused on them one hundred percent. And my addiction to relationships with men certainly did not contribute to me becoming mother of the year.

I was also clear that my emotional life was mine and I had to keep that separate from them. This meant that I didn't control or manipulate in order to get my emotional needs met by them. They were not to feel responsible or any guilt for my choices. They had a loyalty to their dad, and for Noah, Joshua was the significant parent like a gosling following its parent. Though there was an assumption on my part that we had developed some level of bonding—I nursed him for fourteen months—it wasn't the same had I stayed and mothered him as a *real* mother would do.

I knew that at some point they would have to deal with their anger and grief for being abandoned. They would have to sort out their thoughts about what kind of mother would leave her children. They would have to resolve this betrayal for themselves. This reality protected me from any expectation of the happily-ever-after scenario that could have played in my head; that, someday we would bond together and be one happy family. It also prepared me for a time when all of this would begin to unravel. I'd have to love them and myself, no matter what.

Fortunately, for them, they didn't have to visit Nova Scotia, but for once a year—twice at the most. Mostly they came for summer visits, as their dad would take them to Mexico for Christmas. How could I compete with that?

More of Sam

The rollercoaster ride of an abusive relationship is an experience that far too many individuals live with. Both men and women are bashed about without a handhold to steady themselves. Violence is an interesting bedfellow. All of my life I perpetrated violence in so many ways, though I'd only seen myself as the victim of other people's insensitivity and carelessness. At this point in my life, I totally get the value of the time I spent with Sam. Karmic pay off, perhaps; however, over time I strengthened the muscles required to extract myself from a self-abusive way of being and a way of living. For it was only in me that I could come to a place where I no longer allowed myself to be abused, intimidated, or to constantly act out of fear of hurtful words, rejection or neglect.

Inch by painful inch I birthed myself, as I recognized my own desire to feel better in relation to myself. Creating closeness with people with whom I enjoyed being me, distancing me from people with whom I didn't enjoy being me, took years of practice. With Sam, as hard as I tried to create peace I continually set myself up for criticism and rejection. My time with him brought such recrimination as my breasts were not adequate and my vagina didn't smell or taste as nice as other women's. I became more insecure. Where with Joshua, I wouldn't undress in front of him, with Sam I became more obsessed with trying to be sexy and appealing; way beyond the beyond in order to feel accepted, worthy and loved. These seven years with Sam were the most self-abusive.

It took a long time to find my sea legs. I constantly asked myself what I was willing to be with and what I was not willing to be with. I left Joshua because I could no longer endure the lack of presence, the loneliness and isolation. We were two different vessels on this sea of life and neither of us had the communication tools to allow us to find each other's hearts. Children are such wonderful sources of love, but in the world of marriage, when partnership isn't obtainable, children cannot fill the empty space. I thought they could, hence I wanted to fill my life with more children. In my mind, there's little vulnerability with children, and so much more control in one's life.

My projections of who I saw Sam to be continued to outweigh the everyday experience of who he was. I could see and experience his essence, his innocence, and his playful charismatic delight. I loved being with these aspects of him. It filled my soul. Yet who he was in the world fractured the very same soul. I continually looked for ways to change myself in order to be more pleasing, sexy, loving and attentive. I wanted to perfect myself so that there would be no reason for him to choose anyone else, but me. What was I thinking?

As it turned out Sam talked a lot about being sexual, but never acted on it other than to go to strip clubs or masturbate while viewing pornographic magazines. It saddened me to realize that so much of what I'd projected onto him in regard to positive and strong aspects was only a mere hope of who I wanted him to be.

Over the years, I've attempted to understand the enmeshment with Sam. What was it that kept me from leaving? The analogy comes that he represented the only safety line I had. He gave me connection, otherwise I feel like I would have spun off the planet. There were days, then weeks, and then months that I learned to live without him, but like any addiction, once you start up again you've got to go through the cycle again.

Liverpool, Nova Scotia

I worked four years in Liverpool, which had a population of about fifteen hundred people. I lived in an even smaller village called Milton, which was about as beautiful a place as you could find anywhere. My home faced the Mersey River. The view was like something out of a Monet painting.

It wasn't until I was settled in my job in Liverpool that I began to unravel the emotional web I'd woven since leaving the children. Being settled and alone meant that the time taken up with Sam and with anxiety regarding money was now available to focus on myself. There were days every three or four months when I would feel physically ill, enough to take a day off from work. It wasn't as if I *was* sick, it was that I didn't feel well. I would stay in bed sometimes sleeping, sometimes awake. Inevitably, a thought would come to mind; not only were my children having birthdays without me (thinking about *their* loss), but also, I missed being a part of their lives: Halloween, birthdays, proms, and so much more. I began to feel my own deep sorrow and loss. Over time, these few hours relieved the years of emotional build up. Rarely were there words or thoughts. Just deep sobbing for just a few moments at a time, and then it would end. Just like that. I'd feel better, get up and go for a walk with my dog, Hattie.

Rarely did I speak to anyone about this part of my life. I couldn't even acknowledge it to myself. Finally close to being forty years old, twelve years after leaving the children, I spoke to Stan, a psychologist and colleague about what was happening to me, that I was experiencing these bouts of grief after all of these years. This man was the first person to acknowledge me for the choice I had made and for what I had done. He said if I had sacrificed my motherhood by walking in front of a bus in order to protect my children I would have been considered a good mother and a hero. What I did; this kind of heroism; this kind of sacrificing of my motherhood goes unacknowledged and is scorned. This isn't what real motherhood looks like or feels like for ordinary people. He encouraged me to be present to my grief at having given up my motherhood and my children.

This brought on a turn of thinking. I'd been looking at what my children had sacrificed, never acknowledging my own. Stan, through his wisdom gave me permission to take it in small bite-sized pieces; letting the process move at its own speed and that my higher self knew how to take care of me.

Work

Liverpool is ninety minutes south of Halifax. It's a small fishing town and the home of a pulp mill. About ten percent of the population was involved with drugs and alcohol, directly. That meant a larger percentage of people—parents, children, spouses, friends, employees and more were affected by substance abuse.

My clients were those who were serious about dealing with their addiction issues. First, they would go through a recovery program, either a five-day or twenty-eight-day program. They would then work with my co-worker Carolyn Howard to ensure stability, self-care and employment. Once the individual was stabilized then they might consider therapy to support their recovery. This would bring them to me.

It was during my years at Drug Dependency that I began to experience the wonder of people who had a sense of spirituality. In those years, I learned a great deal from my clients, many of whom worked the twelve-step program. Slowly I began to develop an awareness of the potential value of surrendering my will to a higher power, whoever or whatever that was.

The process was gradual enough that I did not recognize that spirituality was becoming more and more infused in my work and in my life. Therapy with clients began to include more of a spiritual perspective and my convictions grew stronger that the spiritual component within the whole recovery process was essential.

I loved my work. I loved my clients. I loved the freedom to work so independently. My supervisor was in Yarmouth, two hours away. I was a good therapist for the most part without that supervision, yet I know now the mistakes I made because I was on my own. In essence, I was a brand new therapist who had a great deal to learn about addictions, recovery, spirituality and life in general.

Small Town Living

Life in a small town has many perks. Being an attractive, single woman in her thirties was advantageous when it came to acting in community theatre in Liverpool. There weren't that many young women interested in doing theatre in Liverpool, so I got to be a star! Even before high school, I dreamed of being the lead in plays and musicals. Living in this small community gave me the opportunity to strut my stuff. I played the virgin Philia, in *A Funny Thing Happened on the Way to the Forum*, a Steven Sondheim Broadway Musical, and also played young Christina Graves in *Murder on the Nile* – an Agatha Christi play. The most challenging role I played in this small community theatre was the lead in a play called *The Last Real Summer,* written by Warren Graves. I had to deliver over fifteen monologues. I played an elderly woman who reminisced about her summers as a young girl. We were invited to the International Multicultural Festival in Toronto to perform this Canadian production. That was pretty exciting! My children came to see their mom on the big stage in Toronto!

In many ways, I thrived in this tiny part of the world. As I've already made clear, I loved the outdoors and the beauty of nature was right outside my door. I could swim, hike, ski, bike and sail if I wanted. It was all so very close. I loved living in my one hundred-year-old home and the close, intimate knit of neighbors. Everyone knew my business, but that was okay with me. I believed people really cared. Maybe there were a few busybodies, but for the most part this was a community who took care of each other in time of need. I liked it!

I Want What You've Got

A few times a week, an old fellow, Big Don, who had been in recovery for many years dropped by our office for a cup of coffee and a visit with Carolyn and Dawn, our assistant. Big Don was not one of the brightest fellows I'd ever met, but over time, I realized he had something I wanted. He had serenity. It was clear that his work with a twelve step program gave him that serenity.

I put two and two together and realized it was time to begin working a twelve-step program myself. Understanding that my life with alcoholic parents created in me certain survival mechanisms that were in a word, dysfunctional, I knew I had to begin to let go of what no longer served me and explore new ways of being that would inevitably bring the serenity that I witnessed in Big Don. Facing what I had been avoiding my whole life was about to take me far beyond the work I did with the *Seth Book.*

Melody Beattie's book *the Language of Letting Go* became my bible. She was speaking to people who were co-dependent and to Adult

Children of Alcoholics, and she was absolutely speaking to me. She gently revealed underlying processes that fueled my thoughts and actions. Little by little, I released patterns of being that no longer served *the me* that was emerging.

Because I was the therapist with NSCDD, I didn't feel comfortable going to Al-Anon meetings. It's one of the downsides of being the Go-To-Gal in town. But, on my own, I was able to unravel slowly many of the threads that bound me to what wasn't working.

Age Thirty-Six

Where Sam had been the catalyst for me leaving my marriage, I became a catalyst for someone else to end his marriage. Funny that life turns out that way.

Chris had all of the charm and delight, the stability and humor. It felt like the perfect match in so many ways. I met him for the first time in the doorway of my own home. He had come to Liverpool to present a workshop on suicide. I'd offered my home as a place for him to stay with his co-facilitator Mark.

I didn't intend for things to go the way they went. I didn't intend to be the catalyst for him to leave his marriage, and I didn't intend to fall in love with him. But my friend Maggie spurred me on. She knew Chris really well and knew how unhappy he was in his marriage. She thought he and I would be a good couple. And that's how it all started.

Chris provided an appearance of stability in the community, since he was a dad of three children with a good job as the manager of a parole office in Nova Scotia. He had people who loved him and respected him. My children loved Chris, and after almost ten years after the separation from Joshua and the children, it felt like I was finally settling into myself. I allowed myself to relax. There was none of the crazy-making elements of relationship that was part and parcel to being with Sam. At least not in the beginning.

We loved to do the same things; hiking, jogging, tennis and we shared so much laughter and fun. I liked his family and he liked mine. The companionship was effortless. He was easy to talk to and because we were in similar professions, we shared in deeper more profound levels then I'd known before. I figured that Chris and I would be together forever.

We had this thing; we somehow knew that we'd have to do everything that we wanted to do together right away. We didn't know why, but through each season of the year, we fully embraced our time together. Both of us expressed such gratitude for what we'd brought to each other.

Slowly, things started to shift until one day, one year to the date of him leaving his wife, Karen, three weeks before Christmas, Chris told me it was over. He'd been having an affair with a woman who he eventually married and then divorced.

Emotional Breakdown #2

I felt like I was hit in the head with that two-by-four about which Gloria Taylor warned me. Though Chris was acting more disinterested over time, I had no idea he was involved with another woman, or that he'd recreate his relationship with Karen all over again.

In no way did I feel responsible for this relationship going south. I saw the cycle that had occurred and realized from a cognitive perspective that being part of Chris's process meant playing out a dynamic, which neither of us was aware. I could see it and clearly understand it; however, it was still one of the most devastating experiences of my life.

I was faced with excruciating emotional and physical pain and like many of my clients, I wanted something to take away the pain; I wanted a fix. I approached my doctor with my circumstance and requested some sort of sedative. He gave me three pills – THREE! I was frustrated with his choice to give me such a small amount, yet respected his decision. I had to walk my talk.

I was pretty sure that this break up was a catalyst for a breakdown that would require that I not ignore or deny my personal reality. I might as well have been in a car crash, because I felt as though I'd been run over by a truck. There was no way I could distract myself from this level pain. I'd never realized the degree to which the body is affected by our emotional reality. I now know very well.

I broke each precious sedative into quarters so that they would last me a couple of weeks. One quarter of a mild sedative wasn't going to make much of a difference, but it allowed me to at least fall asleep at night.

Nothing was going to damn the forces of the dissolution of self. Work was my salve. While sitting with clients, focusing on them gave respite. Between sessions, I would head to the bathroom, which became my sanctuary for tears. I'd break down and sob for minutes at a time; blow my nose, wipe my face then head back to the office for my next appointment.

My belief is that aside from Sam, Chris was the first real relationship after my divorce and separation from my children. Somehow, this breakup opened up large pockets of grief that I'd tucked far away. It was a knockdown for sure and I had no idea how long it would be before I was myself again.

Though my sleep was restful and full of wonderful dreams of Chris telling me how much he loved me and wanted to get back together, waking into life was agonizing. Even before I was awake, I could feel my body in anguish. I knew this to be all the sorrow and grief of wishes and dreams that were dying. This was also a catalyst for lifting the veil of denial of my loss of my motherhood. Though much of it did not have story attached, my body would not hold the lies and the consequences of those lies anymore.

Grief has no limit, and when denied it can be an unforgiving master. Walking was painful. Every step I took brought with it a great deal of agony. I focused on getting my dog, Hattie out for a walk every day. Moving the muscles to put one foot in front of the other was a monumental effort. Walking around the river daily was a requirement regardless of my emotional and physical resistance.

I was doing Tole Painting at the time and it was in these moments of creativity when I would forget the pain and the darkness. These brief flashes let me know that I would return to a time when pain would no longer predominate my conscious, waking life. I didn't share this time with many. My friend Mike knew what I was going through. He was the first person that said as a matter of fact, "Yep, that's how it is. It will get better a little bit at a time."

These flashes of freedom from the pain moved into minutes. What wonder and gratitude came with these moments. Minutes became hours and hours became days.

Now, I know these experiences to be called Spiritual Emergence processes. Our spirit has to whack us over the head with a two-by-four to get our attention. It's probably the only way I would actually pay attention to my real self and heal the wounds of the separation from my children, from my soul, from Spirit itself.

Four months later, I had a Wake for the ending of that relationship. It was a celebration of my recovery. I threw old Christmas wreaths in the ocean as symbols of the dead and old being released. I recovered them days later when I found them washed up on the beach.

Many years later, I called Chris to ask what really happened; what was it that had him leave his relationship with me. His response totally surprised me. He told me that I was smarter than he was and he knew it. And though he left me for a woman in many ways just like his ex-wife, she wasn't as threatening as I was to his manhood. It didn't have anything to do with how I was being. He just couldn't live with someone who was smarter than he was.

Tai Chi

Six months after leaving Chris, my friend Pam encouraged me to take Tai Chi with her on Saturday mornings in Bridgewater, which was about thirty minutes from Liverpool. The class was held at 7:00 a.m., which meant getting up at 6:00 a.m. to be there on time. Pam met me at the highway and we'd drive up together. I'd been suffering with a great deal of lower back pain for years so it was possible that Tai Chi would benefit me.

For the next two and a half years, this class was my sanctuary. The people there became long lasting friends. My back heeled and so did my soul.

This form of Tai Chi was founded by a Mr. Moi, who founded the Canadian Tai Chi society a long time ago. The instructors teach as a service and do not accept money for their time. This was significant to me, that someone was dedicated enough to spend every Saturday morning with us. He always had the water hot and a large selection of tea from which to choose. We would donate money for the space and the tea.

I loved the way my body felt. I loved the flow of movement in the room. I loved the ritual of my Saturday mornings. Over time, I came to do Tai Chi by myself in the mornings before going to work.

The Halifax head office of the Canadian Tai Chi Society began to take a more politically active role. They began to intervene in our little class in Bridgewater. They began to require membership and membership dues. They wanted members to become organizers. Our instructor, essentially, was booted out and replaced with teachers who would come from Halifax. The politics ruined the beauty of this grass-roots ceremony. It hurt my heart to see the demise of what showed up out of love and spirit. I stopped attending the sessions and Tai Chi slowly disappeared from my life.

As beautiful and serene as my life in Liverpool was, it was beginning to feel small. Some friends of mine, who I'd met through Tai

Chi and who lived closer to Bridgewater encouraged me to look for a house up in that direction. The first day of looking, I found my next dream home and moved in the following month.

This house too was more than one hundred years old on twenty-five acres of land, with a small waterfront beach on the estuary of the LaHave River. It would be a forty-five minute drive to work, but for a commute, it couldn't have been more breathtakingly beautiful. I never minded driving to or from work as every turn was an awe-inspiring view of rocky coves, beaches, waterside cottages and amazing birdlife.

Jumping into a Leaky Boat

I believe it was almost a year after the ending of my relationship with Chris when I met Jonathan. Meeting him literally created unexplainable sparks as we both grabbed the door handle simultaneously. It was one of those moments that you wonder what God is up to.

Jonathan was a handsome, brilliant man who was a victim of the Vietnam War. He moved to Canada after serving time in Vietnam. I believe he suffered from Post Traumatic Stress Disorder (PTSD), among other things.

This time it took me just two years before I was done. He was torn between his ex-girlfriend, Melanie and me. This was a confusing relationship. Six weeks on and six weeks off. He needed a lot of solitude and cave time. In the meantime, I learned more and more to enjoy myself in my own life without a lover or partner. I was becoming my own partner.

While I was working as a therapist with recovering addicts, Jonathan decided to grow marijuana in his attic. Hmm! This was somewhat of a dilemma for me, but I wasn't going to blow the whistle on him or break up with him. It was one of those times when I didn't feel out of integrity, yet I didn't feel great about it either. It was a question with which I sat for a long while.

Starting in college, I used marijuana occasionally. It wasn't at all unusual at that time for most of the people I knew to kick back and light a joint after dinner.

As with Sam, Jonathan was not available for my emotional needs, he was too much into his own emotional process, mostly depression and anxiety. To a degree, I allowed myself to be immersed in his life, but I was able to stay afloat without him.

All of this time, my children visited maybe once or twice a year. They were entrenched in their own life. Both Hannah and Noah were in dance and acting classes. As I mentioned, Joshua took them to Europe, Asia, Africa and South America. I wanted them to come live with me and enjoy the simplicity of the beauty of Nova Scotia, but they just weren't that interested. They were used to having fun handed to them. It was really challenging for them to come to what seemed like the sticks and have to create their own fun. Over time, though, they made friends with local kids and began to look forward to their visits to Nova Scotia.

Growing oneself is an endless process. I suspect that this life had been built upon the foundations of past lifetimes, where I was also shackled to guilt, denying not only the gifts of my essential being on this planet, but also denying all of the gifts that are inherently mine. I found a card that I sent to my mom one year for her birthday. It said something like – I've always tried to be normal. Now I know that this is it!

A Promotion

The Commission hired a new director for our region of the Province - Marilyn Keddy. She was clear about what she wanted and whom she wanted for specific positions. The Province was creating a new detoxification center in Lunenburg with new offices. When I met Marilyn, I shared that I was interested in developing a ten-day treatment program for this region. She was thrilled with the idea and gave me free reign to develop the program based on my expertise.

Over the next year, everything was in process and a move to a new office in Lunenburg took place. This shortened my commute to about twenty-five minutes and included a ferry ride across the LaHave River.

My years with the commission were extremely fulfilling. I'd worked through so many of my issues. I'd come to accept that my children had to make their own choices as I had to make mine. Where my choice was to include them, they didn't necessarily need to include me.

A moment that revealed to me how far I had come in my life took place on a sunny Sunday afternoon. I was transplanting some shrubs in front of my home in LaHave. My gardens were thriving and I was digging, hauling, and having a wonderful time. As cars drove by people would honk and wave and I'd wave back. I had a thought: "I wonder if they think I'm lonely, doing this all by myself?" I realized in that moment that I was having the time of my life. I wasn't anxious or worried about men or relationships. And in that moment, I felt anything, but lonely. I was just happy, serene and connected to myself. My life was filled with beauty, which gave me far more joy than I ever imagined.

Peter Pan

I can't think of one man that I've been with as a partner who was sincerely interested in growing up and being adult. A few of them said they were into personal growth, but when it came to exercising the muscles and walking their talk, they just weren't willing to take the first step. Dan Kiley called this the Peter Pan Syndrome. Though I've always been curious what drew me to such men I can only look to myself for what facilitated that attraction.

I wished that I could stay forever young and free of responsibility; at the same time I was doing everything I could to become self-reliant. As a mom in her early twenties, I took my responsibilities seriously. I was accountable and reliable as any good co-dependent can be. And at the same time, I so desired to be with someone who loved me enough to relieve me of any burdensome requirements of being self-sustaining. I believed they would be fulfilled and happy as the sole breadwinner so that I could be free of any concern for surviving. I say that and yet I did have that with Joshua. At that time, I didn't have to worry about financial security—what many women dream of; but it wasn't enough to be a stay at home mom, void of partnership with the man that I'd married. And over the last ten years I'd come to love my work, life and home in Nova Scotia.

Perhaps by focusing on being with men who wanted to stay youthful and immature, I could help them grow up, find their true essential self, leading them to their truest path. Perhaps as a good co-dependent individual, being with men that would never grow up I'd always have someone who would need me—the very underlying reason for having children.

The fact is that very few of us grow ourselves beyond adolescents. Regardless of whether we are in our twenties, thirties, forties; even seventies or eighties, quite often we still act as if we are in our teens. The whole concept of emotional intelligence is to cultivate consciousness of how we allow ourselves and others to maintain a way of being that is so much less then optimal in business relationships and personal relationships. Most television sitcoms reflect this level of emotional maturity or lack-there-of. Have you ever noticed that many of these characters never change over the years? What is so attractive about immaturity?

There are places in life where we are grownup and then there are places where we are not. Generally speaking, personal relationships ignite childhood reactions without a sense of how to do or be any different.

I've met people who in their professional lives are mature, respectful and follow through on their commitments; however, when they go home to their partners and children they revert to the emotional level of an adolescent, ignoring or shirking commitments such as taking out the trash or feeding the dog. I can only surmise that since most of us operate at this adolescent level of maturity we assume we have to allow others the same.

What is it that allows us to continually tolerate and endure immature behavior? Well, because I can answer only for myself, I can say that my attractor beams were set to only one frequency and a very low one at that. I have to admit that theirs were set, most likely to the same frequency, since they found me as I found them.

Meeting the Crew and Mac McKenzie

In 1991, I was thirty-nine years old and I'd created a comfortable and happy life for myself. My home on the LaHave River brought me endless joy. I loved the work I was doing for the Commission. I was settled into a life that was stable and secure, and essentially I did it all by myself! I was engaged in painting classes with a wonderful husband and wife team that were brilliant and fun. It was the first time in my life where I experienced my ability for creative expression to feel fulfilling and satisfying.

I learned to fly fish, and though I never caught a single salmon or trout, standing in the river, witnessing the breathtaking beauty of nature brought such peace to my spirit. My life was ideal. Never would I ever leave Nova Scotia.

In early June, a new member joined our small community of LaHave. An American moved into the big, empty house just down the road from me. He moved in with a crew of artisans to build a seventy-three-foot traditional gaffed-rigged schooner. This brought a lot of excitement and activity to this part of my very small world.

John Steele, a master boat builder in Petite Riviere, Nova Scotia was hired by Mac McKenzie, a fellow from Alexandria, Virginia, to build his boat *Tree of Life*. John and his wife had a *welcome to the neighborhood party* where I met Mac, his partner Cynthia and their crew. As it turned out one of the men was from my hometown, Grosse Ile, and had gone to school with my sister Helene. I vaguely remembered him from those many years ago.

Though John had built many amazing boats, for some reason this one was special. There was a mystique about it. He built a huge building within which to create the frame and structure of this massive vessel. The boat was hidden away from site until the day she was birthed, with the assistance of a huge tractor-trailer, through the doors of the shop with only inches to spare. It was extraordinary to witness. The next day, when she was officially launched and released into the water, hundreds of people came from all over the South Shore of Nova Scotia to watch and to celebrate. Mac had a flair for the dramatics. He always drew crowds.

When *Tree* was launched, she was essentially a hull with a deck. She had no masts nor rigging, and none of the wiring, woodwork or plumbing was in. Once in the water she was towed to her summer birth in front of the famous LaHave Bakery. Here is where she would be fitted in all her regalia; the tall wooden masts, miles of rope, lines and steel cable to secure the masts. Wooden hoops were fashioned to attach the gigantic sails to the masts. Each component of *Tree's* building process was a work of art and it had to meet the specification for a boat capable of sailing around the world.

She was built of wood, epoxy and other specific materials to ensure that her hull was impenetrable to most unforeseen forces throughout her worldly adventures. Though she was a Baltic Trader by design, she looked and felt like a traditional Nova Scotia built vessel, which she was and still is.

Mac's artisans were some of the best on the Eastern Seaboard. And they were all living just a few doors down from me. Like a shorebird, you never know what the current will bring your way. I didn't have to go anywhere to seek adventure; as I've found more times than not, adventure came to me!

Every day, as my dog, Hattie and I walked; we'd witness the progress that was made on *Tree*. The long round masts lying on the ground one day would be lifted into place by a crane the next. All the rigging required to hold the masts in place had to be put there by individuals willing to climb eighty-five feet up in the air to connect the wires by massive screws and bolts. It was a high-flying act for sure. Day by day, while *Tree* was being dressed on the outside a number of crews were down below; one, getting her engine and generators working; another working on the electrical system, laying over a mile of wire throughout the hull connecting everything to the main fuse box. Still another focused on the carpentry. I had never witnessed such an undertaking before and couldn't imagine how all of this was going to come together.

Once the rigging and sails were in place and the engine and generator was working, it was time to see if it all worked as it was designed to.

I was invited to come on her maiden voyage. I'd come to Nova Scotia for many reasons, one being that I wanted to sail. Though I lived within a mile of the local sailing club and watched boats sail on the estuary in front of my house, not until this moment did I feel compelled to bring sailing more into the forefront of my life. Now I was sitting aboard a sixty-ton sailing vessel, feeling an excitement and a resonance with the wind and sea that I'd come here to experience.

Though there were at least twenty people on board for this maiden voyage, I found a secluded spot in the furthest aft corner of the boat overlooking the stern and the wake that followed. I wanted a moment to myself and with *Tree*, to get acquainted with her, one on one. I enjoyed the tranquility of the moment and at the same time I thought to myself that there was *no way* I could be aboard a boat longer than a few hours without going stir crazy. Try as I might to imagine the wonders of sailing around the world I couldn't find one thread of desire that would take me away from Nova Scotia. Besides, I was terrified of sailing beyond the site of land. It made me anxious just thinking about it. So, I let go of that possibility and settled into the moment. I was enchanted and captivated with the experience I was having on such an exquisite vessel. I counted myself among the very lucky to have this opportunity to sail on *Tree* on a perfectly beautiful Nova Scotia breeze.

Over the months that followed, I got to know Cynthia as a friend. I liked her. She shared with me on numerous occasions that Mac was really challenging to live with. She was somewhat concerned for her well-being and wanted a safe haven in my home if need be. I was happy to oblige.

For the whole summer, I enjoyed to company of the crew, owners and *Tree*. As October rolled around it was time for the boat to head south to finish her interior in warm, sunny Florida. I was sad to see them go. I stood on the dock with all of the other people who'd come to develop deep friendships with *Tree* and with the crew. We waved farewell until they were out of sight and looked forward to their return most likely the following summer.

Out of the Blue, Mac Called

One evening, in late January, I received a long distance phone call from Florida. It was Mac. He had been thinking of me and decided to call. It was just sort of a catch up call and it was lovely to speak with him. Among other news about the crew and the boat he shared that he and Cynthia had split up a few months back. She decided after sailing down to Jacksonville that living on a sailboat wasn't for her, so she went back to her home in Seattle.

He also shared that he planned to bring *Tree* back up to Nova Scotia for the summer again, to continue the finishing of *Tree* with John Steele and his crew, and to sail in the annual Mahone Bay Schooner Races.

Over the next five months, Mac called more regularly. It became obvious that he was interested in me. He asked if I'd consider sailing with him around the world. I had no interest in that or in him that way. Especially after talking with Cynthia, I knew enough to know that this would not be in my best interest, but I certainly looked forward to his return and the opportunity to sail on *Tree* again.

Around the middle of June, the buzz was in the air that *Tree of Life* was on her way back to Nova Scotia, and depending on the winds would be arriving in the next week or so. She'd be sailing into Lunenburg to get some specific work done before returning to her berth in LaHave.

Since my work was now in Lunenburg I was there that day with the crowd, anticipating *Tree*'s arrival. There was a hint of romance that Mac shared with a few friends that he was coming back to Nova Scotia to woo me and intended on me sailing off into the sunset with him. How romantic can you get?

A screenwriter couldn't have created a more perfect scene: As the sun slowly set over the harbor, *Tree of Life* sailed into the quaint and beautiful village of Lunenburg. I was standing in the crowd, just as a bystander, but I was goaded to go down and meet the crew personally. On one hand, I wanted to keep my distance from Mac, ensuring that he knew I had no interest in an intimate relationship. On the other hand, my excitement to reunite with my friends compelled me to scramble awkwardly over the fence and run down to meet the boat. The reunion with *Tree*, her crew and Mac was delightful and fun. I knew them all and was so happy to see them again.

The winter in Florida did *Tree* well. She returned to Nova Scotia in her full magnificence as her interior was finished impeccably. Whether on deck or down below, her textures were rich and luxurious. The grains of the teak, maple, pine, mahogany, Hawaiian Koa, purple-heart, and oak beckoned your hand to reach out and touch, exploring the satiny finishes and the diverse underlying grains and tones; like the short, shallow grain of the sun-faded teak, and the long deep, dark brown and red swirl of the Koa, each having its own seduction, each its own magnificence. Mac spared no expense and his crew paid faultless attention to detail so the eye and the soul would be bathed constantly in sensuous beauty. From far away distances to microscopic inspection, *Tree*'s classic lines and beauty were luminous. And she was as safe as she was extraordinary.

The summer was wonderful with sailing and being courted by Mac. I didn't waver in my stand to remain uninvolved with Mac in a romantic way. As I've said already, I had no interest in sailing around the world or having a relationship with someone who would be so unavailable. I knew I would never leave Nova Scotia, never, never, ever.

However, over the summer I found myself falling in love. At first, it was with *Tree of Life*, herself. It's hard to describe what it's like to be at the helm of such a wonderful boat. Her beauty was one thing, but the way she handled under sail was a thrill to say the least. To me, she was a living, breathing being. I felt her spirit. I wanted more!

And Mac continued to be more and more endearing. One evening we went out to a dance with some friends. Dressed up for the event, I felt lovely and sweet and he looked enchanting, even prince-like. I remember the very moment that I allowed myself to be swept up in the magic and romance of Mac McKenzie. I slipped the lines from the dock of logic and reason and began to drift, no float over to where he was dancing with someone else. I cut in. That moment changed my world and my destiny. There was no question that I was saying yes to what he was offering. In that moment, what had been an absolute, that I would never leave Nova Scotia now became a huge possibility.

I Must Be Crazy

It was daunting, to say the least, to think about leaving my home, my career and the family I created. I also had to consider my children. Hannah was fifteen and Noah was thirteen. I'd already moved fifteen hundred miles away from them. What would they think of their mother sailing around the world? I thought they'd just shake their heads and judge that not only had I left behind my responsibilities as a mother, but that I'd given up my job, my home and my dog, for some hare-brained adventure. I didn't know if I could endure more criticism from their father, from my parents or from myself.

Their visit to Nova Scotia that summer included meeting Mac and sailing on a number of occasions. They liked him and the idea that I might sail off to exotic places. They could sail with us whenever they wanted. I was relieved and elated that they supported me in this possible adventure. In my own mind, though, this all seemed too crazy. I didn't know if I could actually leave my life in Nova Scotia.

The winds of change seemed to be carrying me away from my stable and ideal life. I said yes to the voyage with Mac and *Tree*, but I would take the next eight months to make the necessary arrangements to end my work with the Commission and wrap up details with the house and with Hattie. This would give me time to discern whether this was the best choice for me. I had a lot to think about. I had a lot to leave behind. I did it once, long ago, when I left Joshua and the children, my beautiful home and the stability and security that went along with that picture. "What was it that created another choice-point to up and leave everything that was dear to me for … well, I shake my head and wonder, why me, Lord, why me!"

I was wary of Mac and I was wary of myself. When the spark between Mac and I ignited, it was challenging to literally keep my feet on the ground. It was happening so fast. I knew what Cynthia went through and I'd seen Mac be somewhat inconsistent. I didn't trust it all, yet I felt called to take this voyage. Numerous synchronicities at the time seemed to point me in the same direction. But to cover my back I asked Mac for $10,000 to be put in my bank account just in case things went haywire. Along with the money though, we made a contract, which included all the things we would do to ensure this relationship lasted forever. The contract included: the relationship came before *Tree*; if things got rocky, Mac would sell the boat before he would leave me. We would also go to therapy to handle any differences. We both signed the contract, paid off the mortgage on my home, money went in the bank as a cushion and I was off for another huge adventure.

Things started to happen, though; those synchronistic things that seems too strange to be true. Within a matter of weeks, my house had a renter, though I hadn't been looking for one; and even though my ten-day treatment program was barely underway, my work with the Commission felt complete. Something was telling me that now was the time to leave, not eight months from now. Every little detail fell into place, including finding the ideal home for Hattie. My guilt for always leaving her home alone for hours at a time were assuaged by a retired couple who wanted her. She'd never be alone again. She jumped into their car, laid down in the back seat as if this had always been her life. As much as I would miss her, I couldn't have been happier.

Men and Their Stuffed Animals

As for the Commission, I developed a program that brought the best of all I had to offer to people who were ready for the next step in their recovery program. I was passionate about cultivating personal awareness in individuals so they'd experience self-empowerment; they could make choices in service to what they really wanted in their lives. This ten-day outpatient program provided a container within which recovering addicts and alcoholics could discover their ground of being. I was in love with my work and every individual who joined me for this personal adventure.

I want to share with you one of the many highlights of this program that touched me deeply. It happened just prior to my leaving Nova Scotia. I was sharing with the group of ten men and my support person, Carolyn, my plan to sail with Mac and that I was taking my stuffed bear William with me and that I'd found a girlfriend for William to take along on this voyage; her name was Blossom.

One of the men in the group said that he too had a teddy bear. He shared how important his bear had been to him. Then another man spoke up, saying he had a stuffed dog. Nine of the ten fellows shared that each had a stuffed animal that brought comfort to him.

The one fellow, who didn't have a stuffed toy, at first, pooh-poohed the idea of grown men having stuffed animals. No one chastised him or got defensive about this fellow's position. And when we decided we would have a Teddy Bear's Picnic on the last day of our program he said he'd borrow a stuffed animal from his son.

Every one of these men, most of them hardy fishermen and loggers brought in their stuffed animal. Instead of borrowing his sons, the fellow who was reticent went out, bought himself a bear too, and was so glad he did. He shared what a special moment that was for him to give himself that bear.

Sharing my story facilitated such an opening for these men. I was touched to the core of my being with their openness to be vulnerable, intimate and childlike with each other. This is still one of my most precious memories of my time with the Commission.

Chapter Five

Leaving Nova Scotia

I left on a snowy November day. Mac flew up to Nova Scotia to drive with me to meet *Tree* in Florida. We had to leave as soon as possible because a snowstorm was coming in and we needed to catch the evening ferry, if possible.

We drove from LaHave to Yarmouth through the snow. The closer we got to Yarmouth the heavier the snowfall. We were anxious during the drive, but we made it in time to get loaded onto the ferry and find our stateroom, which was a real luxury. Most people sleep in chairs or in their cars during these crossings, so to have a room with a private bathroom and a couple of bunk beds was heaven.

The ferry ride across to Bar Harbor, Maine usually takes about six hours, but this particular passage took hours longer. The storm was bad. Within an hour of leaving the harbor, twenty-foot walls of water were being thrown up against the highest reaches of the ferry. At first, it was thrilling and fun to witness the incredible power of such a storm system. But then seasickness set in, in the worst way. Whatever excitement and enthusiasm I'd been enjoying vanished with the dizziness, the queasiness and the nausea. I felt awful, yet I was afraid to let Mac know just how bad I was feeling. I needed to vomit, but worried he might think me weak and decide he made a big mistake.

We lay together in a single bunk; I was too afraid to sleep by myself. As we lay there being rocked and rolled by the sea, I nonchalantly asked him if he'd ever gotten seasick and vomited. The word yes was hardly out of his mouth when I was up and into the bathroom chucking up the contents of my stomach. I was so relieved to hear that *yes,* and that I didn't need to pretend to be strong in this way. What a relief!

Once that was taken care of, I settled into his arms and rested. We woke hours later as the ferry pulled into the dock. Thank God, that was over. I saw this very short voyage across the stormy sea as an initiation to the world of sailing adventures.

The snowstorm was all along the Eastern Seaboard. We worked our way down the coast; Thanksgiving in New Jersey with Mac's family; to Alexandria, Mac's home, to meet his friends; then down to Jacksonville, Florida where *Tree of Life* was waiting. It was fun to watch as the snowstorm turned to rain and then to sunshine as we drove closer and closer to our destination. The warmth of even the more northern part of Florida was divine; a big difference from the wintry world of Nova Scotia.

Jaime Ebright

Mac put an ad out to the sailing community looking for a cook for *Tree*. This would be someone who had experience living and cooking on sailboats and could commit to a long-term adventure. We got a few responses, one being from a woman named Jaime Ebright, from Southern California. She had the experience we were looking for. When I interviewed her over the phone, I found her to have a lovely balance between professionalism and playfulness. She sounded like she'd be a really good fit.

A week after Mac and I arrived at the boat, I took the dingy over to the dock in Jacksonville to meet Jaime. It felt like meeting a dear old friend after many, many years. I liked her immediately. She was cute and perky, yet grounded and clear. She was a no-nonsense woman who could party until the cows came home. Life would have been unbearable aboard the boat without Jaime. She brought with her a great attitude and was always helpful and caring.

Sailing from Jacksonville to Key West was a two-day trip and the seas were light so we motored most of the way. We stopped over night in Fort Pearce, just a few miles north of my parents' home in Stuart,

Florida. We spent the night with them and they agreed to sail with us to Key West. They actually approved of my relationship with Mac. They saw that I'd be with a man that had character and money. It was nice to feel their approval and for them to share a bit of the adventure with me on *Tree*.

Christmas in Key West

It takes a hell of a lot of work to build a boat like *Tree of Life*. It takes a hell of a lot of work to maintain her too. Though finished on so many levels there was always more to do, especially on a boat that needed to be seaworthy. Electricity, water, engine, safety, food, ballast, technical stuff like radar and GPS. Each of these systems needed to be dependable and unfailing. In many cases, Mac had an extra of everything, just in case there was a failure. Much of the hidden storage space aboard *Tree* was filled with the *just-in-case* gadgets.

Our stay in Key West was longer than anticipated, which in many ways was terrific. There are so many wonderful things about this Key; all of the history, the bars, the local color; it was funky and offered so much fun and Mac loved fun!

This was where I first began to get a sense that my life wasn't going to be better than what I had in Nova Scotia. It was just going to be different. Each day, including Christmas we worked and worked and worked to clean up the boat and get her ready for her sea trials. Maintenance of a boat the size of *Tree* is a never-ending task. Everything has to be checked and re-checked. The sun faded the decks incredibly fast, so there was a constant process of oiling the decks, the railing; everything exposed to saltwater and sun. We had a few play days on Key West; however, we were readying ourselves for the inevitable day when we would leave the security of our berth for the voyage that lay ahead.

It occurred to me around the second week in the Keys that Mac was anxious about undertaking the responsibilities of such an enormous proportion. He was the owner and captain of a million dollar boat, with six crewmembers on board. Though he was an incredibly experienced sailor, his father's voice rang in his head, "You are a loose cannon and don't have the where-with-all to be a grown up man." As sure as he was of his dream to sail around the world, he doubted whether he was man enough to do it. Inevitably, he overcame his reluctance to leave the safe harbor and out we went into the sea of the unknown.

Our first leg of the trip took us to the Bahamas, then to Turks and Caico's, down to Jamaica and back to Florida. Jaime and I were the only women with five men. What a trip!

I was plagued by seasickness. Even before we'd get beyond the break walls, I'd see the open ocean ahead and immediately feel sick to my stomach. I'd take a seasickness pill in order to stop feeling sick, but this meant that I slept a lot. I realized that my seasickness was my attempt to avoid facing the journey in front of me. Like leaving my marriage and children, I couldn't face the reality of my choice. In this case, though, I couldn't deny my reality, but I could take an anti-nausea pill and go to sleep.

I hid in my bunk for the first month or so of the cruise. I eventually chose to come up on deck, and participate fully in the sailing experience. It was the most profoundly frightening experience I have ever been through. At the same time there was absolutely nothing to be afraid of.

It took awhile, but I did realize that my seasickness was my way of distracting myself from my fears of being out of control and in the hands of a man I didn't trust. I was sure that I was drawn to this adventure by the hands of fate. If this was absolutely true then I needed to be present to what it was I was supposed to be doing. As frightened as I was, I decided to choose to be more present to the reality of my circumstances, facing the open ocean, then overcoming my sickness and eventually my fears.

Over the course of the months aboard *Tree*, sailing around the Caribbean I did become acclimated and more self-assured. I took my time at the helm like everyone else and learned to read charts and the compass like an old-salt.

Jamaica was our last stop before heading back to Florida. Friends joined us for a week and we enjoyed the scenery and the new friends we made. We'd been cruising for about six weeks and it was time to get back to the States to begin preparation for crossing the Atlantic, which had to take place within a certain framework of time. Hurricane season would stop us from the crossing if we didn't give ourselves the time we needed. No one wants to sail through a hurricane.

A gentle shower of rain sent us on our way back to the U.S. Quite often we played Celtic music while sailing, and as we lifted the anchor and hoisted the sails I danced a jig while at the helm, blissfully taking in the sensation of the warmth of the rain, the confidence I'd gained over the past months and the joy of facing the last leg of this adventure. It should be smooth sailing from here on.

A few hours out from Montego Bay, while sitting in the wheelhouse with everyone else, I overheard the weather forecast that there was a system coming up from Cuba. It was traveling about six miles per hour, heading north. We were about fifty miles north of Cuba at that time, so I quietly calculated the possibility of this system hitting us. By my calculations, if this storm were to hit us, it would probably hit before dawn.

No one else seemed to notice or be concerned, so I asked if we should be worried. Mac said no, that we would be much further north and the storm would probably peter out before it reached us.

This was one of those interesting things about sailing. You would think that when sailing off shore the captain and crew would have listened to the most current weather forecast, ensuring that we were prepared for what came our way. Sometimes this happened and sometimes it didn't. I assumed that Mac was on top of all the safety precautions and so I let it be, yet at the same time, I realized that if that storm did come through I'd be the one on the helm when it happened.

My watch began at 5:00 a.m. It was still dark. I was replacing Joe, who'd been at the helm for the past two hours. All the portholes and hatches were open, given that is was a beautiful, warm tropical evening, yet this was a real no-no to sail offshore at night with everything wide open. I noticed some lightning off to starboard along the Floridian coast. I could see the lights of the cities and aside from these few lightning strikes everything was calm. At the same time, my senses were telling me that this system coming from Cuba wasn't too far away and I wanted to make sure we were safe. I ordered Joe to close all of the portholes below and all of the hatches too. He looked at me disdainfully and complained that there was no reason to, but did it anyway. He didn't batten down the hatches; he just closed them.

I checked the radar looking for this storm, but it seemed to be alluding me until the thought occurred to me; we don't have to worry about a storm that is moving north if it's ahead of us. We only have to worry if the storm is behind us. At which point I shifted the radar to show what was behind us, and there it was! A huge orange mark on the screen. The intensity of the color informed me this wasn't going to be a light sprinkle of rain. I looked outside the wheelhouse to see if I could see it and there it was. Dark even against the night sky. I called up Mac and shared with him everything I knew. He had no worries and didn't even consider taking down the sails. He was very nonchalant about the whole thing.

I was still at the helm when the wind began to pick up and *Tree* slowly healed onto her side, enough so that the sea began to pour into the wheelhouse. Everyone was calm and Mac told Joe to close that door. I told Mac to take the wheel, that if the boat was going down I wasn't going to be at the helm.

A boat, the *Pride of Baltimore*, similar in size to *Tree*, had gone down just months before with her teenage crew aboard. The conditions were very similar with portholes and hatches wide open. That boat sank in a matter of minutes with all aboard lost.

We had four sails flying, which would take us into the drink in no time at all. I sat in the stairwell waiting for our demise, angry that the person in charge was about to kill us all.

There was a crash and the sound of glass breaking from below. A glass cooking dish fell. Jaime was awakened and came to see what was happening. In her calmest voice, she asked for help. The portholes were taking in massive amounts of water and she needed the bigger fellows to force them down to get them latched. I went down below, but knew I'd be of no use. I saw what looked like six water hydrants wide open. We were in big trouble.

My stomach was upset—the seasickness thing, but it occurred to me that even in the worst weather, I had always been able to find my way back to the aft cabin where Mac and I slept. I knew where the small water pump was under the floorboards and thought that perhaps I could at least be busy doing something while we were going down.

By this point, *Tree* was so far over on her side that her rudder was out of the water. There was no use trying to steer. So Mac left her to fend for herself, while he came down to start the large electrical water pumps. First, he had to remember how to turn them on!

If I hadn't been scared before all of this happened, this was the icing on the cake. *Tree* would not have sustained much more intake of water. We would have sunk as surely as the *Baltimore* had.

It was only a few minutes of ninety miles per hour winds that put *Tree* on her side. She began to right herself as the storm system passed. She had taken on an incredible amount of water and suffered a huge amount of damage to anything that would not sustain a good drenching of saltwater. All electrical components that got a soaking were an automatic loss, so were computers, TV, stereos—you name it and it was destroyed.

I remained in the aft portion of the boat with my little hand pump, pumping out the water in the bilges that I could reach. It was good to keep myself busy. I would have loved to sock Mac in the jaw for what happened, but it would have done none of us any good. Even an "I told you so," would have been fruitless. I knew what I knew and I kept it to myself. I was just glad to be alive and still afloat.

By this time, the dawn was breaking and we were just a couple of hours out of Miami. We motored in, took a nap, and then began emptying out every single item from the boat. Every nook and cranny needed to be rinsed of the corroding effects of the saltwater.

A small squall traveling just six miles per hour carried winds that were blowing ninety miles per hour. It knocked a sixty-ton sailboat over on her side. I witnessed the incredible power and force of Mother Nature. Her profound presence impacted upon me for many years thereafter, for I no longer trusted her to grant kindness and loving gentleness. From then on, I suspected that within each cloud patch was the wrath and fury of another potential knockdown.

Normal Is as Normal Does

No structural damage was done to *Tree* herself, though thousands of dollars worth of stuff needed to be replaced before the transatlantic crossing in June.

From Miami we sailed to Jacksonville to do the majority of the preparatory work for the crossing. I took a few days off to visit my mom and dad. I needed a break. Among everything else, I'd been living with six other people in a space that was approximately seventy feet by twenty feet for the past three months after years of living alone.

It was interesting being on land after months of living on a boat. The first night at my parents, when I got up to go to the bathroom, I nearly fell on my keister. The floor did not heave or lurch, but my body reacted as if it had. It would take a few days to normalize my balance and by then I'd be back on the boat.

Life went on at a normal pace; no more bad weather to sail through, though a hurricane kept us hostage in Charlottesville, South Carolina for a week. I was really happy to have that time on shore and all of the crew said that of all the ports we'd been in, this was the one they enjoyed the most.

Next stop, Rhode Island, and the final preparations for the Atlantic crossing. I had been unsure as to whether I would be a part of the next leg of this adventure. I'd barely been out beyond the site of land and I had been thoroughly traumatized by the knockdown. Mac and I had some hard times, but some good times too. I wanted to go and yet I was really scared. I didn't want to miss the adventure of a lifetime, as if I hadn't had it already. My sense was that this crossing was part of that calling I had in Nova Scotia; that it was important that I participate in this part of the journey with *Tree*.

I had done some research and found very few women at that time had sailed across the Atlantic and there was very little written about their experience. What had been written had to do with what for me seemed mundane: what foods to take, how to store canned goods and fresh foods, how to cook in stormy seas. I couldn't find anything about what it was like for them; how they faced their fears; how they chose to be with the gigantic ocean that surrounded them. I couldn't find the book or article that I would have wanted to read in order to ground myself in the experience of an ocean crossing. I figured, if I make the crossing perhaps I'll have to write the book that I would have wanted to read.

Yes, I made the commitment to sail from Newport to Ireland, a three-week trip across the ocean. Among the many books I took with me was Joseph Campbell's *Hero with a Thousand Faces*. Aside from *A Course in Miracles*, it was my bible – my "how to" manual on doing a hero's journey. I wrote in my journal, read every day, and felt one with those who have also endeavored to take a *bigger journey*.

Sailing on *Tree*

Sailing on the sea awakened me to a spiritual connection with the Divine. On *Tree of Life,* I was exposed to incredible beauty and serenity as well as horrendous amounts of fear and anxiety regarding the ocean of life's vastness and its depths. I was enchanted into this adventure for reasons unknown to me at the time. Through love, beauty, money and a quest for meaning I was compelled to expose myself to emotions and sensations I could deny no longer.

Tree of Life was my teacher. No matter how exotic the places we traveled to, it was the relationship with her alone that made this journey exceptional. It created an emergence of a self I could not know through my normal, everyday, landlocked life. This vessel and this journey brought me into a more sensuous, spiritual and natural world. There were many people who sailed with me through this time on *Tree*, but my story with them will be reserved for another time.

Though there were those preliminary months of training beforehand in the tropical-blue waters of the Bahamas, Jamaica and Florida, my inner journey began in earnest with the three-week crossing of the Atlantic Ocean. Though I was very intent on making this passage, my fear of the ocean was agonizing, exhausting and unappeasable. I went in spite of oppressive thoughts and clenched viscera. The fact that I believed that I was going to die out at sea resounded in my whole being. My goal was to resolve my fear of death and my fear of the ocean. If I were to sail around the world I couldn't do it fearful of every wave in the ocean or cloud in the sky. I had to come to allow a full knowing I was safe regardless of where I hung my hat.

The Crossing

As I said earlier, *Hero with a Thousand Faces* kept me conscious to the fact that this crossing was more than just an adventurous way to get from one side of the ocean to the other. It taught me that death takes many forms, and that what I was on was an archetypal quest. I had no doubt the sacred and profane elements would direct me through this process as needed. In so many ways, the outcome was out of my hands and I surrendered to the journey ahead of me.

We left Rhode Island on the eighth of June. Coldness of the grey North Atlantic did not help to uplift my courage. The sky, overcast with low and melancholy clouds allowed no sun, moon, or stars to appear, but for one, brief, two-hour window in the middle of the eighth day at sea. At night, while on watch I only saw the ocean reflected off red and green running lights on each side of *Tree's* bow. Their purpose was to let other vessels know that we exist and that we were headed in a specific direction. Night waves as high as the freeboard of the vessel challenged my ability to steer. The waves rolled primarily unseen, but their presence was duly impacting. *Tree* pitched and rolled from side to side. Under the hand of a more experienced helms-person, she rode gently and smoothly. Having little experience at what I was doing, I sailed by sensing where the waves *might* come from. For many nights, I cursed and swore as I misjudged wave action and we rolled and pitched good and hard, making it difficult for the crew to sleep.

When not on watch during the nights, I was down in my bunk awake and shivering, not from the cold dampness of the sea, but from the fear of the powerlessness of my life in that moment. The heavens and seas were my masters, and my task was to reconcile the lack of authority over my own life. I felt I was dying into the divine, omnipotence of the cosmos.

The darkness of the cabin and the creaks and groans of the rigging further enhanced my dread. Rolling from side to side in my lonely bunk, as *Tree* rolled from one wave to the next; I clutched and wrestled with my mattress, pillows and sheets. With white knuckles, I attempted to hold myself still, an impossible endeavor, and one that made sailing and sleeping all the less enjoyable. The lee cloth held me in on the port side, keeping me from falling on the floor of the cabin. The leeboard on the starboard side kept me from rolling into my sweetheart nestled in his bunk, if he too were not on watch.

Tree creaked and moaned, and for the longest time I could not rest. I lay awake in my bunk for hours on end shivering with terror. All of me trembled. All of me waited for that one unseen ravenous wave to engulf me into the belly of the sea.

Meanwhile, the rest of the crew was having an incredibly wonderful experience. Fear and death were of no concern to them. They played and enjoyed the rapturous beauty of wind and waves. I was scared and drowning in a sea of fear and I thought they were all lunatics for being as happy as they were. I spent a great deal of time experiencing this overwhelming fear and yet most often it was only in my imagination that the possibility of dying truly existed.

One particular night, while lying in my bunk, my body stiffened and resisted, working against forces pressed upon me by the external world. I contemplated once again my death at sea. Waves of water rolled under me while waves of dread washed over me. Somewhat bored and fatigued with the ongoing struggle with this habitual consternation, I turned onto my belly and tried to settle myself down. I lay there quietly. I felt a sense of comfort as my limbs released tension and my breathing began to deepen. I felt serenity in by body for one brief moment. What is that? I focused within, looking for physical sensations to explain this transitory phenomenon called peace. The external world had not changed; the night was dark and the waves pressed consistently against the hull, lifting then releasing *Tree* to the troughs that followed. Again, I concentrated on my belly, now pressed deeply into my bedding. My umbilicus attached my life's well-being to this womb of a vessel; "I cannot survive without her support," was the thought that surfaced. As I quieted my mind's chatter, I began to experience a larger knowing and sense that *Tree of Life* was at that very moment, completely and utterly blissful; her spirit was soaring in the wind and the waves. It awakened in me an essential knowing that this was her home. The ocean was her world in which to be most expressive and alive. I longed to express such aliveness, but in the moment at hand, I needed to sleep. I settled in some more, pulling one leg up in a semi-fetal position, deepening my physical connection with *Tree*. I found that through my body I sensed her true connection with the night, the sea and the Universe at large. Through my belly in her belly, I too experienced that connection with the Universe. My mind quieted. My limbs and joints relaxed. I inhaled deeply and released my fears into this ship for her to carry. I quieted myself and became present, and a sense of calm washed through me. I felt wonderfully caressed and secure within this vessel and sensed her joy at being where she belonged. Like an unborn child still in the womb, I released myself, abandoning resistance. Enraptured in this moment, I willingly allowed myself to be rocked and cradled into restful sleep.

A rebirth perhaps, but from that night on I trusted *Tree* more and more implicitly. She became my spirit, my mom. She instilled great faith in me. At times, the oneness I had with her was like nothing I have ever experienced at any other time in my life. She had been created to circumnavigate planet Earth, which she was doing. She held her passengers safely and for the most part comfortably, especially those who were willing to let themselves soar and sail with her.

With the sense of her strong, trustful presence, I became more courageous, more honest with myself, and more dedicated to the Divine who brought me to this incredible place of learning. I took a more active role in crewing, participating more fully, more courageously in my night watches.

The transformation that took place that night allowed me to be awake and connected to life in a new way. There has been nothing in my life comparable to being on watch in the middle of the night when I was the only one awake. With the sea calm and my fear resolved, I had time to watch the stars, if they were out, and hear the water washing against the hull. The compass was my companion and guide. The sails talked to me when they needed attention. I experienced the quality of those hours as soulful communion; as rhapsody of sight and sound; as moments of serenity and often, spiritual stirrings.

During daylight hours, sitting on deck, just passing time, I was mesmerized in watching the sea change its dance from total stillness to a slow waltz then to complicated rumbas. The color and texture of the ocean shifted remarkably. In northern waters it is mostly a grey green that does not bring sensations of awe and beauty that more tropical waters bring to mind; that breathtaking blue, that blue that comes to mind just imagining the sea. The North Atlantic is grey, or grey-green, or grey-blue, and it looks cold and uninviting. It carried us across its vastness, sometimes playfully, sometimes with mystery. Sometimes it was remarkably calm, while at other times it seemed stirred by the devil's pitchfork. When open to viewing it in its entire splendor there were incredible wonders to see, taste, smell, hear, and touch: a pod of whales spouting at daybreak, sea-birds that never go ashore except to nest, unusual mollusks clinging to floating objects once attached to man made things. It took time and patience to see the sea as more than just waves and spray; acknowledging that this is only the uppermost layer of an unfathomably deep sea, much like our consciousness is the uppermost layer of a greater being. I came to accept its fathomless depths reflecting the depths of my own being. When feeling overwhelmed by its immenseness though, I broke down this vastness into much smaller increments, holding to an image that land was just over the horizon; much like a child holding a teddy bear when the night feels too long. Sometimes I'd do this for days on end; taking the realities of life in smaller increments. It sometimes helped settle that part of me that could not comprehend and accept the immense task of living this life, on a boat or on shore.

Where are you Bernie Oestebo

A most peculiar event happened in the middle of the Atlantic, something that was completely unexpected. During the normal course of a day on the crossing, Jamie and Fiona, the only other female crewmember, would radio to the tankers they would see on the horizon. This was primarily just for fun, but there was always a conversation about the weather, ensuring that we were up to date with any forecasting.

One particular episode, after the, "Over and out" came a hailing from an American sounding individual, "*Tree of Life, Tree of Life*, come in please." Since I was the nearest to the radio I picked up and said "*Tree of Life* here." Who is this?"

"Who do you think it is out here in the middle of the Atlantic Ocean?" The accent spoke volumes and it was very clear it was a Nova Scotian individual. "Bernie Oestebo?"

Bernie was my next door neighbor in LaHave for all of the years I'd lived there. He and his wife Carol, their son Jason and daughter Kellie Jean were more like family then neighbors. I'd spent some part of everyday with them.

Bernie was the captain of a boat that primarily fished for scallops and he was returning home from Norwegian waters with a boatload of seafood. He heard *Tree of Life* hailing other boats in the area and knew it was me. Anticipating the next step in the protocol of talking on the radio, I suggest we go to another station. I switched over and assumed Bernie did too. "*Tree of Life* here." No response. "*Tree of Life* here, where are you Bernie?"

For the next two hours, I attempted to reach Bernie with no response from him. "Bernie, Bernie Oestebo where are you?" I'd sing across the radio waves? Our radio antenna was shorter and our signal wasn't as strong as the larger ocean going boats. So, after that one brief moment with my Nova Scotian neighbor it was over.

Months later when I called the Oestebo family to check in, I was able to share that moment with Bernie over the phone. He said that I came across loud and clear for the next two hours though we weren't able to receive a response from him. He said he was embarrassed to have his name sung across the airwaves, but we laughed about it all the same. What an amazing coincidence, eh?

Watching storms crawl out of the horizon sometimes brought glorious sunsets or dangerous winds that pushed the seas into dark waves of rage. I learned to know the difference after watching clouds come and go for those three weeks on the Atlantic and the months that followed. A sailor's life, my life, was connected intimately to what was happening in the skies above my head. The relationship with nature became more sacred. Honoring its presences and its power was part of my practice.

We Just Might Make It

Once we sailed over the halfway point of the Atlantic Ocean, I began to believe we just might make it. All in all the crossing was uneventful, aside from my own imagination having us swallowed up by some hundred-foot wave. Nothing even close happened. Sometimes in fact, we were in the doldrums, when the ocean was completely flat with no wind whatsoever. We had to motor or sit out there just waiting for nature to takes its course, which could be hours, days or even weeks. We were grateful in these times to have an engine and the necessary fuel that could have literally propelled us across the Atlantic, if need be. Sometimes, when the wind was light and *Tree* was barely making three knots, we'd get antsy and would want to turn the engine on to make headway toward our destination. We had to remind ourselves that we were a sailboat, after all and turned the engine off.

We arrived in the Aran Islands off the coast of Ireland around midnight on July 1. In that part of the world, in the early summer, there was still light in the sky, which meant we could see not only the islands, but also that we could visually track where we were laying the anchor. After three weeks at sea, this was a lovely event to experience with all of our senses.

Tired yet excited, we celebrated the completion of a very uneventful, but significant event. We toasted *Tree of Life* with rum, for everything she gave us on this journey. We tucked in her sails and said goodnight! We knew we would be greeted by the local customs officers in a few brief hours.

This is My Dream

Living aboard a sailboat is not everything it's cracked up to be. It's challenging and at the same time a much simpler lifestyle. Cramped quarters with a captain and a crew of young men provided very little private time. Moreover, *Tree* was a high maintenance boat. Every inch of wood that was exposed to sun, sea and wind had to be bathed continually in protective oils. The sails and rigging had to be inspected before and after every outing, looking for wearing that could lead to disasters. Lines had to be replaced, bilges needed to be emptied of any water, sweeping, cooking, all the elements of keeping a home with the inclusion of a hull that was constantly submerged in seawater. Corrosion of the prop overtime led to major overhauls.

There were personality challenges, drunken crew, and finicky eaters; those who didn't want to pull their weight. As the captain's girlfriend, I had some power, but not really, and Mac's relationships with these men were interesting. He was like Peter Pan with his band of lost boys. I was sort of the Wendy girl. I was loved, but not respected.

Over the months, my confidence grew and my competence as a sailor emerged slowly. I grew stronger in character and my faith in the Divine became my stronghold; however, the more competent I became the more demanding and intimidating Mac became. I was becoming more of what he wanted in a partner on this journey, but as I did so, he became angrier and abusive. It didn't make sense, but I figured we would work through whatever miscommunication was occurring.

Though there were many instances where verbal fights broke out, one in particular stood out. We'd been sailing between Ireland, England and France, enjoying the summer months. We were trying to decide what would be the best way to sail around the world, which destinations we wanted to visit and how long we wanted to take.

I offered up a suggestion about sailing to Patagonia, on the West Coast of South America. "This is *my* dream." Mac shouted. "Go find your own dream." Now, this was very confusing to hear, as I thought we were creating a dream together. How else do you live on a boat that can only go to one chosen destination at a time?

I realized that perhaps I was once again on the back of someone else's dream and not my own. I thought it was mine—I had at least come aboard *Tree* anticipating the dream, or was it more accepting of the dream. Since I was on the boat and making this my life, how would I like to spend it? Where would I like to go? I started to realize that perhaps I was more like a prisoner than a partner. I was confused yet I was learning to navigate by an internal compass that would keep me on course. It all would be revealed eventually.

Tree of Life and her crew were in Europe for a year and a half, though all headed back to the States for six months during the coldest, darkest days of the winter months. For the duration of our time in Europe, we sailed along the coasts of Ireland, southern England, France, Spain and Portugal. After that, the boat would head back across the Atlantic, landing in the Caribbean before Christmas. We'd take another break from sailing then prepare for the next leg of our world cruise … minus Patagonia.

Hannah, Noah and *Tree*

My time on *Tree* gave me an opportunity to share something extraordinary with Hannah and Noah. Though they were exposed to many beautiful environments on the planet with their dad, such as China, India and Africa, they would not have had the opportunity to be part of a sailing experience like this. Whether we were in Nova Scotia or Europe, they would have an opportunity to participate in sailing *Tree*.

While in Ireland, Noah and his friend Sheldon came for a two-week adventure and the following year we met him in Paris for another two-week stay. As it turned out, he wasn't really interested in sailing. He was more interested in seeing the sites.

Noah really wanted to go to Amsterdam, but I was hesitant to travel there without Mac. Though I couldn't say no, because I didn't want to disappoint him or have him decide not to come to Europe, I told him that we'd go either to Amsterdam or to Euro-Disney, another destination he was wanting to experience. I regret that I didn't just say no to Amsterdam. Rather than doing that, I left him anticipating a trip that never happened. I'd hoped that Euro-Disney would suffice. Who was I kidding? He was a fifteen-year-old boy. He wanted to see the Red-Light District of Amsterdam and all the pot smoking.

Seventeen-year-old Hannah and her friend Shannon also met us in Paris. While exploring the modern art museum a young handsome fellow, Stan, took a fancy to Hannah. They struck up a conversation. He was from Chicago and just traveling around Europe for a few months with his friend, Dan. While in Paris Hannah, Shannon, Stan and Dan hung out together. Hannah asked if they could join us on *Tree* for a few days. As was Mac's way, he immediately said yes. He felt that this boat was a gift in his life and that he wanted to share it with anyone who wanted to come aboard. They joined us on *Tree* for a week and they were a wonderful addition to our time in France.

My hope was that sharing these adventures with my kids would somehow change their relationship with me, but Hannah wasn't interested in that. She was angry that I moved to Nova Scotia and didn't trust me. More often than not, she would side with other people and their opinions over mine. All I could do was do the best I could and hope that someday I could demonstrate what was really in my heart.

The greatest gifts you can give your children are roots and wings. I wanted Hannah and Noah to have a sense of roots in nature through our home in Nova Scotia. I wanted them to experience the essence and beauty of life outside cities and just be present to the beauty all around. They weren't raised to see that beauty. They weren't interested in this level of connection to nature. It wasn't that they didn't appreciate it; it's that they weren't interested in appreciating it. It makes perfect sense to me now, but then, I just wanted them to have that connection to nature.

How Do You Know When It's Time to Go

I started getting headaches daily, which up until then was a rare phenomenon. Clues to the reality of my emotionally demanding situation were beginning to build up and I began to imagine a possible exit strategy if things continued to go the way they were headed. I kept telling myself that I would never leave *Tree*. I was actually afraid for her life if I was to leave, but the more I tried to hold on the more craziness and abuse surfaced. I found it fascinating to witness and at the same time, it was devastating to my soul.

Sailing on oceans means that you've decided to take on the responsibility of your own well-being. You have accepted and actually created an opportunity to challenge yourself on an adventure and you have no way of knowing the outcome. That's what we do in life … until we don't.

I was committed enough to do whatever it took to stay with the boat and with Mac, but over the two years aboard *Tree,* I was taught that I had limits and as much as I loved Mac and *Tree* I decided to leave. I'd come to value myself enough to know I needed to make a change and so I did.

I believed that the next leg of my journey would not have happened without the adventures on *Tree of Life*. I miss her terribly, but I learned to be courageous in living with the missing and the longing for what was never mine in the first place. I learned to trust in my abilities and my strengths and be grateful for the incredible experience given to me through that adventure. I learned that some people dream and then manifest those dreams. Some of us are unaware that we create our dreams moment by moment. We live happily in the present, allowing the winds of change to whisper in their ears "Get ready. Another adventure is ahead".

Chapter Six

A Scavenger Hunt in the Making

It was late October 1994. I was forty-two years old.

My parents picked me up at the airport in Detroit. They were very kind and caring. It was nice. They were okay with me staying at their home in Grosse Ile, even though they would be heading down to Florida in a few weeks. They wouldn't be back for Christmas, but were fine with me staying until I picked up the pieces of my life and figured out what was next.

One day followed the next and I didn't hear from Mac. Every day that went by was one day closer to the end of the relationship. I knew it was the best thing for me to end the relationship and at the same time, I had come to love my life aboard *Tree of Life*. I felt sad and at the same time, I was so relieved. I spent those three months on Grosse Ile getting my bearing on land and pondering what was next.

You'd think I would have headed back to Nova Scotia, since I never wanted to leave there in the first place. I'd lived there for ten years; my house and home were there, and I could most likely pick up my old job with the Commission, but it just didn't feel right to go back. I had a sense that there was more to do before returning to that part of Canada, I just didn't know what it was.

Mac's home was in Alexandria, Virginia. I had spent many months there in preparations for the sailing voyage and made some wonderful friends there. On a practical note, at some point I'd need to return to Alexandria to pick up the rest of my things from Mac's home, and somehow it felt as though this was the first leg of some scavenger hunt I was on.

Quite a lot of my life had been lived by *what felt right* and what didn't feel right. I don't know if it's intuition, a calling or what to call it;

I just knew that for the most part, following it worked better that trying to do what I was supposed to do—acting according to what was right and appropriate—generally speaking, that just made my life unsatisfying. It's like having a compass from which to steer, but using other aids that aren't going to get you where you want to go.

After Christmas, I headed south to Alexandria, not knowing how long I would stay. It could have been just a quick turnaround or longer. As I said, it was like being on a scavenger hunt. I'd know it was time to move on once I'd found a sign or a clue as to what was next.

I ended up staying in Alexandria for seven months. I moved in with my friends, Matthew and Mary and with the help of my friend Lewis, found a waitressing job at a local pub. The effortlessness of finding a place to live and a job told me I was on the right track. This allowed me to settle into focusing on possibilities that were more professional. I considered a Ph.D. in Clinical Psychology, but knew that the rigors of such a dry, academic program would kill my life force. Besides, after working as a therapist with recovering alcoholics, addicts, and their families, I was clear I wanted to study more spiritually based models of therapy. And I knew that I learned best through experiential teaching. Plus, with two master's degrees behind me, the MFT and an MSW, I wasn't sure I really needed another degree.

With a master's in social work, I figured my best bet was to focus on becoming licensed as a social worker, though I wasn't sure what I would do with a license once I had it. I sent for applications, filled them out, sent letters to supervisors for verifications; I did all the right things. But, through months of tremendous effort, what I found was that all roads leading in the direction of licensure were blocked. No matter what I did, who I talked to, who I wrote letters to, I couldn't get what I needed to even take the examination. I was frustrated, but I kept my spirits and my curiosity high. I knew that if this is such a big fat NO, there must be something else in store for me that would be a big fat YES.

I have learned through years of experience that when the doors are open and there is effortlessness in the task – that's the path to be taken. When there is struggle and effort in each step, then I am meant to go in another direction. So I gave up the idea of a license in social work in search of … you guessed it, what's next.

It Takes Faith

Midwestern Germanic upbringing says you have to work hard to get what you want, or at least to get what you need. It might not be fun, but it will be gratifying. I've actually never found this to be true. Anything that I had to do that I didn't want to do, that had no joy, fun, or meaning in it, did not create a sense of value, interest, enthusiasm, or passion for me. It just created anxiety, frustration, resentment and regret. Sure, there was the sense of accomplishment, but the tedium and struggle, the sense of not being good enough, smart enough, or worthy enough, created extenuating circumstances that made the accomplishment even less satisfying.

When I pursued what brought interest, meaning and fun, my studies soared, my grades went to the top, and I earned raises and promotions. I mastered what I set out to accomplish and had a great time doing it. The effort became effortless. This is what I have learned about life; when you are on track in your own life, effort become effortless, fearfulness turns to fearlessness and joy is all over the place.

The Next Clue

While in Alexandria, I took a weekend workshop at The Institute for Attitudinal Healing with Susan Trout, a woman of great wisdom and love. Much of her work was based on *A Course in Miracles* by Helen Schucman and William Thetford. Though there were about twenty people present for the weekend, one man in particular attracted my attention, Francis. Francis drove all the way from Connecticut for this weekend workshop. It seemed like a long way to come, but who I was to judge. I was curious though why anyone would drive so far for just a weekend despite Susan's reputation. Over the weekend, we talked a great deal about the adventures thus far in our lives and enjoyed the level of intimacy we shared. He really got the adventure I was on and my search for what was next in my life.

After listening, Francis said, "Rosie, you belong at ITP."

"ITP? What's ITP?" I asked.

"The Institute of Transpersonal Psychology," he exclaimed with great excitement. "It's in Palo Alto, California."

Now, up to this point, I had no interest in living in California. Earthquakes and groovy-types, over population and pollution was what I equated to that State. I had been living in the pristine Province of Nova Scotia for a decade, and then sailed for two years. I was not interested in living in a huge metropolitan area. But when Francis began telling me about this graduate school, I began to forget about the earthquakes, pollution and population. It was very much like the moment that Steve Hartwell shared with me about his adventures at Outward Bound. I was captivated and listened intently.

Francis shared with me that ITP was a graduate school where people studied transpersonal psychology. "What the heck is transpersonal psychology?" I asked.

He said, "Well, you study Aikido, yoga, creative expression, spiritual psychology, and non-ordinary states of consciousness, Sufism and other extraordinary aspects of being human. Basically, it's studying the whole person, not just egos and personalities like in most psychology programs."

Francis had a girlfriend who was attending ITP and he suggested I give her a call. I felt exhilarated and excited to find a school that had so much to offer, and focused on spiritual psychology, which excited me to no end. I got the phone numbers of the school and his girlfriend and began the process of applying. I had no idea what it would take to get into a Ph.D. program. I didn't know if I had the right stuff academically. I just took one-step-at-a-time to see what would show up.

It was late February. The application arrived and, like all graduate schools, they required transcripts of all my grades from all the schools I'd ever attended. By the time I was forty-two years old, I had attended ten different academic institutions. Because of all of the traveling, my records were scattered between California, Michigan, Ontario and Nova Scotia. Many hours of phone calls and letter writing were required to get all of the transcripts sent to ITP. An autobiography had to be written to indicate my writing ability, as well as share information pertinent to requirements for the school. The logistics of filling out the application was huge. Miraculously, this was in February when restaurant business was slow, and I was laid off a week. Holy Toledo, it was exactly what I needed!

As I mentioned earlier, I had been studying *A Coarse in Miracles* over the past few years. In the section on rules for decision-making, rule number one is, "I will make no decisions by myself." Now, think about what this means to all of us. This doesn't mean looking to others for answers. It means looking to God, Universal Source, and a Higher Power for guidance. It means giving up control of how your life is going to turn out (even though we have no control anyway, we just think we do). It also means giving up judgments, interpretations, and assumptions about life and what it's supposed to mean. Practicing rule number one and making no decisions by myself was a real spiritual practice for me because it meant living in faith, and living in the present moment; however, since my life had been in such transition, I found it tremendously helpful to allow my Higher Self to guide me. I surrendered my will and was open to the adventures that lay ahead.

One afternoon, when I was in the middle of writing my autobiography, I became anxious and upset. I worried whether I was on some wild goose chase. I was forty-two years old with two master's degrees. I was waitressing because I couldn't get a job because I didn't have a license. I just got off a major sailing experience and relationship journey and now I was considering moving to California, where I never wanted to live, to do a four-year Ph.D. program. Was I nuts? My parents sure thoughts so.

So, I sat at my desk and said, "Okay, I will make no decisions by myself. What do I do now?"

I got this answer back immediately, "Go take a nap."

"Take a nap, what do you mean, take a nap? I've all this stuff to take care of. I'm broke and I …"

"Go take a nap."

I wasn't going to argue with this voice since I employed it to support my well-being. So, I lay down on my bed and closed my eyes. Probably within forty-five seconds, I had the most peculiar vision. The vision was of a squad of cheerleaders, dressed in their sweaters and short pleated skirts, white tennis shoes and socks, with pom-poms raised high above their heads. They danced their way across my vision chanting, "GO FOR THE EXTRAORDINARY! GO FOR THE EXTRAORDINARY! GO FOR THE EXTRAORDINARY!"

I was stunned and so delightfully surprised. I got the message. Going to California to a graduate school in transpersonal psychology was for me, extraordinary. It was exciting to consider studying what was truly valuable and meaningful to me. My practice was to continue to trust my inner knowing and the Universe that everything was going to unfold just as it was meant to.

I got up from the briefest of naps and finished the necessary paper work for the application to ITP. It was effortless!

The more I read, the more I learn, the more I experience life on this planet, the surer I become that life is supposed to be fun, effortless, and meaningful, with playfulness and purpose thrown in for extra measure. I think we forget that, if we've ever known it in the first place. We are so caught up in all of the doing that needs to be done every day. My practice at this moment is to live an extraordinary life, intentionally. My life as a mother for the first three years of my children's life, my life in Nova Scotia, my life sailing across the Atlantic was extraordinary, but I didn't plan it to be. I was just following my instincts. What could possibly happen if I intentionally focused my attention in the direction I really wanted to go rather than where the wind blew?

Mac returned to the States and we met after many months apart. We felt the love and affection that we held for each other. He was willing to help me get what I needed financially for school. I don't remember the details, but I do remember feeling an incredible amount of gratitude for all that had transpired with him and *Tree*.

In May of 1995, I found out I was accepted to ITP. I had the summer to work then get myself out to California by mid-September. I applied for student loans and knew I had money from Mac. I was on my way!

The clues from the scavenger hunt in Alexandria brought me to discover ITP and to move beyond limited thinking, deciding that California was where I'd perhaps find the next set of clues.

Revisiting Nova Scotia

From Alexandria, I headed north to Nova Scotia to take care of business around my house. I really had no idea what the outcome of this whole adventure would be. I was open to things unfolding in the moment; that at any twist or turn in the road I might find myself detouring in an unexpected direction. I even imagined that I would find myself staying in Nova Scotia back in my own little house in LaHave.

As luck would have it, Mac and *Tree of Life* were also in Nova Scotia for the schooner races. This allowed me to say good-bye to the boat the way that felt best. I sailed her in the races with Mac and some of the old crew. It felt perfect to be at her helm one more time with more confidence and ease than I ever imagined. I'd grown up over the years and in that moment I felt strong, grounded and full.

I said good-bye to my friends and Nova Scotia and I drove off in my little VW Golf, packed tight with all I could carry in search of the next big adventure. Wahoo!

California Here I Come

I headed west, first to Niagara Falls to see the kids, then to Detroit to see my parents and siblings; to Niles, just outside Chicago, to spend the night with my sister Helene and then on my first cross-country road trip across the U.S. alone. I was forty-three years old and had crossed the Atlantic Ocean, so a land crossing felt like a breeze. I was prepared for any sudden intervention by the Universe to detour me off the course to California; however, I arrived three days later in Santa Cruz, to warm sunshine and the Pacific Ocean.

ITP

I came to ITP to learn how to include spirituality in my therapy practice. I really didn't know any more than that. I felt called to be there and the rest would unfold. Clinical practices and licensure was a possibility; however, I'd already done ten years of practice in Nova Scotia and I wasn't about to retake all of those required clinical focused courses plus another two-year internship. It would feel like a waste of time and money. I hadn't gone through all of this to relearn what I already knew well.

At the orientation to the school, the founders Jim Fadiman and Robert Frager shared that their expectations of us new students were to push the edges of transpersonal psychology beyond where the leading theorists had taken it. That was profound to me. Most educators want their students to remain within the structure of learning already laid down. Not these men; however, I couldn't see how I could possibly out think some of the greatest minds of the world. Jim and Bob also were very clear that they hadn't created the Institute to generate more clinicians. They created it to cultivate new ways of bringing transpersonal psychology to the world. After hearing Jim and Bob speak, I was pretty sure that my path would be taking me somewhere very interesting.

Transpersonal psychology is the study of all of what's possible in our human experience. It includes what we consider to be normal psychology and includes the paranormal—everything else outside what's normal: dreams, near death experience, non-ordinary states of consciousness, the connections of the body-mind-emotions and spirit, connection to nature—you name it; all that weird and wacky, woo-woo stuff that makes people roll their eyes and walk away. For the next four years, I'd be immersing myself in this whole field of study.

This transpersonal world allows the inclusion of all the ways we have of experiencing the world in which we live. Even though the word *transpersonal* sounds unfamiliar to most people; once I explain it, everyone I've spoken to says, "Oh, I know what you mean; I've seen things in my dreams that have come true, or I had a near-death-experience, or I'm sensitive to the vibrational field around people." It's given many people an opportunity to speak about what seems to be too woo-woo and unacceptable.

What this does for the human development field, especially psychotherapy, is it allows clinicians, healers, spiritual guides or coaches to expand their bandwidth to include in their listening what wasn't allowed to be included before. Clients now have a freedom to speak about their personal reality and a transpersonal clinician can hear it in relation to the life challenges they are facing. If in our human potential movement we are excluding the majority of what influences our human potential we remain within the current paradigm with no way out. Through transpersonal psychology, the paradigm shift becomes far more widespread.

ITP provided me with an education far beyond the academic requirements necessary to fulfill a Ph.D. The environment was such that it promoted, at least for me, trust, respect, and safety to express authenticity. In fact, one of the pillars of the school was creative expression. In essence, the process of educating oneself here was a sacred event—one honored by everyone there.

I exercised and strengthened muscles of spiritual intelligence; of faith-leaping and yogic postures that stretched me beyond a reality I long ago resisted; Aikido maneuvers to support distinguishing and refining the practice of connection and detachment. The intention of such an Institute is to seek and transcend *How To* manuals, as each one of us can reveal the rights and wrongs, the shoulds and shouldn'ts of someone else's reality and illusions; suspending judgments; no right, no good; no wrong or bad; just this moment—blindly living into hopes or fears, faith or despair. This school allowed me to explore and discover the truth of who I was from the inside out, only using textbooks and teachers in service to this process. I was given the opportunity to reveal my own *unholy* path and come to appreciate the unique purpose that is solely mine. Here's an example of such a process:

People asked me often, "Once you have your Ph.D. what will you be doing with it." Usually I'd shrug my shoulders and say "I don't know; I'll know when I get there." This sounds ridicules to spend perhaps hundreds of thousands of dollars and not know the outcome of such an investment of time and money, but when stepping into a program like this, I learned not to be attached to the outcome and that the journey is the destination. It is a big practice; one that only continues to serve me well.

In March of my first year, now 1996, I was struggling with what was mine to do; how would I know where to go or what I'm supposed to be? Rather than talking about it with a therapist, I took it into my bathroom where I sat on the floor with a lit candle and some soft calming music. I sat with a small palm-size piece of clay, and with my eyes closed, I began to work the clay—not making it into anything specific, just allowing it to form through the massaging process in my hands. The question I was sitting with was, "How I will I know what is my path; how will I know what's mine to do?"

Every few minutes I would peek through squinted eyes to see if anything was emerging in the clay; if not I'd continue to sit with eyes closed, massaging the clay, gently; allowing time for my soul to connect with this substance. Again, I peeked and instead of finding a nondescript lump, I found a nose. "Cool!" I thought. "I wonder what's next." As I began to allow the form to take on greater detail, what emerged fully was a face with no eyes and no eye sockets! The sobbing began immediately for what was being revealed to me and what I was able to acknowledge was that I was required to live blindly into faith—into life without a roadmap, with perhaps only pebbles of insight or intuition that could disappear in a blink of an eye, if not seized in the moment.

When given gifts of insight like this, which is so common at ITP, it's important to write down the process and allow the full measure of the experience to be brought to life. It's not always comfortable or easy, but if I wanted comfortable and easy I would have been somewhere other than this school, which demanded a level of rigor for which I was looking. It was through a very similar process that the story in the forward emerged, *The Great Little One*.

Through this process and many that followed I came to trust that if I ask, I shall be guided—perhaps not with GPS directions all laid out in front of me, but I will be given what I need. Every day at ITP had the potential for profound personal awakenings like this one if I was up to such an adventure.

I don't think it was by coincidence that my internship at Interfaith and my master's at California Family Study Center (now known as the Philips Graduate Institute) were based on experiential learning. Fifteen years back, when I left my marriage and children, I certainly was completely naive to the whole idea of experiential learning. ITP was a continuation of learning by doing, immersing myself into the moment and then articulating the experience, by either verbal sharing, writing or some other creative media; it could even be through dance, painting or clay. ITP required the use of our body, mind, emotions and spirit as well as participate as a community and creativity. These were the six pillars of the school that brought about the development of the whole person. I was happy!

The school was very small with about sixty students. I felt as though I was among like-minded people, which to some degree was true, however, as time went by it was obvious that though we were all here together for this unique style of education our paths would for only a brief time keep us walking together. Each of us had to explore our own path, our own style and just maybe some of us would remain colleagues or friends.

During my first year, to earn money I worked at the school, in the library and doing odd jobs for different departments. Everyone was friendly and kind. It was an atmosphere of kindred spirits. It was fun and a great way to get to know people. It allowed me to cultivate relationships with so many influential people. I was available, accessible and they could count on me to follow through with my commitments.

The academics per se weren't that challenging for me because of all of the schooling I had previously. What was challenging was that the school required us to be self-directed. Personal accountability and responsibility were foundational to getting the education each of us wanted. I could take it to whatever level of mastery in which I was interested. My experience was that most individuals continued to live and work within the box, though there were others who were so passionate about exploring the far reaches of reality, where it became very clear to them that the box was just an illusion.

ITP was extremely challenging in another way. Each student was required to bring their *entire* being to the learning process. The physical discipline of Aikido was required for two years as were the courses in creative expression, community development, group process, spiritual emergence process, and journal writing to record what it was like in each of the classes. This notation required one to bring mindfulness to each class. These plus normal academic courses cultivated awareness far beyond what normal psychologists study.

At first, I expected the usual critical form of evaluation, but found that the instructors were far more interested in supporting and enhancing their students own thinking and creative processes, as opposed to telling them what they should think or learn. The foundations for a transpersonal education were laid out, but it was up to each one of us to build the platform upon which we'd create our realities and our work in the world.

More than Survival

Up until this time, I'd wondered how people made it in this world with work, traveling or just in transition as I had been, without any visible means of support. Before this journey that started three years prior when I left Nova Scotia, I was terrified of being homeless and destitute. The thought of being in transition without any real financial support was unfathomable for me.

Some of the best insights come to me when sitting on the john, mostly in public washrooms. It came to me there, just a few weeks into my coursework at ITP that for the past year God had provided for me, through family, friends and strangers. I had no idea how life would unfold for me, but it worked out just fine. This past year's scavenger hunt was a lesson in itself. I was so grateful for what I experienced.

It was also no coincidence that it was almost a year to the day that I'd left *Tree of Life* that I moved into my own space, sharing a house with another woman. It was the first time in a year that I had my own bed, desk, chair, telephone and bathroom. I had a place I could call home. One year later, with my student loans in place and part time work to fill in the gaps; I breathed a sigh of relief and I knew I was where I belonged.

Sister Denata was Right

I wrote a spiritual autobiography for one of my courses. Through the writing of that paper, I realized that at the age of six, I had made a monumental decision. At the age of six, I decided to leave my innocent self behind, because I came to believe through my experience at school, at church and at home, that she, my innocent self, wasn't going to survive the ordeal of being on this planet. I promised that I would come back someday and liberate her, once it was safe to do so. It took nearly thirty-seven years to do that.

I realized too, while writing this paper, that Sister Denata was right about everything. God is everywhere and in everything; he hears and sees everything and is omnipotent, not in a bad, violent, authoritarian way, but in an all-loving way. I also realized that Sister Denata was right about another thing. If I am in alignment with my Divine purpose, "God's Will," my life is full and rich with love and amazing abundance. I won't be punished if I don't live the vocation I came here to live; life would just be more challenging, more difficult, unfulfilled with very little meaning. There was struggle and resistance when I tried to live my life my way. Now, one of my favorite prayers is, "Not my will, but thy will be done."

Spiritual Guidance

When I first arrived at ITP, though the school had some courses directly focused on spiritual guidance, it had no internship through which students could actually practice this form of work. This was frustrating to many of us who had no interest in clinical training; we wanted to specialize in spiritual guidance and we wanted a program that was going to deliver the goods! ITP required students to create the learning program that would best serve their needs. I took ITP at their word.

At the beginning of my second year, I was told that there was a new director of the counseling center coming and he would be the person to talk with about starting up an internship program in Spiritual Guidance. This was Dr. Paul Roy, and he became one of the most significant mentors in my life. He was an ex-Jesuit priest and though he was hired to teach and run the program for psychologists in training, he was very excited about my desire to create an internship program in spiritual guidance.

I wasn't the only person at ITP wanting such an internship, but it was easy enough for me to get the ball rolling by just asking Paul if he was willing to support such an endeavor. With Paul's essence of playful wisdom, and a *why not* spirit, he was open to seeing what we could create. I loved that about him. I still do.

We called a meeting of anyone interested in creating such an internship program. Bill Kippers, Genie Palmer, Kat McGiver, Elyse Green, with Pat Luce, Paul and myself as mentors and supervisors. We had a wonderful time creating an outstanding program. Each of us had an enormous amount of experience that we brought to the process. We met weekly to cultivate the foundation for the program. It was through our own process that we discovered the roots of organic spiritual guidance and how different it was from psychotherapy.

Spiritual guidance is a beautiful practice of sitting with people who want to deepen their knowledge and experience of their own unique relationship with spirituality. How this is different from therapy is that there are no problems that need fixing. The individual is seen as whole, and while in session, the presence of a higher power is recognized.

There are all sorts of reasons people seek out a spiritual guide. Some come for spiritual guidance because they're unsatisfied and aren't finding the essence of a meaningful relationship with God. Some think there is something wrong with themselves; others find that their own religious tradition is no longer fulfilling. As interns, we were learning to understand and follow the lead of the people who were seeking, and in doing so, we found incredibly rich and profound territory of life that could be revealed just by being present and listening.

We didn't really understand that chasm between spiritual guidance and psychotherapy until one day, when we were invited into the therapist's group supervision session. The idea was that we would be able to support each other in our unique practices. That turned out to be a very bad idea.

Even though all of us at the counseling center took the same foundational courses in transpersonal psychology at ITP, it became clear that somewhere along the line a split occurred. For those following the clinical track, they were required to learn about and focus on the pathology of our psyches. Those of us following the spiritual guidance track were required to learn and focus on how people were in alignment with their higher truth, where they weren't, and what needed to change to bring them into alignment. Also, we were required to be aware of a higher power that was always with our clients and us and that whatever the client was going through; it was related to their spiritual development. This was a very different approach to traditional psychotherapy.

This was important to distinguish as new interns in this fairly new field. We were all concerned about when we were guiding and when we might be doing therapy. Over time, it became obvious. Our job as spiritual guides was to listen to the client and to a higher guide to support and empower, not to fix or heal. From our perspective there was nothing broken.

The psychology interns were somewhat threatened by us non-psych interns. They remarked how we didn't have to be licensed, which in their eyes somehow made us less qualified than them, and they considered us a threat in that we could *steal* their clients. This was such a fascinating situation because it was generated from fear and lack; this was so non-transpersonal, from the perspective of spiritual guidance. We'd all gone to the same school to immerse ourselves in a larger perspective of humanity.

This entangled me in a conflict between what was right and what was not right – the normal paradigm we live in yet of which we are unconscious. On the one hand, the *right* thing to do would be to be licensed as a therapist. On the other hand I wasn't called to be licensed or do all of the work it would take. I kept hearing Robert Frager and Jim Fadiman's encouragement to step out of the box and into other ways of supporting, empowering and healing. And wasn't that what those little cheerleaders were encouraging me to do when they danced across my visions chanting, "Go for the extraordinary!" Along with my fellow interns, we were bushwhacking a different way to bring transformation to the world.

Shifting one's paradigm is very much like this – in that it takes time to recognize that you are immersed in a reality that has rules and ways of being that we are unconscious too. Once I began to get clear that from a transpersonal perspective, there was no right, wrong, good or bad, I was able to find my own path. It was challenging, but I was by now getting the hang of it – how many years ago did I start this journey?

Olympic Circle Sailing Club (OCSC)

I found myself teaching sailing on the San Francisco Bay through a school and sailing club called OCSC, in Berkeley. It came about synchronistical and was an internship for me, in and of itself. I had to integrate all of my sailing skills with the skills of courage, compassion, and acceptance. It also allowed me to integrate transpersonal psychology with sailing.

The sailing school needed women instructors and I was a great candidate; after all, I'd sailed across the Atlantic. The fact is that, although I had a lot of experience I didn't have the book learning. I actually knew very little about sailing.

You would think that someone who sailed across the Atlantic Ocean would know how to steer a boat. A large boat steers with a wheel, much like a car. Smaller boats use a tiller and it takes some getting used to. Basically, I had to start from scratch.

In the initial stages, all I could see was my hand on the tiller and the other hand on the main sheet (the rope that controls the large sail). There was a vast world I was sailing in, but I first needed to understand the mechanics of the push and pull of the tiller and how it affected the boat, and how pulling on the main sheet or letting it out controlled the speed and angle at which we sailed. Once I became comfortable with the mechanics, I could expand my reality to include the others in my boat who controlled other lines and sails. I could then begin to work collaboratively with them to create smooth sailing.

It was a good year before I could sail without looking at my hands. I could just feel what was happening. I was literally sailing by the seat of my pants, how it felt in my body, how the environment and the rush of the water, the stillness of the sail, with wind on my face informed me. This is when I was truly being present. (Yes. This is the same person who sailed across the Atlantic. You wonder how I could have sailed so much and known so little. Me too!)

This is a piece I wrote in 1998, for an embodied writing course at ITP. The intention of embodied writing is to bring to the reader the quality of sensation of the experience being had by the writer. Three years of sailing on the San Francisco Bay brought me to a level of mastery of sailing that I never imagined.

When the Student is Ready

The experience of sailing can be very complex. I must hold in awareness the mechanical workings of the boat in relation to wind, water, sails, rudder, boat, the sky, seascape, and landscape, while at the same time holding my students safe and fascinated with the rudiments of sailing. Intuitively I balance and center, tuning the boat to outer forces, tuning my body to inner forces. Sailing for me is a metaphor for harmonizing with another, with myself, with the Universe.

Realities unfold within me while sailing that if wise enough, I will practice in my land-based living. For instance, I know that I am connected with all of the Universal presence, that the Divine is embedded within everything, and that I need to stay centered in the moment and in my body if I am to witness and experience my inseparability with my surroundings. Yes, these are big realities and they present themselves daily if I am open to connecting with such wisdom.

Awakening to my body's knowing, in the present moment, brings to consciousness experiences that just moments before seemed so separate from me. Ordinarily it is difficult to stay awake long enough to register experiences and sensations of being here in my body, whether on land or water. While sailing though, the heeling motion of the boat, as well as the boiling, turbulent water, fresh winds, beautiful landscapes and the warmth of the sun peeking out between broken clouds keeps me present and awake. Yet, in the midst of the rich multiplicity of this aquatic environment, I still fall into thinking sleep. Abandoning ship, as if tossed overboard by my incessant thoughts, I leave students and myself for a world of memories from the past or worries and fantasies of the future.

By its very nature though, sailing easily shakes me back into the present by a wave heaving the boat about in such a way as to knock me conscious. It might take a flick of brilliant white and black seagull's tail, or a gust of hardy wind to pull my awareness back into the boat and back into my body, sensing again the union that is experienced only in the present moment.

I am an addict to worry and concern, and sailing gives me plenty to worry about. Keeping track of the comfort and performance of the students, other boats and the direction of the wind all at the same time can be overwhelming. And, it provides a form, a practice for staying open, aware and grounded in my body, mind, heart and spirit as I move with the boat through the wind and sea. When I call myself back from my worries, which through practice happens more and more often, I am free to be fully present. In such moments, I glimpse my inseparable connection to the Divine, to my boat, and to my students. I don't want to forget these experiences so I take a snapshot in my brain; not to validate my heroics to family and friends, but to substantiate a recognizable moment of interconnection. I remember myself in that moment of tumultuous waters, reefed mainsail and clear, cerulean blue skies. I want to stay wide-awake to the omnipotent sea, the boat's sturdiness and the resiliency of its qualities that make it alive, like me, with a character all its own.

My bodily senses yearn to play and enjoy the physical manifestation of momentary oneness with this world. My vision inhales the mountains of Marin, the Golden Gate Bridge, the cityscape of San Francisco, and the Berkeley Hills. My hearing tunes in to wind in the rigging, waves rushing against the hull, bubbles and foam seething and breaking. Buoys gong and bird-life sing merry sea chanteys. My body plays with the motion, swaying with waves as if the boat were no longer there. Standing on the stern, sailing downwind I sometimes pretend to surf the waves to their completion. My students think I'm silly, but the exhilaration that comes with the lift from the sails raising us higher and faster through the water ignites giddiness inside that needs to take expression. It proves too irresistible. In these moments, I feel alive fully and free to take flight the only way I can.

Sometimes though, I just feel terror. The dark, ominous clouds that appear in the winter sky carry not only rain, but also more wind than I want to imagine. I sail with students as their instructor and guide, teaching them how to prepare for all types of weather, from light winds to gnarly squalls. I teach them how to sail, how to read the wind and water. Yet at times, my mind wants to numb my bodily senses, my body-knowing. Cellular memories surface of that hair- raising squall that knocked Tree of Life on her side. My mind says don't go there! It's too dangerous to succumb to feeling those fears again, but the memory cannot resist reliving the story. I see clouds like that today and instead of succumbing, my mind says we're okay, but I begin to shake and tremble inside my foul-weather gear none the less. I look down at this body, which responds so quickly to the environment. I smile at it as it tries to direct the boat and me back to the safe shore. I cannot allow that familiar old fear to defeat me. Not only is it my job to work with such adverse conditions, but it is my path to freedom, my path out of the bastion of fear. Here I connect with the Divine, with my own sense of belonging to and with the wind and the sea. I connect to me too. The me *who is fearless, who is courageous, powerful and responsible, and loves living this life.*

Exposure to the elements of wind and water, in this inescapable venue demands clarity of thought, physical presence, emotional stability and a keen sense of the obvious. I benefit greatly only by harmonizing my skills with the power of the Earth. I taste moments of union and joy amidst the tremulous grey-green waters and the rolling earth-toned, burdensome clouds. It is ominous. It is frightening. And in staying present, even while shivering in my boots, I experience a relationship with nature I cannot find on land. This is what I seek. I share a very strong bond with this world that non-sailors find difficult to understand. If respected and honored, this union reveals treasures to my senses, to my soul. I remember solace, connection and oneness. Nature is reverently married to a sailor or maybe it should be stated the other way around. Life at sea is dependent upon such a marriage. Sacred union creates consciousness, at best, all the time. Certainly, if I could hold that same level of this reverence and sacredness in all my human partnerships, less conflict would arise.

Surrendering to fear and just witnessing its presence are two different experiences. I learn through this practice of sailing to detach from the fear and terror remembered in that knock down where life truly was threatened. But it has not come easy. Months and months of coming to work when I know there will be strong winds on the Bay. Driving in my car with my heart beating harder then I would like, feeling the tension in my arms, hands and fingers as I clench the steering wheel of my little red car. My gut is tight and breathing is difficult. I cross the broad expanse of the Richmond Bridge toward the East Bay. My destination is the sailing club in Berkeley another fifteen minutes away. It gives me ample time to scan the horizon for evidence of hazardous wind conditions. Are there white caps on the waves this early in the morning? Which direction is the wind blowing? What's the cloud conditions like? How will I ____? I fill in the blank with a thousand questions. I feel dread for having to be the responsible one, the leader, the teacher. But I know that I too am the student, and this is my apprenticeship.

I am also aware of the other variety of fear that keeps my crew safe and me alert. There is logic in holding a respectful level of this fear when sailing in twenty to twenty-five knots in a twenty-four-foot boat. I have been sailing for four years now and I succumb to generic fear and anxiety far less often than I used to, though it plagues me far more than I would like. This fear is no longer a necessary part of my repertoire for survival. I have been in enough critical situations that I know my boat and I know my capacity to handle challenging situations effectively. I question the bodily fears that overwhelm me at times. They no longer have validity. The boat will not capsize or sink unless under extreme circumstances, which I do not allow myself to think about. I know this and I have proven my competency to myself countless times. Weather brings uncomfortable and extreme conditions sometimes, but nothing I have not seen or handled before. I am beginning to think my fear is a mask for something deeper within myself yet to be explored. Perhaps it is the fear to dive deeper into the depths of life, no longer clutching to the surface of the knowable and foreseeable. Uncovering meanings and metaphors of this sailing journey will be a lifelong process.

Looking out of the clubhouse windows facing west, across the Bay toward San Francisco, I search for clues for the advisability of sailing today with three beginning students. I am struck by the sight of the deep and dark, grey mass of clouds hanging over the City and Marin. My heart sinks deep into my chest. I do not want to take that on! Is it coming this way? At what speed and what sort of winds will it yield? Worry descends upon me and all kinds of dreadful thoughts go through my head. Thunderstorms are in the forecast today. No one in their right mind would set out for a sail with a sky like that looming so close. Thoughts of the knockdown come again. The wind indicator on the wall to my right says the winds are coming out of the southeast, from

Berkeley, toward the Bay and San Francisco. That means it should keep those storm clouds away from us. The knot in my throat loosens a bit realizing this. I have been on the Bay with similar winds that have kept rain and heavy winds out a mile or two offshore; far enough to allow us space to sail in comfort. I find it striking at times like this that there can be such predictability in the weather. And with that predictability, I feel safe.

The wind is only ten knots; it's a nice breeze in which to teach. The other instructor does not hesitate to move her students out onto the boats to set sail for a good, hardy, morning's lesson. I take a deep breath, brush away the doom and gloom thoughts. Attempting to be encouraging and enthusiastic, I herd my students in the same direction.

The winds are light enough right now. I ask myself if I should shorten the mainsail by putting in a reef, just in case. I question my own reasoning. I look to see the other boat off in the distance. That instructor has her sail large and full. She has years of experience to support her decision. I follow her lead, still holding doubt as to the wisdom of doing so. My heart beats harder and faster than I'd like. It is annoying. I want to feel an inner calm, not this nagging and distracting tension. I need to breathe deeply to relieve some stress. I need to stay focused on my students. They need to feel my presence, comfort, patience, and satisfaction with their performance. I'm aware that my mind's eye is watching the dark sky come closer to where we are sailing. If it comes any closer, it will not endanger us; it will just get windier and drench us with rain. I notice though, how those clouds just turned toward the north and scuttled out of our way. I feel the wind on my cheek reassuring me that the southeast wind is still holding and keeping the clouds away.

I listen to words come out of my mouth all wrong and clumsy. Potential problems preoccupy my mind. Too many details in the environment to be fully present to what is happening in the boat. I take another deep breath and settle myself down, relaxing my belly and opening my chest. I go into slow motion, slowing everything down in my mind so that I can discern what truly is happening: in the boat, in the sky, in the water, in myself. Again, I look up at the sky. South of San Francisco, I spot intense clouds coming toward us. My heartbeat quickens and my face draws on signs of dread and worry. I take in my position on the water. How close are we to shore? How large are the waves? What does the water's surface look like one hundred yards away? Where is my sister-ship? But then again, I notice that these clouds too are not passing overhead. They are circling around and being pushed by the wind toward the northwest, toward Marin.

Near the Golden Gate Bridge, dark grey fingers of rain extend from the sky just barely touching the water. San Francisco is in a deluge. We have been out here for nearly an hour and only a few sprinkles have made contact with us. The students look concerned as they watch the darkened clouds creep nearer. I am now calm and in awe by what I have witnessed for the past hour. With poise and confidence, I point to the furrow of clouds coming in our direction from the southwest. "Feel the wind, and look how its pushing those rain clouds over there," pointing toward Marin. "We're okay." I pause; taking in a deep breath, feeling grounded, centered and connected to the natural unfolding of this day. "Isn't it magnificent to experience the weather so close to us? Feel the tension, and yet knowing we are safe. We could sail out further from shore, but we don't need to. Who wants to get wet anyway?" I relax and smile. We all take a moment to reflect on the incredible beauty within which we play. Countless people are indoors, or on their way, insulating themselves from wind and rain. We sit quietly in our little boat, sailing amidst this rapturous splendor, witnessing the drama above our heads, and we are awed by the stability found in the here and now. Later, I am able to reflect on this metaphor for living my life. While tension and danger seem to loom overhead, when I am willing, I can find strength and equilibrium by staying in the present moment.

After completing this rigorous morning of practicing maneuvers, the boat is tucked into her slip at the dock. We head up to the clubhouse for lunch, sharing the excitement, concerns, gratitude and exhilaration of the day thus far. We are all very energized by our time on the water. Within seconds of being under shelter of the clubhouse overhang, the heavens let go with a torrential downpour. The sound and the smell of the rain makes my eyes close as I lose my mind to my senses. We smile at each other, speechless as to the significance of such a happening, if there is any at all. I feel grateful, as well as a sense of awe, at being part of something greater than myself.

There is something unspoken among us, a knowing or maybe just a wondering about what just took place. None of us is willing to put words to our inner dialogue. A warm cozy fire awaits us in the lunchroom. A variety of sandwiches and hot soup soothe the chill and satisfy the hunger of the body.

For the rest of the day the rain poured and the wind died away. We substituted sailing with lectures all afternoon. I shook my head in wonder as I watched the weather change outside the window. I feel brilliantly enlivened by witnessing and experiencing the drama of these days on the San Francisco Bay. I feel my strength and competence cultivated by this practice of sailing. I am privileged and honored to work and play with the elements of nature. Flutters in my chest stir childlike feelings. By letting go of fear and concern, I no longer feel alone.

My spiritual internship as an instructor at OCSC required me to suit up, show up and empower individuals to find their own capacity to steer their own boat, while at the same time I was learning to steer my own.

My apprenticeship at the sailing school lasted four years. I loved it all and at the same time, I couldn't wait for it to be over. I became a masterful sailor and loved the relationship I created with the boat, the water and the wind, and the people with whom I sailed, and a part of me was terrified of the responsibility every single day.

Some of us choose more safe harbors in which to sail. Until we get older and wiser and begin to get the bigger picture, we don't see that some of us are sailing only in our own bathtubs, yet it may feel as though we are sailing across the biggest ocean on the planet. It doesn't matter. Overcoming the fears of sailing in a bathtub creates the capacity to sail in a pond, then perhaps a lake or an inlet, each preparing us for the next big adventure.

Being pushed out of the nest of my own making with husband and children required me to become responsible for metaphorically sailing my own ship. Years of denial and attempts to climb into someone else's boat continued to be my personal process until I literally and figuratively had to captain my own boat.

I grew up through the sailing club. I had great managers who truly respected their employees. I physically faced my, "No I can't," taking beginner sailors out onto the Bay, returning with, "Yes, I can." I faced all of those "You should be something other than who you are." I faced my own false humiliation until I actually saw the evidence that I really was great at my job. I saw how I was an artist, a master at my craft. I would say this was the first time in my life that I actually realized this level of mastery. Though my work as a therapist was good, I hadn't the capacity then to show up, fully present and be so connected to who I was inside my own skin.

The Beginning of My Financial Reclamation

While living in Canada, I had a good financial life. Great job, my own home, a retirement savings plan—I was hooked up. Being in the States, all of that changed. I was a student with no credit record—no one cared about my past in Canada, especially as a student. Thirteen years later, as I recount this story to my dear friend Jimmy, a twenty-nine-year-old just starting his career development, wondering how it's all going to look, I tell him that at forty-five years old I started from scratch. The only way I could get a credit card at that time was to give the bank $2,000 from which to draw. For a whole year, I wasn't allowed to charge more than that. I had to demonstrate my ability to manage money. On a student's budget, working most weekends teaching sailing, my lifestyle really didn't require more than that; however, I felt humiliated chained to this process, after all I'd lived on a million dollar sailboat for two years, and before that owned my own home and had a car loan, just like everyone else—well, sort of. Therefore, I started from the bottom and worked my way up.

Telling Jimmy this story made me realize I've grown a lot in the past thirteen years.

There were many times in my life that I was so humiliated and embarrassed that my life looked so different from other women my age. Being a sailing instructor on the San Francisco Bay, heck, I was only one of three women at OCSC. Not married, no security, building a huge debt on my student loan and I had no idea what this was all leading toward.

What I did know was that I was happy. And if nothing else, I was modeling for my children a choice in lifestyle that fulfilled me in so many ways. Though financially I was living like a student, in every other way my life was charming, fun, unique and adventurous, deep, full and rich. I believe their father was giving them roots in Niagara Falls; I wanted to give them the wings with which to soar into unimaginable worlds.

Commuting from the tiny town of Mill Valley across the Bay every morning to the sailing club in Berkeley, where I sailed every day in front of the Golden Gate Bridge, while studying the non-ordinary side of being a human being. How great could life get! It's always the *both-and*. Both great *and* challenging *and* painful.

Cultivating Mastery

Over the years at ITP, I went from being a student and intern into a supervisory role with new interns. My background in marriage and family therapy, my internship at Interfaith, my years working in the field of addictions had all prepared me for this role. Paul would supervise my supervision. I loved this work as it sharpened my listening and my ability to focus on how the spiritual guide was being with their client. It brought another dimension to this process.

My colleague, Genie Palmer and I, with Paul's support, created a Spiritual Guidance Training Program that we hoped would be taught by us through the Continuing Education Department. Over many months we created a beautiful curriculum, but it never got off the ground. The field of spiritual guidance was still fairly new and we had no marketing budget to get the word out. We had to let it go. By then, I had found a field of work that would integrate my therapeutic experience, transpersonal psychology and spiritual guidance in such a way that would empower people to empower themselves and others—Transformational Coaching.

Coaching

One of my positions at ITP was as the Coordinator of the Spiritual Guidance Certificate Program. Aside from doing administrative work, I put together colloquiums on Spirituality in the Workplace. For one of these events I invited a friend of mine, Andrew, who was doing life and business coaching. Andrew suggested he bring Hans Phillips with him, as he would add to the discussion in a dramatic way. Boy, did he get that right!

Hans was dashing, brilliant, charming, charismatic and funny. Not only was he a coach, but he trained people to be coaches too. When I watched him work I was clear I wanted what he had; a way of being with people that moved them outside the reality of their current and unexplored contexts in order to have what they said they wanted. Hans' philosophy embraced the transpersonal and the spiritual that took my work to the next level. I could see how this philosophy would allow coaches to take this into the work place.

I trained with Hans and soon after he and I created the Transformational Coaches Training Program at ITP. Paul Roy gave the nod of approval to provide this program through the department of Continuing Education. I was thrilled to bring such a dynamic, integrated process into the school that had given me so much.

While all of this was unfolding, I was working on my dissertation. It came to be about sailing as a transformational experience. It never would have occurred to me in a million years that I would be integrating all of my learning, my working and sailing experiences together in one document that informed the world of the importance of sailing as an activity that brought about transformation. When I discussed the topic with my sailing students they knew, without a doubt that is was important and valuable. It was innovative and cutting-edge research in the field of transpersonal psychology.

It took me six years to complete my Ph.D. I graduated June 2001.

I've had many learning environments and opportunities in my life, but these years in California, at ITP and OCSC were the finest opportunities for learning I'd ever experienced. They pushed my edges to listen to my calling and engage with life whole-heartedly. Between these two schools, I was immersed in environments that supported and encouraged the full potential of every individual with whom I connected. I loved it!

Life with Men and Children

While all of that was going on – being a student and a teacher, there was my personal life occurring as well. If I left this out, I'd be remiss in allowing you to think that I'd gotten my act together when it came to men and children.

For the first year at ITP I was on my own, no romantic involvements, though heaven knows I tried. Though I'd grown more comfortable being without a man, I still had an obsessive way in my thinking process, and continually tried to fulfill myself through a significant relationship. But the transition from my adventurous life on *Tree* with Mac, through Alexandria then out to California required of me some settling in time.

The second year began with meeting Collin. Collin was just beginning his Ph.D. at ITP so there was hope that because he was at ITP and interested in the transpersonal we both would be mature enough to grow a relationship together. But only weeks into the relationship, I said to myself, "We have nothing to talk about!" Similar to my relationship with Sam, though part of me wanted out, there was something else that kept me in.

Collin was six years younger than I was – I was forty-five and he was thirty-nine. He'd graduated from Berkeley University with his law degree; he'd been in therapy for many years, he was athletic and charming; and wouldn't you know he was another Peter Pan, who refused to grow up in the way that allowed full engagement with another human being.

Though there was that chemistry thing that kept us together for two years, I had more clarity of my patterning. It was like being a junky, still using my preferential substance, yet knowing it was no longer working. I was no longer in denial about my addiction, yet I just wasn't able to stop. And though I wasn't able to stop, I was far less desperate. It was easier for me to say what was true for me. It didn't change anything, but at least I wasn't just pretending everything was hunky-dory.

Distinguishing Smart from Wise

There was no doubt about it, Collin was smart. He'd become a successful lawyer prior to choosing to shift professions and become a psychologist. He read books and could discuss the contents of each one brilliantly.

I on the other hand had a different way of being with smarts. Where Collin had a knowing because he read it in a book or heard a famous professor expound about it, my way of knowing was more intuitive and integrative, through my own kinesthetic and somatic experience. I was conceptual too, in that I couldn't tell you the details of what was said or written, but I could give you the gist of it, seeing the bigger picture within which the details took place.

I learned at ITP that I was one of those individuals who needed to get the learning through my body; I was a kinesthetic learner. That's why all the learning institutions, like ITP, used various teaching methods, tapping into all of the various learning modalities each of us utilize in order to integrate information. By using all of the channels, body, mind, emotions, spirituality, creativity and community we are able to absorb far more of what's available than using just one channel.

My different way of learning and knowing created a rift with Collin. He would degrade me because my thinking process seemed so irrational to him. Sarcastically, he'd ask me, "How do you know *that*?" I'd just respond, "I just know." He didn't trust my knowing; however, what became clear for *me* was far more important than his precious opinion of me. I came to understand that there is a certain feminine process of knowing that is different from the masculine way of knowing. A feminine process of knowing uses all of my channels and allows me to fully experience my own knowing, where Collin used the more masculine model, based primarily on logic and rationality, which was great, but somehow felt limiting in its capacity to explore beyond what has been already captured. I came to trust and truly enjoy my learning experience.

The other rift between Collin and I was that he was looking for the epitome of beauty and youthfulness in a woman, and he wanted to have babies someday. Obviously, with me in my mid-forties I wasn't such a candidate. I knew I didn't measure up, but this time I didn't take it personally. We'd either find a path to loving each other in a more sincere and caring way or we wouldn't.

Again, much like with Sam, from the moment I was in this relationship I was in the process of extricating myself from it. I loved him and was in love with him, but didn't like him much. When we finally broke up, my friends as well as his friends shared that they just couldn't understand why I stayed with him as long as I had.

I could think only that there were residual ways of being that I had to work through and Collin was a perfect man with which to work it out. He had all of the entrapments: money, status, charm and like my dad and all of the other men in my life, he may have been charming, but not sincere.

Because I was far more fulfilled in my life than ever before, as a student and as a sailing instructor, my relationship with Collin wasn't as important as in the past, when I made men the most important part of my life.

The other significant piece of this was that by this time, I'd been working with *A Course in Miracles* for about ten years. I was able to identify how I used special relationships not to cultivate love and compassion; I used special relationships to generate a sense of worth and value. By doing so, I essentially devalued my self-worth and my relationship with God. My priorities had men over God. I was learning there wasn't a lot of wisdom in that! Growing myself spiritually liberated me from my fear-based attachments to men as my saviors. In so doing, I gently extricated myself from the belief systems that held me captive. I could love, but not be a slave to love.

Hannah's Visit

It was at the end of my second year at ITP, the day after Mother's Day that Hannah chose to visit me in California. She was twenty-one. I was finishing up requirements for graduating with my masters at ITP, looking for a new place to live, and teaching sailing, and struggling in this relationship with Collin. Her timing couldn't have been worse.

Hannah and her friend Shannon arrived the day after Mother's Day because even at twenty-one years old she still couldn't celebrate me as her mom. The intention of her visit was to get clear that I wasn't the selfish, self-centered person she had heard about from my brothers and sisters. She came to redeem my character in her eyes.

Because of all of the elements of my life in place, there wasn't much room for her during her stay. Just a couple of weeks later I would have had more time to spend with her. As it was, I couldn't be the mom she wanted me to be. I was frustrated that she chose to come at a time when I couldn't be there for her. And she really didn't come to be there for me. Her needs were a priority, and from her perspective, why couldn't I see that.

I totally understood what she wanted and what she needed, but I wasn't able to fulfill either. She left convinced that I was all of what my family had said I was and more.

By now, though, I knew who I was and though I was disappointed she'd arrived with so many expectations of me, I didn't feel bad. I felt sad for her because she came wanting to rectify what felt like a mistake, that I was indeed a good mother. But when she left, her experience told her that there was no mistake.

I was able to remember back when I was her age and older, and I'd visited my parents with the same hopes Hannah had; that my parents were everything good. Every single visit though, left me with an angry and shattered heart. I empathized with Hannah and her plight to find rightness about me. As much as I empathized though, I couldn't and I wouldn't try to reconfigure myself in order to look good in her eyes. Hadn't I been learning that through my relationships with men?

I didn't go out of my way to be mean and disconnected, I just wasn't able to put aside my present priorities because she decided that this was the best time for her to visit and I should make time for her. It was a dilemma for both of us. Both of us were unsatisfied with the outcome. That's how life is sometimes.

Mill Valley

After graduating with my master's, I no longer needed to be close to the ITP campus. Most of my class work was over and I'd be focusing on the requirements for the third year practicum, which was the integration of everything I learned in the first two years. Our options were to work or volunteer in places where we'd practice integrating the six pillars of the school with real life. Because I would, in essence, have a year off from school to participate in a practicum, I decided to move closer to the sailing club in Berkeley and work full time teaching sailing, while fulfilling my requirements. What better way to incorporate body, mind, spirit, emotions with community and creative expression? At the end of the year, I'd write a paper detailing my experience and my learning.

My search for a new home took me to the charming small town of Mill Valley, where Collin lived. It felt like a perfect place for me; close to Collin and only about a twenty-minute drive to the sailing club.

It was challenging to find a decent rental in Marin that was affordable. I used an apartment finding company. This paid off very quickly. In fact, they called me the next day after I registered, with a unique opportunity. There was a three hundred square-foot cabin in the redwoods only $800.00 per month. That sounded crazy to pay so much for so little, yet the call back to nature compelled me to check it out. And I figured that if God really wanted me to live there, He would provide the money for me to stay there.

I had to hoof it up to Marin as early as possible the next day to get a chance at this cabin as there would be many others wanting a chance at it too. It was a ninety-minute drive from Palo Alto to Mill Valley through San Francisco and then across the Golden Gate Bridge. The morning was magnificent and the drive through the City was easy.

Once through Mill Valley, I drove up winding streets until I found the address. The cabin was seventy-five steps up from the street, along what locals know as the *Dipsey Trail*. It was another ninety-eight steps to the street above. If I got this place, I'd surely be getting my exercise and keeping my figure.

There was a wood stove on the bottom level with natural walls of stone. There was a skylight over the bed and the kitchen and bathroom were just the right size – not too big and not too small. Every window looked out into redwood forests. It couldn't have been more perfect for someone who would be writing her dissertation. Rustic, but charming and very secluded.

I was among many who were interested in renting the cottage and as luck would have it, John, the landlord, was from Hamilton, Ontario, Canada, very close to Niagara Falls, and his mother, who just happened to be visiting, was from Truro, Nova Scotia. Very few people on the West Coast of the US would know of Hamilton and of Truro. Of course, I shared that I'd lived close to both places in my past, which I believe put me in their favor. They said yes and I was thrilled! Though it was beyond my budget, it felt very right for me. Again, I figured that if God wanted me there the money would show up.

John couldn't have been a better landlord. He was generous when I was late with the rent, always trusting that I'd pay within the month and I always did.

A Somewhat Effortless Breakup

The break up with Collin was, in some ways effortless, but not without sorrow and grief. I'd been inching my way out, as I said, from the very beginning. I kept in mind that what was true was this was probably as good as it was going to get, so every time more evidence presented itself I would take another step back, and then another. Finally, the day came when it felt as if I had just stepped off an escalator. I was done with that ride.

I realized that he was just another man onto which I'd transferred all of my daddy issues. He was a catalyst for change by being someone who was delightful, smart and wealthy. Like the others, I grew not because of him, but in spite of him. He contributed to my personal and spiritual growth by being someone who had all of the entrapments without the substance that I required of a partner.

My experience is that true partnership is exceptionally rare in relationship. Many people hook up, marry and are committed for life, yet they aren't available to each other; they aren't collaborating in a way that deepens the sense of trust, respect and ability to be vulnerable, which translates into intimacy. Commitments and *I love you's* don't often translate into deep partnership. It's important to learn this if true partnership is what you are wanting.

Another Bout of Cancer

I had settled myself in my cozy cottage in Mill Valley, was teaching at the sailing club and in the beginning stages of my dissertation. I was in my element; surrounded by nature, physically active and engaged with my creative expression through so many portholes.

I'd had a sore on my upper lip for a couple of years, probably since my sailing adventures on *Tree*, but didn't think much of it. Sometimes it would bleed, but more often, it was just a tiny reddish spot. Finally, I had it looked at by a dermatologist. Yes, it was skin cancer and yes, it needed to be removed. The surgeon, when looking at it said, "You know you will be disfigured." He delivered the prognosis with no compassion or empathy. He scared the living daylights out of me, so much so that for another few months I sought alternative methods to dealing with cancer, but in this particular case, the bottom line was that there wasn't any alternative.

Of course I didn't want to be disfigured and at the same time I didn't want the cancer to spread, I had to make a choice. In choosing the surgery, I had to release my attachment to what my face would look like afterward. No one would know the degree to which the cancer had spread until they went in and started cutting. I could have ended up with half a face.

Everyone who is diagnosed with cancer faces the powerlessness of having to be with the unknown. Cancer is an incredible spiritual teacher that way. I had to let go of my beliefs about myself, about my body, about what's important. Cancer brought me to a choice point that no one wants to confront, but by doing so, I explored the depths of my being, beyond my beauty, my identity, beyond my powerlessness to have it be different. Through sobbing deeply, I surrendered my will. There was nothing else I could do.

I believe that this surrendering process shifted the course of the cancer. As it turned out it was contained within a half-inch diameter. The surgeon removed a small part of my upper lip and the cut was called a cupid's bow – a cute name for a sad and ugly procedure. I was relieved and hopeful that the scaring would be minimal.

Hannah volunteered to come out and support me after the surgery. I was pretty self-sufficient, yet I so appreciated her willingness to come out to care for me and I hoped we could do some reparation of our relationship.

She arrived a few days after the surgery. By then I didn't really need that much care or rest. The wound was ugly, but it beat the alternative. I'd done my grieving prior to the surgery so that whatever the outcome was I could live with it.

I'd created a space for Hannah down in the tiny, but cozy living room. Eight by eight feet with a chair, a woodstove, a small bookshelf, that ran below the windows and the futon that would be her bed. It was cold down there, especially since it was February. But we'd do our best to make her comfortable.

Neither of us had any privacy as the only doors were those that opened to the outdoors and the bathroom. There was no insulation in the floor between us, so when she was on the phone I could hear everything. She'd want to be up at night talking with friends on the phone when I needed to sleep. I'd be up early to work on my dissertation and she would be disturbed by that. We were both frustrated!

It didn't take long for us to see that if she was going to stay, she'd have to find something to do – like work. Very quickly, Hannah found a job working at a Montessori School, which got her out of the cottage during the day. She loved children and was happy. She knew she wanted more for her career, but for the moment was good.

We lived in that space for about a month before it was clear that the only way to make things better between us was if she lived somewhere else. Again, she was angry with me that I wasn't the kind of mom that could make things better or different. I was living on a student's budget and there wasn't anything left after living expenses. It wasn't any different from my anger towards my mom for having her life, which couldn't accommodate my needs or wants. I was sad Hannah was so disappointed with me, but I always knew she would have to deal with her feelings about me. Thank God, I had the therapy, the therapeutic tools and the wisdom to prepare me for all of this. I took it in stride and hoped that at some point we'd eventually find peace.

Hannah moved to an apartment with a friend she met at the Montessori school. She lived there for just a few months before deciding to go to graduate school in Oregon. She had studied journalism in Toronto and wanted to specialize in sport journalism. University of Oregon in Eugene was the only school that offered such a specialization.

Before leaving for Oregon, when she was suffering with a cold and was in bed. I told her I'd pick up whatever she needed. She wanted a particular brand of cough syrup. For the sake of a couple of measly dollars, which at the time were very dear, I bought a generic brand – same ingredients, but not what she asked for. That was a big mistake. She was so upset with me that I hadn't gotten what she wanted. She couldn't understand my financial situation, since her whole life was spent with a father who had all the money in the world. I couldn't understand that giving her what she specifically asked for would have said, "*Mom cares*". We just couldn't seem to see eye-to-eye on these types of things.

Hannah also seemed to find many different ways to let me know that I was, well, wrong about everything. She took every opportunity to shoot sarcasms at me. For a long time I let that be her way to work out her anger; however, it didn't seem to help. I finally had to say, *"Enough!"* She'd either have to stop her criticism or stop being with me. She seemed to become more conscious of her criticism, which helped. Soon after, she went off to school in Eugene.

My mom died in 1998. She had cancer for a couple of years. I called Hannah to tell her that her grandmother died and to see what her plans were for going back to Detroit for the funeral. This was soon after she'd left Mill Valley for Eugene.

Rather than talking about my mom's death, we began talking about us. Hannah expressed her anger and disappointment with me; that I was indeed selfish and self-centered. She said she was through with me and that if I were her boyfriend she would be breaking up with me. It was one of those talks I would have liked to have had with my mom when I was Hannah's age – just telling it like it is with no yelling, or disrespectful and shaming tones. Just, *"I don't like you, I don't like what you did and I don't want to know you."*

I'd prepared myself for this moment since I left her twenty years before. My anticipation and compassion allowed me to encourage her to do what she needed to do. I told her I understood that she was angry for the choices I made; to give her up in the custody process and my choice to move to Nova Scotia, so far away from her and Noah. My empathy and compassion only made her angrier.

She told me she didn't want to talk to me, maybe forever; she didn't know. She said I could call or write to her, but she wasn't necessarily going to pick up the phone or write back. I was really okay with all of this. I understood that she had to find her own resolution to our circumstance. I so loved this about Hannah that she could be clear about her feelings and tell me how it was for her. It didn't happen often, but when it did, she delivered her message without accusations.

While in Eugene she struggled with her studies – it was harder than she anticipated and her emotional life was getting the best of her. She worked with a therapist and took some medication to help with some depression. She came to realize that this graduate school wasn't the place for her.

She decided to move back to the Bay Area with a fellow with whom she'd been in relationship. With her so close now, after almost two years of silence, perhaps it was time for us to clear the air. I wrote her emails, telling her I wanted to work things out and perhaps we could see a therapist together. She wrote back, telling me that she'd be willing to see a therapist with me, but that I'd have to first honor her demands – one of them being that I had to admit that leaving Ontario and moving to Nova Scotia was a mistake.

I couldn't do that. If I admitted that as a mistake, I'd have to admit that everything that followed from that choice on was also a mistake – that the life I had had and the one I was creating was just one big mistake. I could lose her forever if I didn't honor her demands. On the other hand, I'd be dishonoring my life and myself by capitulating.

I was at a choice-point. The dilemma was clear once again. The ever-present question was on the table, "Who do I honor?"

I could create a lie, saying that I was wrong and I made this mistake, but again, that would be totally dishonoring of everything I've come to believe in and to practice. There's no integrity or accountability in lying. She may never understand what it was that had me make the choices I made – the ones that were in service to the well-being of my children. It took me weeks to discern the truths of my choices. I revealed to myself, over and over again the desperate, wounded woman-child who attempted to find love where it wasn't available; how that person wasn't a good mother. At the same time, I consistently found the ground of my being, my knowing that I loved my children and wanted them so much. I acknowledged that I sacrificed my motherhood so they could have the stability and the life I wanted for them. Though I had led a dysfunctional life, I've never wavered on that one truth.

I was also clear that having stayed in the Niagara region would have meant limiting my education and all of the experiences that have added up to incredible growth for my children and me. I had to remember that my move to Nova Scotia was not intended to distance myself from my children, but was to cultivate an environment that would deeply nourish them and myself. Had I lived in close proximity to them I more than likely would have alienated them in other ways. There was no guarantee; there is only the interpretation that that would have been the right thing to do. I risked it all by creating the life I did in Nova Scotia and everything that unfolded from there.

I wrote Hannah back. I shared all of my regrets; missing birthdays, Halloweens and proms. It was a lengthy letter and I was truthful with every word I wrote. As much as I regretted not being there for them I knew that the path I took was one that was required if I were to be any sort of real mom for them. What was more important to me was that I, in my own way, modeled for them the kind of life I'd want for them; however, it was hard and often frightening. I'd want them to have the courage to live their life the way they needed to – not for me, not for their dad, not for anyone, but for themselves.

After receiving my letter, Hannah agreed to see a therapist with me. I'd gotten a referral to a therapist in San Francisco and met Hannah at the office. We were both genuinely happy to see each other.

The single most important moment of that session was when again Hannah required of me that I admit that I was wrong to leave her and Noah and move to Nova Scotia. The therapist asked me, *"Were you wrong?"* I had to declare in front of Hannah that I wasn't wrong and much like I'd said in the letter, to think I was wrong about that would say I was wrong about every choice I'd made since leaving Niagara Falls. I knew that as tough as my life had been I hadn't been wrong about the path I chose.

Somehow, Hannah was able to hear this and in that moment let go of her demand. The obstacle between us shifted and there was a free flow of energy that brought a sigh of relief. She was willing to have another therapy session with me, after which we both felt that we no longer needed the therapist to mediate for us.

Over the next few years, while we both lived in the Bay Area we saw each other more frequently. Her priorities have always been friends and other family first. So I had to get used to being in the back seat of her life. I don't know that many parents get to have a choice about that with their children.

Hannah has worked with various therapists over the years. I so appreciate that she's willing to reach out for support and not hide behind stories and thoughts that would interfere with her life being the best she can make it.

As a therapist myself and then as a coach I had a lot I could offer my children. Yet, in one conversation with Hannah, she shared that she and Noah wanted me to stop playing coach all the time and just be a mom. I told her that it was really vulnerable to be a mom. I could make mistakes. Hannah said she'd prefer I be real and make mistakes then to be the coach.

I've given my children the freedom to choose the relationship they would want to have with me. I believe a healthy parent-child relationship will always be unequal in that the children want parents to want them and want to be with them, while the children only want that sometimes – mostly on their terms. This is something that I've come to learn and slowly accept. I'd love to be closer to Hannah. I'd love for her to confide in me the way some daughters can with their moms. At times, we've been there. But, mostly I feel inadequate in her eyes. As with my relationships with men, I've come to define myself by my standards – not someone else's. I'm proud of both my children. I'm proud of what we've cultivated over the years. Thank God, we have more to come!

Todd, My Sweetie

My relationship with Todd began when I was forty-seven years old. At that time, his name was Dreamwalker. That says a great deal about what was important to him eleven years ago. He was in a mystery school for six years and his spiritual life took precedence over just about everything.

I fell in love with him a long time before I ever knew anything about him. I met him the night he facilitated a breathwork for a group of my classmates from ITP. The essence of his being was heartfelt. He was playful, soulful, wise, strong, very cute and had an innocence too that made me want to be with this kind of man. He showed very little interest in me that night, and the same goes for the next five times I met him over the next five years. Our story is one which people really enjoy hearing about.

After the first meeting, I met him again at the mystery school for a preparation for a vision quest, another ITP event. He would also be one of the facilitators for a sweat lodge the next day. I was sitting on the ground near the fire with my friend Scott, when Todd walked past us. In a tone of admiration and awe Scott pointed up at Todd and said "that's Dreamwalker." He had a coonskin cap on and to me he looked seven feet tall. I felt like a young, giddy schoolgirl looking up at some popular guy in high school. I too was in awe of him as he passed by. He didn't notice.

Again, at the mystery school, during the vision quest, I had a tiny window of opportunity to make an impression on Todd. Again, he didn't have eyes for me. I was with Collin at the time, but it's always nice to think I've made some impression on a guy. But Todd just wasn't getting it.

In September of 1998, I met him again at a wedding for Scott and his sweetie Jennie. He was the officiate for the ceremony. Though I was only a vague recollection of moments shared at the mystery school and the breathwork, he actually spoke to me as if I were someone he knew.

He seemed very happy and shared that he was engaged to be married. Though I'd been dating Collin, I'd had a crush on Todd since that first moment I met him four years before. Now, I felt that my chances were over to be with this man and I just had to let the fantasy go. I sincerely wished him happiness.

My breakup with Collin occurred shortly after this. I had some healing to do and wasn't ready for another relationship. But about nine months later, in June, Scott and Jennie said they wanted to introduce me to someone. When I asked who it was, they said Todd Zimmerman. "But, he's married!" I said. I was shocked that they would want to introduce me to a married man. They shared that the marriage never happened and the engagement was broken off. I was so excited about the chance to get to know this man. Scott and Jennie said they would call me in a couple of weeks once they had spoken to Todd and arranged a dinner for all four of us.

About three weeks later, I checked in with them about this potential dinner. They said they hadn't gotten around to talking with Todd, but would call him within the week. Again, I didn't hear anything back. A few weeks went by and I called once again. They said they'd been too busy to connect with Todd, but would do so in the next couple of weeks.

During the summer while I waited for dinner with Todd, I dropped the need to think about, worry about or be anxious about being with a man. In essence, I went on the wagon. I got clean and sober and it felt really good. I felt a clarity and groundedness within. I no longer allowed distraction. I imagined the qualities of Todd being everything I wanted in a partner. I also imagined all the qualities I'd need to be in order to be with someone like the Todd I imagined. I really had no clue who Todd was, other than all of my own imaginings, but what this did was bring about clarity. I no longer wanted to waste time on cultivating relationships for the sake of my own fear of loneliness. My life continued to be full and fulfilling and I could let go of chasing a dream that somehow things would be better with a man in my life. Just like that day on *Tree of Life*, I came to accept that it wouldn't be better, it would just be different.

It no longer made sense wasting time or energy on anyone less than extraordinary. My brief meetings and imaginings of Todd gave me the grist for this mill. I experienced a quality of presence and connection with Todd, in my imaginings that were deeper than what I ever considered possible. I had a knowing that as deep as he was as a spiritual teacher I could meet him there and be that for him too. I imagined kissing him and it was exquisite!

I knew nothing about Todd other than he was a massage therapist, facilitated breathwork groups and sweat lodge ceremonies. He was well thought of in the ITP community since half the population knew of him and his amazing healing work. He seemed to be my kind of guy!

The whole summer came and went without a meeting with Todd. So I gave up on the possibility that we would meet.

Because I'd always been the initiator of most of my relationships I'd promised that I wasn't going to initiate another one again; however, I thought I needed to take the bull by the horns, just one more time. So, I called directory assistance in the San Jose area and asked for the listing for Todd Zimmerman. Wouldn't you know it – there were two listings. I asked the operator to give me one of the numbers since I knew nothing more about where he lived other than he had lived in San Jose. When I called, it was the wrong Todd Zimmerman. I took that as a sign!

About a month later, sitting at lunch with my wonderful friend Joan, I shared the story about Todd and that I didn't want to initiate another relationship. "Oh, but you have to call him," was all that Joan said. I didn't ask her why she was so adamant about calling him. I just took it as another sign. I called another friend that was a client of Todd's and asked for his number. This time it was the right Todd Zimmerman. I left a message regarding my relationship with Scott and Jennie and my interest in maybe going sailing with him.

He called me back that evening and we had a lovely conversation that ended with a plan to go sailing the following weekend. Though we'd had some brief meetings he actually didn't have any idea who I was, so it was very much a blind date for him. Once he saw me, though, he did recognize me at once.

Sailing made for a good first date. There are a lot of details to attend to and talk about, which meant if there was any discomfort or lack of interest on either of our parts, the sailing itself would carry us through until it was time to put the boat to bed and say goodbye. However, we had a lovely time and very quickly – more quickly than we anticipated we became inseparable. But …

His name was Dreamwalker for a reason. On one of our walks together he asked me if I could be with someone who was a dreamer, indicating that if this relationship was going to work it meant letting go of my attachment to him being a breadwinner. I'd have to love him for his capacity to love and to provide a sanctuary for deep spiritual work for people and for me. I had to accept that he wasn't going to be financially stable, maybe ever. This isn't to slight him at all; it's just a matter of getting my own priorities straight; that financial security wouldn't be the foundation of this relationship. Spiritual development and connection would be.

I told myself during those summer months when contemplating the deep relationship I was wanting, that a soulful connection was far more important to me than having someone provide for me. And it was challenging work for me to live actually into that truth, but that's what I was committed to do.

After only four months, I moved in with Todd who was living in his sister's home. This decision was based on the basis that we wanted more time together and with me in Mill Valley and him in San Jose; it was very much a long distance relationship. This move would also create convenience for me: I needed to spend more time at ITP and letting go of the cabin meant I could reduce my living expenses significantly. His sister Barb was happy to have me move in. She was a generous person in that way.

Very quickly, I let go of the independent me; the one that was free and clear about priorities. I began my whole co-dependent, nurturing thing again. Todd would have none of it. He could sense that my loving actions were controlling, manipulative and not authentic. He stopped me at every turn. He'd always made his own meals and didn't like to be told what to eat and when to eat it.

He was emerging from a relationship with a community where the women were not only assertive, but dominating, making men wrong for being men. He was angry and grief stricken and at the same time didn't realize the depths of the wounding that occurred during those six years. He was in love with me and at the same time was very angry with women. He wasn't going to placate or show overt kindness just because I'd wanted that.

And though he said he wanted to spend time with me he continually was wrapped up with clients and emails. He wouldn't come to bed until the wee hours in the morning. This really aggravated me. I couldn't control or manipulate to get my way. At forty-seven, I'd slipped into using the same old strategies and they weren't working.

So, here I was with a man who'd indicated incredible capacity for deep intimacy and spiritual depth, yet he wasn't emotionally available. It's as though those two years with Collin added up to a hill of beans of growing and maturing on my part.

One evening when I wanted Todd to come to bed and he said his normal, "I'll be there in a minute." I rethought the situation. When living in Nova Scotia, wasn't I happy and content? And when living in Mill Valley wasn't I fulfilled and satisfied? So, I liked my life without having to pull someone into the center. I remembered that I actually enjoy sleeping alone. From that night on, I started enjoying my life again doing what I liked and loved, and learned to let go of my attachment to Todd and what he was doing. Either we'd find our way together or we wouldn't.

As I had heard from my friend Aniesa, I had to learn to live on my side of the street. I needed to let Todd live on his too. Through this practice of walking solely on my side of the street, I sloughed off so many strategies to try to be important, special and in control. More and more I walked my talk, practiced what I preached, had far less anxiety and more calm than in any other relationship. I gave up my expectations that this guy was going to fulfill me. With my perspective clearer than ever, I had to assess whether Todd and I were compatible enough to have this relationship work.

It's so fascinating to realize that some of the sweetest, wise and mature people, while in their practice as a therapist, just may not have the same capacity in their personal relationship. It's safe to be open and accessible with clients for an hour, but then to go home to partners, quite often we aren't the same person. It's too vulnerable! Both Todd and I struggled with the challenge of being amazing caring people with our clients, but being crazy and dysfunctional in our own relationship with each other.

A key moment came when during a relationship coaching session with Hans, he asked, "Are you killing your relationship, growing it, or letting it die?" Both Todd and I, with incredible clarity were able to admit that in spite of the love we had for each other we were continually trying to kill the relationship. Our unconscious survival mechanisms that we'd learn to use very early in life kept us from stepping beyond our comfort zone towards the intimacy we so desired and the vulnerability we so wanted to avoid.

That night we got clear that we were both killing the relationship and we both got clear that we really wanted to begin growing it. The question we sat with was, were we each committed enough to do whatever it would take to grow the relationship.

Like every recovery program there is a great deal of conscious awareness that has to be exercised in order to reveal patterns of being that are no longer working. Growing a relationship means letting go of these patterns and practicing new ones. It's a lot of hard work.

Through the years, both Todd and I continued to practice staying on our own side of the street. This has allowed me to focus on my way of being that in the past interfered with growing myself and growing my relationships.

As much as I loved Todd, I came to accept that my need for solitude was as great if not greater than his. I became more and more conscious of that fact that I couldn't stay with him and be impacted by behaviors that seemed too crazy-making.

I realized that I'd lived on my own far more years than I'd lived with others. Because of that I'd become emotionally self-sufficient. I didn't need or want the hardship that this relationship was continually contributing to my life. I continued to work the serenity prayer: accepting the things I couldn't change, being courageous enough to change the things I could, and cultivating the wisdom to know the difference. I asked myself, "How do I be with the most amazing man I know and still extricate myself from the dysfunctional aspects of our relationship?" I wasn't sure I could do it for much longer.

Looking for Home

Todd and I struggled for four years together – two of those years, we lived with his sister, Barb, and the next two we lived in two other homes. By this time, I'd finished my Ph.D. and had finally finished my work at the sailing club. I found a full time position at ITP as an admissions counselor. It was stable work and I was content yet, I knew I just didn't want to stay in the Bay Area. I was looking for home. I'd lived in the Bay Area for eight years, but was looking forward to being back in some rural area that would feed my spirit.

In 2002, I got a call from a new acquaintance I'd met through the admissions office at ITP. He called to say he was on Orcas Island in the State of Washington. "Rosie, Orcas is calling your name. You've got to come!"

Orcas Island is part of the San Juan Islands in the Puget Sound. The Island is fifty-five square miles and is very close to the Canadian Border. Though there are mountains and farmland the population is a wonderful mix of cosmopolitan, hippy-types with a few conservatives thrown in to the mixture. I knew of Orcas through an old friend of mine in Nova Scotia. I knew how beautiful it was. So, when James said those magical words there was no stopping me.

I thrive in the northern climates with the dark cloudy days, but Todd wanted nothing to do with that kind of weather. He's a native Californian and just felt he couldn't handle all of the rain of the Pacific Northwest. After James' exclamation that Orcas was calling me, we did some research and found that Orcas Island had sun at least two thirds of the year. That was enough for Todd to take the next step with me to go see the Island.

It was March of 2003 when we went for our big adventure. We flew into Seattle, rented a car, and then drove up to Anacortes to meet the ferry. The ferry ride from Anacortes to the San Juan Islands alone was magical and when we arrived at Orcas, there was nothing more to be said. I was coming home.

Even though Todd and I were partners, my requirement for nature overrode my need to be connected at the hip – this much had changed for me. I decided that one way or another I would be moving to Orcas in August. Todd could or would come when he could or would. It didn't matter to me if or when he moved up; in fact, it was my strategy to extricate myself from the relationship. Because he'd always had overriding priorities and he hardly had time for me I expected that with my move to Orcas, he would slowly, but surely forget about me. I wouldn't be constantly demanding quality time and he could be happy doing what he wanted. This felt like the best solution. He never knew that this was my plan. He didn't need to. I figured that we'd gone from killing the relationship to just letting it die. There was no need to use any further life-support system. Either it would die or it would somehow begin to grow again. I didn't really care.

Somehow, once I began to implement my strategy to move to Orcas, Todd began to act more like the partner I wanted him to be. He was becoming the man I fell in love with. It didn't stop me from moving away from the Bay Area, but it did give me hope that perhaps we could work this out. That was eight years ago.

Chapter Seven

Home at Last – Really

I had no idea how it was going to work, to move to Orcas while my work was in California. I'd been facilitating the transformational coaching training program, running coaching groups and working with individual clients for four years. My intention was to live on Orcas and fly down once a month for a week during which I'd see clients, have the groups and facilitate the training weekends. I could always do coaching sessions on the phone too. I'd just have to try it out and work with whatever showed up.

I settled in to my new lifestyle on Orcas effortlessly after years away from rural living and the appealing solitude that often adjoins it. I rented a small house on East Sound, which is a small finger of water that essentially splits the Island in half.

The silence of the space provided another dimension to this time, which is so unavailable in the middle of Silicon Valley. The crackles of the wood burning in the stove were sounds of life and connection to nature; it was so different from the noise of traffic, forced air heaters and all.

Having this time to myself brought all sorts of feelings and thoughts to the surface of consciousness. "Here I am, all alone, isolating myself to a degree from life's distractions, mostly because I really enjoy a great deal of solitude. And it's offering me a chance to spend time writing. Yet there are a great many chores that need attending to. Bringing wood in for the fire that in this moment is only for me."

Living with Todd for four years, I'd focus much of my energy on caretaking; my nature to care for others in spite of myself was effortless, but was depleting my life force. On Orcas, everything I was doing was for me alone. I grasped the idea that I was being solely for myself and wondered of the value of that. I found that thought curious, wondering about the value of being for myself. I felt sadness that I'd become so immune to opportunities to live for myself, being for myself. After all, none of us can be for anyone, but ourselves, in relation to others and to things in general. When I am not living for myself, I am living for money, for love, for freedom from debt, for material goods. Being there on this particular Saturday in November 2003, my thoughts were only of my being comfortable, warm and rested. I think about indigenous people who lived their lives in a way that sometimes meant being alone was necessary to survive or thrive. Did they question their being of value? I doubt it.

I had opportunities to chase away my solitude with dinner with new friends or a walk with a companion. I relished this time alone and enjoyed this opportunity to experience this being with myself. I was able to hear the different voices in my head and get to know the unmet needs of aspects of myself that desired nurturance. I brought a whole community of voices with me. Gratefully, we agreed about warmth and sitting so we can watch the sunrise in flannel pajamas, with the wool blanket from Ireland doubled across my lap, a warm cup of tea and this computer.

Being is a practice. The doing of my being is so distracting that often I'm unaware of how I am being. I ask my clients, "How are you being?" Initially, they haven't a clue about what I've asked them. I am familiar with that state of cluelessness when it comes to my own being. I'm exploring all of that for myself. I believe it's one of the reasons for showing up on this planet - to be; yet, the business of the world I've created often blurs my connection with my being. Even in sitting meditation, where the practice is to sit and just watch thoughts and feelings come and go, there is still a doing required. When do we give ourselves permission just to be?

Living among the trees and water I am reminded that that is my practice. Not to rush off to make new contacts with potential clients. My job is to make time just to be.

One night, when I arrived back from California, I was scurrying around unpacking, checking mousetraps and all when I was startled by a bright light shining outside the window. Oh, my God! It was an incredibly full moon and it was reflecting radiantly off the water. I had moved in eight weeks before, while it was cloudy and rainy, and had just a few days here before going back to California. So, my shock at seeing the moon was laughable. I wrapped myself up in my blanket and went outside to be with the beauty of that moment. As I'd noticed many times, it was challenging to be present to the beauty at hand. As much as I wanted it in my life, I observed how often I distracted myself from it.

I took the phone out to call Todd to share this precious and rich moment with him. A thought in my head said, "Why are you doing that?" I struggled just to be in this moment with this beauty by myself. I'd been alone before, chosen the solitude of Nova Scotia, Mill Valley and now Orcas. Sometimes sharing these moments deepens the experience; however, my sense is that I was wanting to lessen the degree of presence I brought to this moment because, quite frankly, being that engaged in beauty makes me feel raw and open; my heart aches and feels like it will shatter. To me beauty is an essential element of the Divine and sometimes to expose myself to this experience overwhelms my circuits. It feels too much – too big. Too often, my distractions allow me to diminish the fullness of being me in relation to the Universal Oneness of all that is. To expand my capacity to be with such beauty and with the expansiveness of the Divine; this too is a practice.

A Christmas Present from Noah

I got a Christmas package in the mail from Noah. Along with some candy, Christmas candles, a book and a CD of Abba's best, there was a white sheet of folded paper. Among the usual Merry Christmas and I hope you enjoy ... came this, "You are one of the best grownups I know." It's what I most cherished in that box. It's what I wanted most in the whole world as a present from my son.

You do the best you can with what you got. You can't get it right, you can only get it. You can't foresee how your actions will affect your children. You hope and pray that someday they will love you and more importantly, respect you. Noah's words carry more weight than any other gift, recognition or reward could ever do.

The vulnerability of a child is bounced between parents and grownups with little recognition of how they are being affected. I no longer take the blame for the choices that bring them pain and disappointment in their adult life. I can hold their hands while they are facing the bleakness and let them know I believe in them and they will find their way.

My own Place ... Once Again

With my parents' passing, my inheritance allowed me to purchase a ten-acre parcel of land on Turtle Back Mountain overlooking Crow Valley, only eight months after moving to the Island. Though I've dreamed forever of building a home, I've lived happily in a twenty-six foot travel trailer for seven years. With a yurt for guests and a sweat lodge for ceremony, life on Orcas has been very comfortable and very simple.

Todd visits maybe twice a year, but most of our time together happens when I return to California, where we live comfortably in a townhouse in Mountain View, just a mile from some of Silicon Valley's biggest players. The juxtaposition between Orcas and Mountain View provides me with all of the benefits that life has to offer.

The deep friendship and deep commitment to walking our spiritual paths together keeps Todd and I connected and continually engaged in each other's journey. We understand that we walk separate paths side by side. I love that we are still very much in love too – that hasn't changed in the eight years we've lived separately. I believe he'll be my sweetie forever.

Living on My Own

Slowly I put the pieces together; inch by inch, extricating myself out from under a context that required me to be a certain way in order to supposedly feel fulfilled as a woman. Part of me still wished I could believe that to be true, but the fact is I'm actually living more happily without sharing a home with a man. Relationships have not been a means to self-fulfillment for me though I always thought that would be so. More often than not, I've grown in spite of the men I've been with. Perhaps that will change as I continue to change and grow. With Todd, my fulfillment comes when we share our unique truths and opinions; when we hear and acknowledge each other for the gifts that arrive with just being; knowing that, I'm the best I can be with this person. I continue to grow up by meeting him and by meeting myself.

We were married five years ago here at Eagles Heart Sanctuary – the name of our property. Though Todd had asked me to marry him many times over the years, I just didn't want to be trapped in a marriage, which if again found unsatisfying would take incredible effort to untie all of the knots. But somehow, in a split second something unexplainable happened.

In one of these conversations about marriage, I said to Todd, "I'll marry you if I get to die first." He thought about it for just a few seconds before saying "Okay." He loved me enough to endure the grief of losing me, his wife, someday in the future. That said a lot to me. For some reason an enormous burden was lifted and it was as if some archetypal energy rushed into my body; much like that magical moment with Mac on the dance floor in Nova Scotia when I allowed myself to fall in love. This moment with Todd became exhilarating and playful. It would mean another new adventure, one we would be sharing while continuing to walk alone on our own side of the street.

Long-term relationships provide a spiritual practice that short-term relationships can't. We have a piece of driftwood painted with the words, "Forever, for Always, No Matter What!" The degree of personal work one has to go through in order to live this motto is monumental. We can capitulate and compromise, which mostly results in suffering, settling and surviving, or one can surrender what no longer serves the growing of a marriage. The outcome is never known, but the practice itself is what it's all about, anyway.

We decided to have a spiritual wedding ceremony that would be more about the celebration of our love and less about the legally binding contract. That it was a spiritually binding contract was far more significant. There was no doubt in either of us that this event was bigger than both of us together. Eagles and hawks circled above our heads and the very late sunset of July on Orcas allowed the celebration to go on and on.

Letting Go of ITP

ITP has been my home for fifteen years. For the ten years following graduation I've been contract faculty within their academic departments and in their Department of Continuing Education. My expertise in coaching provided me an opportunity to create and facilitate the Transformational Coaching Training program for the past nine years. I felt so blessed and lucky to integrate all of my learning and experience in Marriage and Family Therapy, Transpersonal Psychology and Spiritual Guidance with the Coaching, providing a huge bandwidth within with to coach and train coaches.

I loved my work and found my niche as a facilitator. I came to understand the true meaning of the practice of facilitation, which for me is empowering people by engaging them in discussions and conversations, which reveal their own knowing and understanding, and letting that be the basis and foundation of the learning upon which they build more learning. This form of facilitation allows people to share their wisdom and to be heard. This, to me allows everyone to cultivate and live into dignity.

Each of the yearlong trainings brought ten to fifteen people together. We had a revolving door entrance so people could come in just about any time of year. This was a really valuable process that was taken from the model used by the martial art Aikido. The trainees who've been in the training longer, saw that they had to build experience and knowledge. They could see their growth and share that with newcomers.

The success of the first four years I chalked up to luck; the fifth year, I got very anxious because it became obvious that this wasn't just dumb luck. I was actually providing a training program that was rich, deep and profound. Much like when I was a sailing instructor at OCSC, I had to acknowledge that I excelled in my art. As much as each of us wants that for ourselves, it was so challenging to accept my abilities. My childhood learning stayed with me; don't be too visible because someone is likely to take potshots at you if you do.

It was frightening to acknowledge my own abilities, and yet it was essential. I'm constantly empowering my clients to empower themselves through self-acknowledgement. In doing so what no longer serves, concerning archaic beliefs and judgments fall away.

The sixth, seventh and eighth years were probably some of the most exquisite of my life. The quality of presence in that classroom year after year was remarked upon by visitors and trainees. People returned month after month to participate in a level of presence and consciousness that they did not have outside the training.

The training program taught the fundamental skills and tools of life coaching. There are programs that do this over one weekend. Our coaching program focused on the domain of humanity from which all of our choice making originates. And you cannot train individuals to be transformational coaches without including the Domain of Oneness and Universal Source of All that is. The field of transpersonal psychology contributed greatly to my knowledge and my ability to navigate in such expansive waters. Month after month, Todd, who co-facilitated the program with me, the trainees and myself, together as a collective, explored how as humans we choose to choose what we choose in order to have the life we have, and how to choose differently in support of having the life we say we want. Easy, elegant, yet one's willingness to traverse and explore in a sense the rabbit hole meant cultivating courage and compassion for self and for clients. It's a big practice – one that takes a year to begin to grasp. Heck it took me so many years to get that I was getting it.

Halfway through the seventh year and while facilitating in the ITP Global Department's Transformational Life Coaching Training program too, I realized that I was done with teaching in the Global Program, and I felt like I would be completing the other program at the end of the year. I felt a calling to do something in the bigger world. I could see the trajectory heading somewhere out of sight. It was a very powerful pull – to what I couldn't say. But it was strong enough to have me seriously consider letting go of … well, essentially letting go of everything.

Todd, who had been co-facilitating with me for a majority of these years, thought he was interested in taking it over, but as life unfolded, it was obvious I wasn't leaving; at least not that year.

The eighth year of the training rocked my socks off. The brilliance and compassion that each individual brought into the room was palpable to all. It was interesting because we had more corporate trainees than in previous years, yet they had something beyond the corporate mentality that engaged all of us in a much deeper conversation than imaginable.

The calling to something else was still incredibly compelling so again I declared it so. The ninth was to be the final year of this training program. We had only three fulltime trainees plus a few individuals here and there that were fulfilling incomplete requirements. Though the group was small, these three women showed up and required us to show up just as if we'd had twenty individuals.

When the training ended September 2010, it was done! I felt done and have yet to give it another thought. No regrets, no unfinished business; it's over! I'm not missing the weekends, nor am I pining for what was. My sense is that the quality of those weekends will be a part of other trainings and seminars. There is nothing to miss as it will come around again.

For all of these years, I'd been able to maintain my livelihood commuting between the Bay Area and Orcas. Now, with the end of the training came an end to the long string of clients that had come through the training program. I knew, as I'd experienced in the past that following the calling would lead to something extraordinary. I took the leap.

Next

Days after ending the training program, I returned to Orcas to wait and see what was next for me. I had a lot of panic and anxiety because I'd let go of my main source of income. I really had no idea if I'd be able to pay my mortgage from one month to the next.

There was a large part of me that looked at this experience as one of the most stupid ideas I'd ever had. From a logical, rational perspective, it was insane. No business plan in place, I leaped off into an abyss with no visible parachute or safety net. I'd be free falling for who knew how long.

I had to remember the many times in my life where I'd leaped into the abyss sans parachute and safety net. I had to reread the spiritual teachings that revealed that the logical rational world, to a large extent is one big illusion and is held together by the reality each of us is attempting to create. And what shows up is a co-design between Self and Universal Consciousness.

I had to reframe my past experiences of being supported by others. I had to see that the Universe put those people there to support me – that it was God, in essence that was the foundational support and empowerer of all that is. When I got this, it was easier to let go of my fear and anxiety.

I had enough evidence from my past that said that this is the reality in which I want to live – to trust that I am always held safely.

I also had to remember that I continually empower my clients to take the leap. I tell them that I'm right next to them as they take flight. But this time, I was taking the leap and I felt all alone. No matter who tells you they are right next to you – you have to leap on your own – no one can hold your hand. It doesn't work that way.

"... when you leap, you will either land on your feet or learn how to fly."

This Is It

I received an email that was forwarded to me from a person I did not know. It was an announcement that ABC's Good Morning America show was looking for an advice guru. From what the email said, they were looking for me!

I did a quick inventory of myself, my experience, my book, education – you name it – The TV show wanted what I had. And based on the calling and the trajectory of that calling there was no doubt in my mind and my heart that I was meant to have this position.

I filled out the very brief application and sent it off quickly. I knew that if I was meant to have this position it would all go effortlessly and I'd hear back probably within a week or two after the closing date, mid-October. That meant I'd be going to New York City probably in November.

The process of instant manifestation requires a degree of commitment that goes far beyond any level of faith I'd known thus far. I witnessed my past leaps and said, "Well, this is the same process just a different leap." Yet, I was far more conscious to the process I was undertaking. This time I was more of the generator and the rocket boosters than just a passenger.

As part of my self-empowerment process, I began using dowsing and muscle testing to talk with God. For more than ten years, I've been finding incredible wisdom through using a pendulum or by letting my fingers to do the talking as a form of muscle testing. The more I understood quantum physics the more sense it made that a pendulum or the various forms of muscles testing works. I've learned to trust my ability to dowse and continued to follow in faith the path that seemed to be laid out before me. Much like the clay face with no eyes that I made while at ITP, I was being asked to go forward blindly. I let my fingers do the talking and I'd do the walking.

I was called to take this journey. And as in the past, when called to such a journey – leaving my innocence in first grade, leaving the Catholic Church, leaving my children, leaving my home in Nova Scotia, leaving *Tree of Life* and now, leaving ITP, there is a releasing of what no longer serves my spiritual development.

Each ending had been done with more and more consciousness and more clarity of the intention, the trajectory getting clearer and more visible – the destination, though, was still out of sight; however, this time, I'd never been surer of anything in my life. While I was waiting for the call from Good Morning America, I figured I had better begin to clear any patterns or processes that could interfere with being one hundred percent available for this position.

I let myself believe I could achieve a goal bigger than I ever dreamed of before. I got confirmation from the Universe through muscle testing that indeed this was my path and that I was chosen for this particular position. I dreamed big dreams about what it all would be like. It was a wonderful experience.

As part of the preparation work for this position as America's Advice Guru I was called to write this book. I started it a number of years ago, yet for some reason it was time to bring it to the center of my attention. What this meant was that I'd have to touch into any unhealed memories that made themselves obstacles in my path to my goal. I had no idea that there was so much unresolved sorrow and grief within me.

As each memory revealed itself, I became present to its own unique gifts to my life and allowed it to free itself to its next higher incarnation. Day after day, I spilled myself onto paper with my writing. I'd then walk with Gracie, my dog, in the woods, talking to God, to Jesus and other guides and angels. I continually muscle tested on this goal and continually got a yes. I kept the faith, walked my talk and purged myself of addictive patterns of worry and anxiousness. I knew these patterns had to do with past experience and choices I made. Why worry about the future – there's nothing really to worry about in the unknown – only what we make believe.

October 2010

Through my writing, I got that I created my life as it was. Only in relationships with my parents and with men did I feel I was a victim. Everything else I could take like water off a duck's back. Once I got clear that I wasn't a victim in these relationships either and that these were all of my most dedicated teachers, I began to take myself and my current circumstances more seriously. I empowered myself to acknowledge, then relinquish my burdens, surrender my grief and sorrows, forgive myself and others for our humanity and allow the grace of God to shine upon me. This has been the journey worth living for.

Motherhood and Moments of Disappointment

Every day I was gifted with revelations, insights and truths I'd read about in other people's books. Now in my own life and through my own writing I was experiencing what it truly meant to let go and let God.

At the same time, I continued to come up against storms of my past. Time and again, I relived the moment of letting my children go, letting go of my dreams of making my children happy. Over and over, I went through those memories in search of something I didn't know.

Each day after the last day in which applications would be accepted by GMA, I had to choose how to be. I could feel disappointment, anxiety, worry, rejected and more, which I did to a degree. At the same time, I stayed clear about the course I was on, knowing that I was living into my life purpose in the way I was meant to. I was strengthening muscles that allowed me to stay true to my course, wavering less often and enjoying the adventure. I was learning so much about myself, letting go of what no longer served me and I continually watched my thinking process; stopping when I was going in the direction of the past. This was much like a sitting meditation process, but this practice was a living-my-life meditation – mindfulness practice.

As I held to my course, I had to be with the reality that the shores of my destination might not look like what I imagined. Perhaps I'd have to give up my attachment to Good Morning America as the destination. Just like sailing across the Atlantic, I'd have no idea of what it would be like to land in Ireland until we actually arrived.

Invisible, Lost, Confused

My writing practice took me back and forth from young to old, to adolescence to family; this book wasn't written chronologically. I followed my intuition through dowsing and knew that whatever would show up on the paper was the next element of my life to be revealed.

Over and over, I saw my attachment to the idea that I was and still am invisible to the world. I witnessed how I created patterns in order to avoid feeling lost, invisible and confused. I manipulated and controlled in order to maintain a façade. Divorce – more deception, more facades – little by little learning to reveal myself to myself – creating incidence after incidence, which over time created cracks in the façade and armor. I came to a place where denial was no longer possible. I saw time again how I had to choose which pain to be with – the anguish and agony of aloneness, o the agony of a painful partnership, betrayal and abandonment.

Choosing Agony

I was done with suffering for the sake of reinforcing the beliefs that imprisoned me, the one's that dictated that I was a victim to my circumstances. When I got to this point of self-empowerment, I then had only one choice; to recognize self-betrayal, self-abandonment and self-annihilation in order to recognize all of my survival strategies including procrastinating and avoiding agony. Choosing self-realization meant acknowledging that I am betraying, abandoning and annihilating myself; choosing self-actualization meant exercising atrophied muscles in support of walking through Hell for Heaven's sake; no longer betraying, abandoning and annihilating me. What it meant was that I'd come to the realization that I had nothing to lose. At the same time, I had everything to lose.

Walking through Hell for Heaven's Sake

Meeting myself, following the thread of agony, meant experiencing the full monty. The quality of experience of agony took me down various rabbit holes. Sometimes it was loss and grief, sometimes it was anger, and sometimes it was despair, hopelessness, helplessness and powerlessness.

In late October, I experienced a breakthrough. At twenty-six when I chose to leave my children, my armor, which held the agony in and more agony out – that armor cracked. Hairline fractures began to appear. I didn't acknowledge them, hence the denial. I wanted to find someone outside myself to hold me together, someone who would continue applying the glue that would keep my façade together. I wanted life not to be hard any longer. I also wanted to have realizations turn in to actualizations without the agony of these damn birthing processes.

That cracking and splitting of my various false selves occurred many, many times in my lifetime. To sever attachments to what I believed gave me my identity and security in service to allowing full recognition that I am already what I want – that practice has been incredibly liberating, so much so that I began to pull willingly back the shell because the revelations were so freeing.

I was cutting the umbilical cord to those moments that in the past were painful. I willingly chose to choose to be in my life differently.

The severing required a dying off. I'd been harboring my wounds, hoping that someday something or someone would come along and take away the pain, the memories, and the misery of that moment. That something, in this moment was the Good Morning America position as Advice Guru. If I got that position, I knew the rest of my life would be on easy street. No more angst or worry; no more worry about being special or visible. My life as I'd known it would be finished. I was so looking forward to the relief of that moment.

There came a moment after weeks and weeks of anguish, when I realized that none of it mattered: the invisibility in my family and marriage; giving up custody of my children; the ongoing obsession with men; no money and no visible means of support; I could die today and I'd be okay with the fact that it's all over. It was an interesting moment, one that has repeated itself over and over again. I realized that most of what I was having to be with were just energy patterns in which I was swimming. Through the weeks of workouts that strengthened my courage-to-change-the-things-I-can muscles and my accept-the-things-I-cannot-change muscles, I was able to swim against the currents of unconsciousness that in the past had drowned me. Swimming against the current now had me fight hard for life itself, though I didn't know what that really meant. I just knew that what had been, no longer was, and no longer mattered.

Am I Worthy of my Own Expression

A few weeks passed. I struggled with more angst, more worry and sadness than before. I rarely blamed it on menopause as the reason for these shifts in my emotional state. Though hormones can cause emotional shifts, rarely am I affected that way. And my experience is that when I stay intentional about being with myself and my emotions – just like a mom with her child who isn't feeling well, the source of the emotions would make itself clear.

Then, I had a series of dreams, one night that were very deep and profound. Usually I don't remember my dreams so I took it seriously that something was being shared and I had better pay attention.

In the first dream, I was a musician on the back alleys of Las Vegas. I'd hit rock bottom, been cast out and now was on the shady side of all the neon lights of the Strip.

In the second dream, I was a homeless woman in Central Park, New York. I was sitting on my sleeping bag in a tent. A lovely man came by to check in on me. He brought me a piece of fruit and some water. He wanted me to consider leaving my tent and begin making it back to a better life. As I considered what he was suggesting, my mind swirled around a lifetime of challenges, heartbreak, loneliness and disappointment. Though part of me wanted to follow this man, there was another part of me who couldn't meet or express a sense of worthiness that seemed essential to returning to the life he was suggesting I return to. I wasn't ready to leave the comfort of the nest I'd built for myself.

A third dream followed with the same sense of living in squalor yet somehow feeling that this was good enough for me. I wasn't in pain. I wasn't depressed. I didn't feel like a victim. I felt that I was where I belonged.

The next morning, I sat with my cup of jasmine tea and thoughtfully approached the content of these dreams. More than the content, I was intrigued with the quality of being each individual lived with. None of them were unhappy, neither were they happy. They lived within a degree of worthiness and to move out of this state of being would cause too much anguish and exposure, to what – I don't know.

An image of a young girl standing in front of her father came to me. Her words would elicit either a warm embrace or a slap across the face. She had no idea what her words would elicit from her father. Her sense of worthiness was in the hands of her father. "Am I the father who passes out slaps or embraces to myself based on my own response?" I asked myself. "Good Girl!" "Bad Girl," just for being me. And the question came, "Am I worthy of my own expression?"

My dreams began to make sense. Each individual in this series of dreams had experienced enough negative judgment that their sense of worth was essentially zero. Their level of self-expression matched their sense of worth as well as the environment within which they existed. These dreams reflected back to me what millions of people live within – a life that meets their sense of worth. No one knows, because we aren't allowed to know that we are far more worthy than how we are treated by others – and here's the important piece – how we are treated by ourselves. Inevitably, it becomes obvious that because we are part and parcel of the Universal Source of all that is worthiness is a non-issue and it becomes a bankrupt concept.

Am I worthy of my own expression seemed like a crazy kind of question to ask, and yet I got that only I can assess my worthiness. Only I can decide what is mine to express.

For the past seven years, my home on Orcas Island has been a small travel trailer. I am definitely worthy of this expression of myself. And I can definitely rationalize that it's given me my lifestyle: traveling back and forth to California, where I stay in a cute little townhouse with Todd. The question is, "Am I worthy of my own expression of myself in a beautiful house with a real kitchen and bathroom and space for real furniture? Am I worthy of the work that I know is mine to do where I have more influence in domains where more is at stake? Am I worthy of my own expression of prosperity, comfort and generosity? Am I worthy of my own expression as healthy, strong, agile, energetic and active? Am I worthy of my own expression as playful, passionate, creative? Am I worthy of my own expression as peace, love, presence, compassion, truth and dignity?" Only I can answer these huge questions. No one else can decide for me.

I've attained three masters degrees and a PhD.; I've been a life and corporate coach for ten years; I've written a book, *Self-Empowerment 101*; and I've directed the Transformational Coaching Training Program for nine years. These are just a few of my achievements and yet each has been an arduous task because I'm always assessing my worthiness of taking each one as an expression of my own self. Am I worthy of this expression of myself? On and on, and on and on I go, assessing my own worthiness to have, to do and to be.

Todd and I have had the plans and the permit for our house on Orcas since 2006. It always seemed that the issue was about money; there just wasn't been enough of it to build a house. I'm now seeing that it's not about the money (It's never about the money). It's about the quality of being that will allow the house to be built. By holding on to the belief that I am somehow unworthy of this expression of myself, I will not attract whatever it takes to bring the house into form. Only by allowing myself to be worthy of this expression of myself will I allow the house to be built and then to actually live in the house – knowing that I am worthy of that too.

This worthiness business is deep, deep, deep, deep, deep! For each of us to allow the conversation to live within us would mean a shift in how we be in our own skin, as well as how we be with our families, our communities and our work environments. Are our children worthy of their own self-expression? How about our communities? How do we each decide who is worthy of their own expression and who is not? What happens when we begin to ask these questions? I wonder what is possible.

In each of these dream scenarios, there was something I couldn't bring myself to admit. Like a bubble, rising from the bottom of a lake it came to the surface, but disappeared again, never letting me know what I wasn't ready to know.

I suspected that at the bottom of it all was the belief that I had been a total failure as a human being. I am less than I should be in God's eyes. I'm a disappointment and worse. I am unworthy of my own expression. If I said what was true everything would change. The denial of that truth keeps me alive, but not thriving. What the heck is it that keeps me not wanting to know?

The Truth Revealed

November 3, 2010, I decided it was time to reveal what I needed to reveal. By doing so, I would exonerate myself from thirty years in a prison I built for myself. Thirty years of carrying guilt that was not mine to carry; thirty years of holding back for the sake of protecting my children and many other people too. I let myself believe that I was guilty of my worst sin – being selfish enough to leave my children for personal gain.

Thirty years ago, the divorce from Joshua proceeded on the grounds that I had an extramarital affair with Sam – he was named in the suit. This was inaccurate, but I had nothing to gain by fighting or being righteous. It allowed the divorce to go through effortlessly.

Today, like a detective, investigating the scene of a crime, I rewound the tape for the millionth time looking for some evidence that I'd missed. This time I allowed myself to see what I'd never been willing to see before.

I saw that for the sake of personal gain I *could have* made so many other choices that *could have* made me look like the good guy and not the bad guy; I *could have* chosen to take Joshua to court for alimony, custody, the house the whole kit and caboodle. I *could have* been truthful about my *lack of indiscretion* with Sam during my marriage; that nothing happened with Sam until I was separated. I took the fall to make things easy.

If I'd been selfish in my leaving my children, I *would have* made a monstrous scene, court proceedings, etc. I *would have* left with scads of money and whooped it up big time. I *wouldn't have* worked for minimum wages at an A-1 Hamburger Restaurant. I *wouldn't have* ended up on welfare.

It looks so different from the inside than from the outside; family labeling me as selfish and self-centered and telling my children that this is who their mother is. From the inside, I was doing only what I needed to do to survive, nothing more. I *would have* been more selfish to stay in a marriage that was unfulfilling for the sake of security. I *would have* been more selfish to take the children with me. They would have had to leave the comfort of their home, and routine. I *would have* been selfish if I had taken my husband to the cleaners for a larger share of the restaurant. I settled for potential collaboration then litigate. It took over twenty-five years for Joshua and me to be on speaking terms. Joshua would not accept my choice as a valiant way to be a mom or to be me. He has only slightly acknowledged his piece in our separation and divorce.

It wouldn't have done anyone any good to point fingers or to be righteous about Joshua's indiscretions, about his lack of presence in our marriage, our inability to communicate in a way that expressed connection and love - all of it. What was most important was to stop the bleeding and the pain of a six-year marriage between two people who lacked the maturity, the tools and the wisdom to do it any different.

Thirty years ago, the Mother's Day following our separation, which would have been almost twelve months to the day of our separation, Joshua presented me with a bottle of wine and a card. He told me he was grateful for the way that I handled the previous year, traveling back and forth to be with the children. He told me he couldn't have done what I did, and that most likely he would have left and never come back. He told me he appreciated that I didn't fight or make it hard on everyone.

I realized that when I took on being the bad guy, leaving my children behind, I took the fall for the relationship. I've played the bad guy so Joshua could be the good guy. He was the one the children were going to need to count on and trust. They did not need any doubt about their dad's capacity to care for them. His parents, his employees and friends didn't need to be burdened by all the shit that is so easy to spread around.

Joshua didn't need to do any finger pointing. I did it for him with my own choice making. His mother did it for him with all of her, "My poor son, my poor grandchildren." My mom did it for him, by taking his side. He and the children were the victims of my *adulterous* and *unmotherly* conduct.

I blew the whistle on my own lie, that day in November, the one I told to protect the innocent. It didn't occur to me the day I took the rap that I'd be carrying the weight for decades and that my children would never truly trust me ever again – I think this is the deepest wound of all.

By finally revealing to myself what previously had been hard to see, up until then, I exonerated myself from this prison by forgiving myself for this *lie of omission* the one that had not allowed me to be worthy of my own expression.

I spoke to myself, "I'm sorry that I've committed these sins against myself. Please forgive me."

I sat with the disappointment that life doesn't turn out the way it should and at the same time accepting and being grateful for the way life does turn out. Without this process I couldn't have found myself; I couldn't have transmuted the disappointments into miracles of revelations.

In twelve-step programs, you take inventory of your life, intentionally acknowledging all of the ways you've harmed yourself and others. You come to accept yourself and forgive yourself, recognizing yourself not as this or that, but as the Divine Spirit who's played itself out through this game of life. Inch by inch I was birthing myself into this realization, with miles to go.

I Am Not That/I Am Not This

For over a decade on rare occasions, I've suffered from a pain that appeared out of nowhere in the area of my rectum. It would last about an hour and then dissipate, without a shred of evidence of its reality. It never seemed to be connected to anything in my physical body so I concluded that it came from either an earlier time in my life, for which I have no memory or from perhaps a past life.

It doesn't matter what I do, nothing helps to relieve the pain. Massaging that area, taking aspirin, sitting on the toilet or doing child's pose; it all leaves me empty of options and helpless, until whatever it is runs its course. All I can do is endure the pain. I have no doubt that it is related to some sexual act perpetrated by someone upon my poor little anus. I have no recollection of such an episode in this lifetime, but who knows? Perhaps my memory won't allow me to remember the details, but as I said, on occasion, it's as though my body is experiencing the experience right then and there. What's missing is the perpetrator.

This last episode took place a few nights ago. It was in the middle of the night. I'd just come back from going to the bathroom and suddenly that familiar sensation began to make itself known, very close to my anus. I know to anticipate the worst, though still hold the possibility that I could do something to stave off the agony and frustration that I should be able to do something. I walked back to the bathroom to sit on the toilet, hoping that perhaps a *poo* was actually the cause. You never can tell – hope springs eternal.

The sensations of the experience is challenging to describe as it could only be described in relation to nerves attached to muscles that were being asked to do what they weren't meant to do. If I touched the skin or the muscles, it had no effect. It was something else entirely. This time too I experienced the same sensation in my vagina and uterus. It makes sense that perhaps this could be part of past lifetime experiences. To my recollection, I've never been raped or molested as a child, so to experience the sensations of such an experience is not rational nor logical.

I found myself most comfortable lying partially on my side and partially on my belly with my upper leg pulled up a bit, while my lower leg was straight down. I became aware of two realities occurring simultaneously. There was the physical reality of me on my bed, experiencing the pain of again, what must be a body memory of lifetimes of rape and abuse. I was at times the rapist and at other times, I was the abused. As the rapist, I was a man, always a man. I was a soldier, a father, an angry man who was out to demoralize and debilitate, to leave whoever I was abusing nothing of themselves.

As the victim, I experienced myself as a man, a boy, a woman, a little girl; even as an infant. To fight or resist was futile. I knew that nothing, but time would end the attack. I laid there with the knowing that this may go on and on and on, as if it were happening to me in that current moment.

About five years ago, for the theatre group here on Orcas Island, I was part of the *Vagina Monologs* written by Eve Ensler. Curiously enough, I played an Bosnian woman who describes in vivid details what it was like for her during the war. How she had been raped with guns, bottles, sticks and filthy penises. This night as I lay in the dark I couldn't help, but know some of the horrors of her experience.

As I said, I was in two realities simultaneously; the first being the physical sensation. The other reality was one where I was in my body, but was not my body. In this reality, I could experience the pain, but be separate from it. This was the first time I was aware of this phenomenon, of being separate from what Eckhart Tolle calls my pain body. In this place, there was a sense of peace and surrender. I focused on praying to a higher power that would help me endure the physical and emotional experience of the violation. It was clear to me that nothing would stop the assault, but I could pray to a universal source, to guides and to angels, who could comfort me during this time.

In my prayers, I asked for forgiveness for all the acts of abuse I ever committed upon another living being. As the victim, I forgave my perpetrator for he knew not what he was doing. Being with the pain and the many lives touched by this act of violence I prayed for all of us who've had to endure injustices in any form that men and women have found to violate life itself.

A moment of clarity came when I realized that I was not the body that was being violated; I was not the emotional being humiliated while pummeled with assaults. This being that I experienced, could not be harmed even if my body was killed. I was not that! I worked hard to stay in this state, exercising the muscles that could hold back the waters of victimization. I was not that! Each place that my mind wanted to take me to I could say I'm not that either. Over and over, I could acknowledge I was not that.

Slowly the aching pain dissipated. I rested with myself, nurturing all the me's that have ever gone through such horror. Comforting myself with Gracie by my side, I fell asleep.

This episode was just one of many of the ongoing spiritual emergence processes that have been escalating over the past few months. This one in particular led me to believe that the twelve years from the onset of this rectal pain brought me to the realization that I am not that. It has taken maybe twenty of these episodes before I came to the realization that I can be separate from the pain. That I am not that.

The following day I realized that if I'm not *that*, then I am not *this* either. I'm not my circumstance, my worries, my anxiety and fear, my beliefs and judgments. It was an amazing realization that has been talked about in just about every spiritual book I've ever read.

I walked in the woods and talked with God. If I'm not my circumstances, the pain, the body, then, what am I. What came was the realization that all I am is the essence of Spirit. And I am here to live in my essence and live my life purpose.

The allure of the circumstances that surround me makes it challenging to sustain the knowing that I'm not this or that – I'm only the essence of Spirit here on Earth to do what I came here to do. Slowly, but surely though, I remember my commitment to be *this* – my essence, and to live into my life purpose – what I've come to this planet to do. Everything else is superfluous.

It's been over two years that I felt the calling to launch myself out of a secure, well-established life as the facilitator of the Transformational Coaching Training Program, for work that took me out into the world doing what, I did not know. Now in December, with the Training now complete, it appeared as though I am now without a parachute or safety net. Fear, panic and anxiety of losing everything, along with my faith that I am following a calling greater than I could ever imagine, were with me every moment of my days. Until yesterday.

Sitting with the episode from a couple of nights ago and sitting with my dilemma of whether I am on the right path or whether I'm being a complete idiot and should go looking for a job, I knew in many ways, it just didn't matter. What mattered was that I practice walking my talk, be in integrity and accountable for a life that is worth living.

No Regrets, No Hard Feelings, Its Over

The day came when it was obvious I wasn't chosen as even a finalist for America's Advice Guru.

On one hand I knew the odds were against me; there were over ten thousand other people who also thought that they were the chosen one; however, I also knew I had the credentials and the experience to be exceptional in the position. I could laugh with myself about not getting it and knew that something else was in store for me. I was disappointed that I was set up to think I was going to get the job. My muscle testing said that God/the Universe wanted this for me one hundred percent. Me, I wanted it about forty percent. I was willing to will God's will to do what I came here to do – to live in my essence and to actualize my life purpose. I guess I was attached to my interpretation of what *yes* meant and what *chosen* meant.

What was really challenging to consider was that God had been lying to me all of these months - Intentionally lying to me. I know this wasn't meant as a cruel joke, but that it was an opportunity for me to let go of more of what I was attached to. So, more than the disappointment of not getting the job, I was disappointed that I was lied to by God.

I realized quickly that it was only my interpretation that God lied to me and nothing more than that. Yet, even this took me to another thought process I was attached to. I began to feel the grief of not being *chosen;* something, it seems that has been really important to me for my whole life. We are talking here about being special, like being chosen as a cheerleader or Homecoming Queen or in second grade at Sacred Heart School, when I wanted to be the one to crown the Virgin Mary in our little Catholic Church, but Theresa Oulette got the honors. I don't know why I thought I'd be *the one* to crown Mary, but I wasn't and I guess I never got over that. Because here I was in this moment, sobbing with disappointment over not being chosen.

Anger bubbled up. For the next few days, when I looked around, I saw that everyone had everything they wanted; every *thing* I saw reminded me of all the things I didn't have. I'd look at the credits at the end of a movie and resented that each individual was *chosen* for their part as an actor or support in the production. Me, I was left out. I didn't get what I wanted. I was left feeling less than, just a tiny, little, piece of poo. I knew this wasn't true. It was just another part of me that needed to be acknowledged and held while I let go of what never happened.

God has some plan that I'm not yet aware of. It's all good, whatever transpires. I get that I'm more attached than I thought to being special and being important. More and more I recognize all of the various aspects of me that give me an identity. On the one hand, I'm coming to drop my armor in order to be my most essential self; letting go of all the meaning and significance I give to all of my wants and desires and all of that which is undesirable. I'm flooded continually by experiences that have me shed more and more and more and more and ... Heaven only knows where this is leading.

Why Stop Now

It has taken a very long time to become the mother worthy of my children. I do not mean this in any way to sound self-deprecating, only that the person who gave birth to my children wasn't like the woman I am now. What woman is after thirty-plus years? Life changes us, hopefully for the better.

Nine months now, I've been on my trajectory towards my calling. I had no idea it would take so long. There are times when I'm really frustrated with not knowing. My bank account is hungry and I'm beginning to consider what I should do to find work and what to let go of bookkeeper, student loan payments and a phone line. Muscle testing indicates a no to letting go of anything that would shift where my money is going. This feels insane and absurd. This morning I awoke not knowing what's to become of me. I said to myself, "If I have to make a choice here *without* Divine Guidance, it will feel CRAZY". I haven't made a major decision by myself, for, well ... I paused to figure out how long it had actually been and what was it? Here's the list of decisions I've made with Divine Guidance:

Outward Bound	1968
Leave the Catholic Church	1969
Leave my children	1976
Enter Interfaith	1976
California Family Study Center	1978
Move to Nova Scotia	1980
Nova Scotia Commission on Drug Dependency	1982-1991
Tai Chi	1984
Course in Miracles	1988
Sail on *Tree of Life*	1991
Go Back to Virginia	1994

ITP	1995
Teach Sailing at OCSC	1996
Take the Coaching Training	2000
Facilitate Transformational Coaching Training	2001
Move to Orcas	2003
Leave the Training	2010

It's fascinating that all of the choices that led me down the unholy path were those in which I felt inspired and called by the Divine.

Each of these choices took me across the grain of what society considers to be normal and right. Each had me leave the security of my comfort zone for something extraordinary. This moment is no different. I'm perched on the edge of my nest ready to soar once again.

The significance of this moment is that I can point to evidence in my life where I've listened to Divine Guidance. My belief is that as challenging as it has been, the consequences of each decision has taken me further from my roots. I believe that I've stayed the course, navigating by my own charts with the Universal Source of all that is as my co-pilot.

A friend of mine says, "If it's not a hell yes, it's a hell no." Evidence, my own and others reminds me of what it's like to know the "NOs" and what it's like to get the "YES!" The experience of "Go for the extraordinary," still guides me. It keeps me from lowering my sites to what's not mine to do.

Looking at the list makes me excited about what's next. My life has been thrilling in so many ways. So, why stop now?

Addendum

January 2011

Hannah is eight months pregnant with a little boy, Andrew. Today is the day that I officially turn into a grandma. It's the end of just one more era and chapter, and just one more new beginning. It's most likely not the last.

I got the call yesterday from Hannah saying her water broke three weeks early. It was time for me to fly out to Niagara Falls to support her through the birth of baby Andrew and to care for her, her sweetie Patrick and the baby for a few weeks. Hanna and Patrick moved back to be near her dad and his wife Nancy, and where her lifetime friends are too.

I've been wintering with Todd in California. He was as excited as I was and came home early from work to spend some special time with me and help me get ready. Both of us needing some serious snuggle time meant we fell asleep probably close to 11:30 p.m. The choice between sleep, which I desperately wanted and the snuggle time, which we both needed brought me to this moment. I'm happy to be able to accept and to allow what is. We have to find balance between what's important and accept the consequences. I knew I could catch up on sleep on the plane and that with the three-hour time change I'd be going to bed early and very happy about that.

I've been pretty subdued and aloof about being a grandma. But today getting on the flight in San Francisco I found myself tearing up for no apparent reason. In the security line in conversation with a young woman who was empathizing with a young mom trying to manage two small children while getting through the security line I mentioned that I was on my way to becoming a grandma. I began to cry. "Pull back, pull back!" I said to myself. The tears subsided. "What the heck was *that*?" It happened again while sitting on the plane waiting for departure. I mentioned to my row companion that I was heading east to support my daughter; again tears. "What's with the tears?"

It's somewhat like the turbulence of the flight I'm on while writing. We can't see the bumps that are causing the shaking of the plane. I just feel the results of those invisible bumps. I'm sure over the next few days I'll find the words to describe the quality of the experience of becoming a grandma. I'll have a space where I can allow my emotional self to express freely what is hers to express.

These life transitions, these phenomena far surpass the logical rational thinking of what this is. A child is being born to my daughter. Practically speaking, this has little to do with me. But it's as though some sort of magical spell has been cast upon me. Archetypes have once again shaken the ground I walk on. Deciding to marry Todd, I felt that same sort of whoosh being swept up into a revelatory experience that is beyond the logical and rational, taking me into the transpersonal realm where the unexplainable is allowed, accepted, and understood as ineffable, but nonetheless real.

I'm unsure whether I've attempted to resist the grandma syndrome because I don't want to be one of those that become so absorbed in my grandchildren that I lose myself in them. With that said though, I can't tell you the number of times I've had conversations with my grandchildren who are still in the spirit-dimension. I walk with them and talk with them while driving or sitting looking out over Crow Valley. I ask them many questions and they do the same. We wonder about life and I wonder how to answer some of their questions; if I'm too woo-woo how will that affect them? What is the best way to support them in being who they are in a world that can put enormous pressure on them to assimilate; knowing that for many, resistance is futile.

My intention for this trip is to not only to meet the new human being Andrew, my grandson. My intention is to be of service to Hannah and Patrick. I want to do and be so she has more time to be with Andrew. I want to serve by cooking and cleaning. It's a good feeling. It isn't coming from some need to make up for, or show what a really good mom can be.

I want to be (tears) available to Hannah as she has always wanted me to be; I now have the time and space for her. It almost feels like, that whatever that is, that's so natural for women to be nurturing of their children; what I had been so essentially *me*, a very long time ago, but turned off, in order to save my life, thirty years ago, it's time to embrace that part of me again.

Instead of being nurturing to my children I became nurturing to men and to clients. As natural as it was, there was a difference. Returning to my daughter with her well-being in mind, I have come full circle (tears) to me. I return to Niagara Falls where I raised my children for those few brief years (tears). I will live with Hannah, Patrick and Andrew for perhaps a month to be there in the wholeness of motherhood I started out so desperately wanting. I'm ready to be present in the way I can be now, and perhaps as a consequence, as a family we can transform the wounds of us all into something capable of flight.

####

Acknowledgments

In writing an autobiographical piece, it would take pages upon pages to acknowledge everyone who contributed to the writing of this book. I guess the fact is this book is one big acknowledgement and testimony to every human being who contributed to me being here, now, and to this book and me going through this gestation period, bringing us both out the other side.

Specifically though, I'd like to acknowledge my editor Lynne Krop and her company The Write Well. I've so appreciated Lynne, her commitment to this project and the integrity she brought with her to the very end.

I also want to acknowledge the brilliant Fabian Espinoza for his cover design. Fabian, you bring so much wisdom and creativity to your projects. I'm grateful that I get to witness your creative process and be rewarded in the end with a cover that speaks to the heartfelt story of this reluctant adventurer.

I want to acknowledge Great Mystery in sneaking a spiritual emergence process into my life just when I thought I'd left that all behind. We never know when we will be sharing your magnificent gifts in any one of the million arrays. You kept me on my toes for the past nine months and I have a feeling you have more surprises up your sleeves.

Todd Zimmerman, Slammer, Dreamwalker, My Sweetie – I would be remiss in not acknowledging all the ways you've supported me though this process. The many moments when I felt like it all had no meaning; you could hear me, listening with the biggest heart I know. You walked me through this without wavering for a moment. That's the best part of having a partner that has navigated the spiritual depths of humanity; you take in strides what most of us fear is the end of reality.

Though my children aren't happy with me for writing this story about my life and the choice I made that impacted them to the degree that it has; I acknowledge them for supporting me to write it nonetheless. I so appreciate their love and support and am enormously grateful to have them in my life.

Dr. Rosie Kuhn is the founder of the Paradigm Shifts Coaching Group, author of Self-Empowerment 101 and creator and facilitator of the Transformational Coaching Training Program. She is a Life, Spiritual and Business Coach to individuals, corporations and executives, known for empowering her clients in making rapid, transformational changes to their lives and relationships. She lives on beautiful Orcas Island where she runs Wonderful Women's Retreats every summer.

Please visit her website and discover how Dr. Rosie can impact your life in ways you may never have thought possible. http://dr-rosie.com.